COUNSELING PSYCHOLOGY IN COMMUNITY SETTINGS

Donald H. Blocher, Ph.D., is Professor of Counseling Psychology at the State University of New York at Albany. He has held professorships at the University of Minnesota and the University of Western Ontario, and has been visiting professor at Utah State University, the University of Colorado, the University of British Columbia, and the University of Keele in the United Kingdom. He received his doctoral degree from the University of Minnesota. Dr. Blocher is past president of the Division of Counseling Psychology of the American Psychological Association. He has authored or co-authored several books, including *Developmental Counseling*. He is also the author of numerous journal articles and is a Fellow of the American Psychological Association.

Donald A. Biggs, Ed.D., is Professor of Counseling Psychology and Student Development at the State University of New York at Albany. He received his doctoral degree from the University of California at Los Angeles. Dr. Biggs was formerly Professor of Educational Psychology and Assistant to the Vice President for Student Affairs at the University of Minnesota. He has also served as Fulbright Visiting Professor at the University of Aston, Birmingham, England. Dr. Biggs has authored or co-authored a number of articles, chapters, and books.

COUNSELING PSYCHOLOGY IN COMMUNITY SETTINGS

Donald H. Blocher, Ph.D.
Donald A. Biggs, Ed.D.

SPRINGER PUBLISHING COMPANY
New York

Springer Publishing Company, Inc.
200 Park Avenue South
New York, New York 10003

83 84 85 86 87 88 / 10 9 8 7 6 5 4 3 2 1

Library of Congress Cataloging in Publication Data

Blocher, Donald H.
  Counseling psychology in community settings.
  Includes bibliographies and index.
  1. Community psychology. 2. Counseling. 3. Community mental health
services. I. Biggs, Donald A. II. Title. [DNLM: 1. Community mental health
services. 2. Counseling—Methods. WM 30 B651c]
RA790.B5566 1983   616.89'14   83-344
ISBN 0-8261-3680-X

Printed in the United States of America

Contents

v

III Diagnosis and Assessment of Individuals and Environments

Preface

Counseling Psychology in Community Settings provides an orientation to the role of counseling psychologists within the human services professions. It differentiates the unique contributions of counseling psychology and explains them in terms of the needs and goals of a community-centered approach to human services.

In one sense, the book represents an effort to define a set of goals, commitments, and approaches that have emerged out of the history of counseling psychology and to relate them to similar concepts and values that are central to the practice of community psychology. The book is heavily ecological in its theoretical orientation. Indeed, it holds the view that the emerging field of developmental human ecology is our best present hope for a unifying and integrating intellectual and scientific force that may finally help to bring together the often fragmented and competing ideas from clinical, counseling, and community psychology.

Our ideas about the future directions of the profession are presented without wantonly discarding the intellectual and technical legacies of our past. Considerable attention is devoted to vocational counseling, for example, and to the significance of diagnosis and assessment to the counseling psychologist.

We have described the operation of a variety of models of individual and group intervention. From that standpoint the book is unabashedly eclectic. We believe that the scope of the challenges confronting the counseling psychologist in community practice can be best met by a critical but open-minded approach to all of the hard-won theoretical and empirical resources generated out of modern psychology.

The book introduces the reader to a variety of intervention models and points out the relevance of these models to the problems encountered in community practice. Major attention is given to interventions such as consultation, training, psychological education, and organizational development. We believe that they have a clear and special relevance in community practice.

Three pervasive and unifying themes run through the book. One is a constant commitment to goals of *facilitating human development*. For us, this is a central ethic that defines and distinguishes counseling psychology. The second theme is an affirmation of the basic utility of a *systems approach* in conceptualizing and intervening in human needs, concerns, and problems. We see human beings as social organisms engaged in patterns of interpersonal relationships that nurture or inhibit their basic humanity.

Our third theme is an interactionist view of the significance of *person–environment fit* as a central dynamic in human functioning. We believe that fixation upon intrapsychic aspects of human behavior has tended to obscure the immense importance of both nurturing and potentially damaging forces at work in the environment. We see the counseling psychologist as one who addresses efforts both to individuals and to the social and organizational factors that define their environments. Out of this dual concern with person and environment emerges the distinctive contribution of counseling psychology.

PART I
COMMUNITY SETTINGS AND SERVICES

1
The Challenge of Community Practice

Changes in the Human Services Professions

During the past twenty years we have seen remarkable changes in the scope and nature of professional roles and settings related to the practice of counseling psychology. Although many counseling psychologists continue to practice in settings that are primarily educational in orientation, or are concerned heavily with vocational rehabilitation, many others have moved into a variety of human services agencies and settings that engage in varied activities and offer an array of services to a number of publics.

Even more important, however, is the fact that within those settings that have been the traditional domain of counseling psychologists, changes in role concepts and expectations have steadily proceeded. Increasingly, counseling psychologists have engaged in activities involving "indirect" helping roles of consultation, training, and organizational development that have supplemented their activities in individual and group counseling.

In many ways these changes in focus and priorities have grown naturally out of the value commitments of counseling psychologists and out of the increased recognition and appreciation of their contributions that have developed in organizations and communities.

These changes have undoubtedly been accelerated by a set of dramatic shifts in fundamental notions about the theoretical and empirical foundations for the human services that have become prominent in recent years. While these changes are not yet fully crystallized, and are certainly not yet at their ultimate state of development, they nevertheless represent powerful and dynamic forces that are shaping the development of human services professions and delivery systems.

These new ideas are best represented outside of counseling psychology itself, in the thinking and research that have emerged

3

from community psychology and the exciting new field of social and developmental human ecology. These fields have exerted, and will continue to exert, tremendous influence over the future of the human services professions. The nature of psychological practice in community settings will largely be shaped out of the developments that are defining the emergence of these fields.

A number of factors are responsible for the impact of these newer approaches upon the practice of professional psychology. Perhaps the most potent reason has been the steadily increasing feeling of disillusionment with traditional theories and models that has characterized the helping professions over the past two decades (Sarason, 1981; Schulberg, 1972; Tharp & Wetzel, 1969). For a number of years a wide variety of critics including Hersch (1968), Albee (1970), and Sarason (1976), for example, have warned of the impending bankruptcy of traditional theories and delivery systems in the mental health field. These criticisms have pointed up a number of critical deficiencies in these approaches both on practical and scientific grounds. These critiques have called into question basic assumptions about our ways of conceptualizing, organizing, and training for human services programs (Hobbs, 1966; Iscoe, 1974; Kelly, 1966).

Major dissatisfactions have been expressed in regard to quite fundamental issues. These can best be summarized in terms of several basic questions.

1. *Is the illness model derived from medicine a sufficiently comprehensive and useful concept around which to organize human services programs?*

The basic concept of "mental health" is an increasingly controversial and perhaps not very useful notion. The concept itself is heavily based upon the philosophical premise of the separation of mind and body. Even in philosophy this position has been less than fully accepted and is today more a remnant out of the history of philosophical thought than a basic tenet of modern epistemology. Out of this questionable and somewhat antiquated dichotomy, however, was born the notion of "mental" health as parallel to the concept of physical health in traditional medicine. Even within a medical model, this view has obvious limitations. The concepts of holistic medicine, of course, would firmly reject the notion of separate and isolatable mental and physical states within a single organism.

In traditional medicine, health has largely been conceptualized in terms of the absence of specific symptoms or identifiable pathology. An individual is commonly seen as healthy when he or she is not sick, that is, experiencing or reporting bothersome or significant symptoms. We often speak, for example, of "passing" a physical examination when the examining physician is unable to find evidence of any specific disease. The usefulness of this kind of concept of health and illness hinges upon the ability of the science of medicine to identify disease entities that have known symptoms, causes, and cures.

Despite many years of truly remarkable medical progress in the pursuit of such goals, we are all too well aware of the limitations of this approach even in medical science. Much that happens in regard to physical health is not yet fully explainable within a disease-entity framework. The fields of holistic, behavioral, and psychosomatic medicine give ample testimony of that fact.

In the area of psychological dysfunction, the shortcomings of the disease-entity approach are even more apparent and dramatic. For years psychologists have pointed to the fact that in the behavior disorders, or so-called mental illnesses, the simple identification of neatly defined disease entities was clearly the exception rather than the rule. Some psychologists such as Eysenck (1960) called for the whole notion of disease entities to be banished from the realm of modern psychology. While this may represent an extreme remedy, it seems clear that a simple illness or deficit model around which to conceive and organize human services is a constraining and inhibiting, if not intellectually bankrupt, approach.

2. *Who is the consumer or client for human services programs?*

Nearly a half century ago Lawrence Frank (1936) wrote a seminal paper that he called "Society as the Patient." The human services professions have failed to this day to resolve the basic issue that Frank raised. He pointed out that without doubt many of the woes and ills that afflict people in our society are the result of our imperfect ways of organizing and managing human affairs, or in other words our society.

Caplan and Nelson (1973) contended that person-centered notions of mental health and illness are counterproductive in our society in that they tend to divert attention away from the real sources of difficulty, and instead foster a person-blame philosophy that sometimes results in blaming people for social problems of which they are the real victims. Even more radical critics of mental health philosophies such as Szasz (1961), Halleck (1971), and Sharma (1970) have viewed the concept of mental illness as a myth invoked to explain more comfortably the failures of society, or even as an essentially political concept used to stigmatize those who are powerless or otherwise disadvantaged in a society. These views are extreme, but more moderate observers such as Sarason (1981) have pointed out the fixation that American psychology has had for individual rather than social interaction models for explaining human behavior. As Mischel (1973) has amply documented, a wealth of seemingly overlooked research evidence exists to challenge the primacy if not the actual relevance of traditional personality theories and models. Only in relatively recent years have these findings been utilized to reshape our professional goals and practices.

It seems clear now that psychological interventions of a purely intrapsychic nature, that ignore the context in which behavior occurs and is caused, are primitive and partial remedies that may merely serve to perpetuate sufferings and injustice. For fifteen years critics such as Hobbs (1966), Iscoe (1974), and Sarason (1976) have pointed to the need for a massive reconceptualization of our human services programs to reflect the revisions in theory and research discussed above.

3. *Who are the healers and helpers?*

Perhaps the most telling criticism of traditional models and theories of mental health services has been pointed up in their failure to grapple with the issue of the identity and characteristics of the service providers themselves. One of the most disturbing and damaging results of this stubborn attachment to the discredited and dysfunctional analogy of mental health has been the way in which it has chained the human services professions to outmoded delivery systems. The traditional therapeutic team headed by the psychiatrist has tended to dominate the human services professions and the psychological delivery systems. The tendency toward dominance of the field by a single model has limited progress in the human services in several ways. It has obviously resulted in a systematic discounting of the important contributions of a variety of other human services workers. The great bulk of human services upon which the well-being of our society depends are provided, not by a handful of specialists, but by many thousands of teachers, counselors, nurses, social workers, police, corrections workers, family practice physicians, foster parents, and volunteers. Perhaps the most important single task in the human services field involves facilitating, supporting, and encouraging the work of these often unrecognized people. A continuation of unilateral control of the mental health establishment will not help to advance the work that needs to be done.

4. *What are the goals of human services programs?*

The final and most dramatic inadequacy of the traditional mental health approach has been its inability to articulate a sensible and feasible goal structure around which to organize resources and programs. The reduction of inner distress or tension was the most obvious and mundane goal for treatments derived out of traditional intrapsychic theories and models. Unfortunately, the various competing theories generated little agreement about the nature, source, or even symptoms of intrapsychic disturbances.

Another perhaps overly ambitious goal borrowed from traditional approaches to medicine was the cure of mental illness. Unfortunately, it is difficult to cure illnesses that we cannot clearly define and recognize. Psychodynamic theories pointed to the total reorganization of personality as the ultimate goal of psychotherapy. Understandably, such goals appeal more to therapists than to patients.

Each of these goal structures has fallen into disrepute in terms of both feasibility and desirability. Few people really seem to come into treatment to have the dents pounded out of their psyches. The great shortcoming of the mental health approach has been its failure to establish a reasonable consensus regarding definitions of what constitutes good mental health. Without this consensus, mental health workers have been in much the same situation described in the old proverb of the blind men and the elephant. The goals and results of treatment generally depend on what part of the elephant the therapist touches.

It seems clear, as M. Brewster Smith (1961) pointed out long ago, that concepts of mental health are inevitably intertwined with value judgments about what is good and true and beautiful in the natural world and in human society. Real dangers of abuse and misunderstanding arise inevitably when these definitions and concepts are viewed as emanating from purely scientific analyses and investigations, rather than from fallible human or social judgments. Indeed, the most patent mark of a pseudo-science is its calculated and persistent efforts to carry on this type of masquerade.

For these very reasons White (1973) argued persuasively against the basic utility of the concept of mental health or healthy personality. He argued that mental health is purely a metaphor and a poor one at that. Given the relative absence of scientific credibility for the concept of mental health, it is hardly surprising that definitions have been both vague and varied.

Jahoda's (1950) definition of more than thirty years ago has been a classic if somewhat simplistic view. Briefly, she described the mentally healthy person as one who actively masters his or her environment, demonstrates a considerable unity or consistency of personality, and is able to perceive self and the world realistically.

Such a person is able to function effectively without making undue demands upon others.

While this rather commonsense and simplistic description would probably still get considerable support, it is not without difficulty. The Jahoda definition has little to say about prosocial functoning as an aspect of mental health, for example. Shoben (1957) was one of the first to go beyond the criterion of self-sufficiency to propose that the healthy person is one who extends his or her functioning beyond self-control and personal responsibility into the area of social responsibility and commitment to some set of general social values.

Even such an expanded definition of mental health is still centered almost totally within the person, however. It assumes that the locus of functioning is situated primarily within the individual and is largely independent of the environment. Such assumptions are probably not even tenable for concepts of physical health. Occupationally related diseases such as the dreaded "black lung" of the coal mining industry, for example, are obvious products of the interaction of the individual organism and the environment. As Hinkle (1968) points out, in the area of psychological dysfunctioning many crucial person–environment interactions exist.

A number of writers have espoused the view that the goals of modern human services programs must transcend the boundaries established by traditional theories and concepts of mental health. Nearly twenty years ago, Karl Menninger (1964) called for a concept of what he called "weller than well" in psychological functioning. Many prominent psychologists have attempted to define such concepts of higher level functioning.

These include "self-actualization" (Maslow, 1968), the "mature personality" (Allport, 1963), and the "fully functioning person" (Rogers, 1962). All of these models provide somewhat greater flexibility and elaboration than those generated out of the traditional mental health view. They share, however, many of the disadvantages of mental health models in that they tend to be rooted in rather thinly disguised value judgments, and to view human functioning as almost totally intrapsychic in origin.

In any event, the lack of clarity, consistency, and comprehensiveness that has characterized the goal structures generated out of traditional approaches has been a severely limiting factor in the development of modern human services programs.

We have identified and briefly discussed four major questions or issues that have confronted the human services field. The deepening dissatisfaction of the field with the answers or solutions generated by traditional approaches has provided much of the impetus for alternative views of these problems offered by community psychology and social ecology.

An attempt to represent fully the contributions of a field as extensive and many faceted as community psychology in a few pages is, of course, very difficult. A brief overview of that field, however, sketched primarily in terms of basic issues, seems useful at this point.

Although the roots of community psychology can be traced much further, Zax (1980) points to the 1961 report of the Joint Commission on Mental Health established by President Kennedy as the takeoff point for the community mental health movement. The subsequent establishment and funding of community mental health centers on a relatively large scale, coupled with a tremendous outpouring of published research and reinterpretation of theory and research, marked the advent of this innovative approach to human services problems and programs.

In the past fifteen years community psychology has attempted to promulgate alternative approaches to many of the problems and challenges that had seemingly eluded the grasp of more traditional theories and models.

During the past two decades the impact of research in cognitive-behavioral psychology and experimental social psychology has been tremendous in terms of its onslaught on traditional intrapsychic personality theories. It has been, as Zax (1980) puts it, an era of idol-smashing.

One focus shared by the behavioral, cognitive-behavioral, and social psychological approaches is their common emphasis on behavior as arising out of interaction between the individual and the physical and social environment. Increasingly, attempts to study or assess the behavior of an individual in isolation from his or her transactions with the environment have been seen as fruitless (Ripley & Beuchner, 1967). This emphasis was echoed and amplified in the community psychological approaches to mental health or human services problems.

As this approach developed it differed from the earlier intra-psychic frameworks in several notable respects. First, it tended to refute the validity of the disease-entity model of mental health and illness. The community mental health approach tended to view psychopathology or inadequate psychological functioning, not so much as a result of a maladaptive personality style or deep-seated psychic conflict, residing within the individual, but rather as a set of responses to a series of immediate situational problems demanding practical solutions (Lehman, 1971). This approach, then, focuses on helping people solve practical problems of everyday living in the natural environment. The value orientation that accompanied this view of human functioning also differed from the traditional approach in major respects. It asserted that the prevention of pathology is more important to human and social welfare than is the intensive or in-depth treatment of emotional disturbances (Suinn, 1979).

As a consequence of these perspectives and value orientations, community psychology treatment programs have tended to be concerned with a variety of factors that affect the immediate and practical functioning and performance of an individual in his or her own community setting. These may include the client's attitudes and competences, family interaction patterns, and educational, social, and vocational skills.

These concerns are not limited, however, solely to processes occurring within the client (Hersch, 1968). They include problems and resources inherent in the client's environment such as housing, employment or educational opportunities, health care, financial security, and physical mobility. Also included in these concerns and variables around which treatment may be focused are the attitudes and actions of the community or society itself toward the identified client (Iscoe, 1974).

The community psychological approach recognizes that some of the causes for so-called mental health problems may reside in the less than optimal features of the society itself, such as racism, sexism, poverty, unemployment, or restricted educational opportunity (Greenblatt, Emery, & Glueck, 1967; Kelly, 1966). Considerable empirical support for this position is found in the mounting array of evidence that indicates that the incidence and severity of mental health problems are inversely related to socioeconomic class. In other words, psychopathology tends to occur with greater frequency and severity among members of lower socioeconomic groups (Dohrenwend & Dohrenwend, 1969). One view derived from these findings is that to some extent, at least, what we call mental illness is a not unexpected reaction to the stresses involved in living in disorganized, disadvantaged, and insecure environments (Bradshaw, 1969). Since the community psychology movement has grown out of approaches to the study of human behavior that stress the importance of interactions between the individual and the environment, the relationship between social status or disadvantage and mental illness is important in designing programs and services.

The community psychology movement represents a step forward from the impasses reached by traditional intrapsychic approaches. It is still saddled, however, with a conceptual allegiance to the ill-conceived metaphor of mental health, with resulting ties to health service delivery systems and medical models of diagnosis and treatment that are limiting to its ultimate development and contribution. These ties seem to be maintained more out of economic and political expediency than scientific credibility. As Sarason (1976) has pointed out, community mental health is in danger of joining its predecessors in the same kind of intellectual oblivion from which it was supposed to rescue the field of mental health.

A major movement that has to some extent paralleled yet now promises to move beyond the community mental health approach is that called social and developmental human ecology. The social ecological approach is designed to investigate the intricate relationships between human beings and their environments without needing to invoke the limiting and dysfunctional metaphor of mental health.

A model that transcends the community mental health approach yet offers a direction for goal-orientation is the ecological model for studying human development (Bronfenbrenner, 1979). This view conceptualizes development as the product of a lifelong process of engagement between the individual and the environment. It views behavior as fully understandable only within the natural person–environmental context in which the behavior occurs. The appropriate unit for analysis is the ecosystem—that is, the system within which the transactions between individual and environments are structured (Warren, 1977). From this perspective, then, disorders or dysfunctions that are barriers to development are best understood and most effectively prevented or remediated within the natural environments within which they occur. This perspective is extremely important in the design of interventions.

As Kelly (1966) has pointed out, an ecological analysis of mental health problems generates different sets of basic questions and goals than those that arise from intrapsychic approaches. One of these involves an analysis of community systems and how they interact with each other. The second is the careful study of the relationship between the physical environment and individual behavior. Finally, the ecological approach focuses upon the relationships between the individual and the immediate social environment. Similarly, the ecological view leads to the framing of goals largely in terms of what Hobbs (1966) termed the "goodness of fit" between social institutions and the people whom they are ostensibly intended to serve. Such ecologically based goals inspire both interventions centered directly around individual–environment interactions and interventions aimed directly at social institutions or agencies (Roe, 1970).

The changes in thinking about human functioning and the human services professions that we have so briefly summarized above have constituted what Suinn (1979) has termed "a quiet revolution." This quiet revolution has had important consequences for counseling psychology in community settings. Masterpasqua (1981) described two basic premises around which a new developmentally oriented community psychology might be focused. Considerable support for these premises exists in contemporary developmental theory and research.

The first premise is the view that *human beings are characterized by a basic and inherent drive toward competence or mastery of the environment.* Theoretical support for this view has long existed in a variety of sources in developmental psychology (Piaget, 1952; White, 1959). Failure to achieve some sense of competence or control over one's life has been related to breakdowns in psychological functioning. Support for this view is found in the work on self-efficacy of Bandura (1977) as well as Maier and Seligmann's (1976) research on learned helplessness. As Masterpasqua (1981) documents, the drive for competence phenomenon is well supported in empirical studies throughout the life span. Indeed, the building of competence as a kind of psychological inoculation against psychopathology has been seen as a viable alternative to the "uncover and cure" approach of traditional clinical psychology and psychiatry (Bloom, 1979).

A second premise around which community and developmental psychology can join is this: *There is a need to study the development of competence as it occurs in natural settings.* As we have seen, this theme can be noted very clearly in developmental social ecology. Drawing upon the pioneering work of Roger Barker (1973), the research on environmental psychology has been compelling in drawing attention to the need for ecologically oriented studies of a wide range of developmental and behavioral phenomena (Gibbs, 1979). The joint emphases on the importance of competence as a factor that reduces vulnerability to psychopathology and on the impact of the environment as a factor in the development of competence puts into sharp relief the nature of the basic problem to which community and developmental psychology must address themselves. That basic question concerns the nature of what Overton (1976) termed developmentally responsive environments.

Sundberg, Snowden, and Reynolds (1978) defined the problem in this way:

We define competence as personal characteristics (knowledge, skills and attitudes) which lead to adaptive payoffs in significant environments. The notion of adaptation points to the need to assess the demands and resources of the environment. Competence suggests an ecological situation; individuals are actively moving through settings which provide "nutrients" or support for certain kinds of coping but hinder others. . . . Consideration of competence raises such questions as, "In which situations can a person best function?" It moves from the "how much" question of traditional trait psychology to "where" and "which" questions concerning the surroundings people will encounter and their coping resources and active interests [p. 196].

Clearly, at both basic scientific and applied practice levels, psychology needs answers to the kinds of questions posed by these challenging reformulations of theory. We need essentially to move toward "an ecology of human development" (Blocher, 1974b).

By now, hopefully, it is apparent to the reader that the developments in theory and practice in the human services that we have traced have brought its mainstream of thinking much closer to the basic traditions, perspectives, and commitments that have distinguished counseling psychology. The antecedents of counseling psychology going back into the guidance movement at the turn of the century were, as Rockwell and Rothney (1961) pointed out, very much a part of a social reform movement. As that movement merged over time with powerful ideas drawn from vocational psychology, developmental psychology, and the psychology of individual differences, the field of counseling psychology evolved around a set of commitments and concepts about human behavior that were very similar to those we have just described in community mental health and social ecology. Many of these concepts were articulated in the counseling literature well before they were reinvented in the area of community psychology.

Counselors were busy working with developing human beings in the natural contexts of school, family, and work place, and dealing with practical problems of daily living while other mental health professionals were still engaged in warehousing human misery in so-called mental hospitals. Consider, for example, the following quotation from E.G. Williamson's book *How to Counsel Students* published in 1939:

All individuals are subject to psychological and social stresses and strains which may produce erratic or unusual behavior, sometimes called abnormal. Sometimes an individual will be alarmed or even terrified simply because he differs from his associates in his reaction to life situations. . . .

When the stresses and strains besetting an individual become too much for his psychological structure to endure, he is forced to find release from the pressure. . . .

Frequently, the counselor can assist in changing the external conditions which may have caused or aggravated the student's disturbance.

. . . The counselor must also have acquired some understanding and appreciation of the possible effects upon the student of social, educational and occupational situations . . . in the future. The counselor will need to predict the effect which these situations will have upon the student. Will they help him grow intellectually, socially and emotionally, or will they lead to maladjustments, wasted efforts and emotional conflicts? . . . The effect of the occupation upon the student, for example, is as important as are the student's chances for success in the job [pp. 174, 175, 176].

As we can see, the rudiments of developmental social ecology were present in the counseling literature more than forty years ago. The notion that the well-springs of both development and pathology are to be found in the interaction between individual and environment, and that the counselor must be able to understand and intervene constructively in that interaction, was articulated clearly and persuasively some twenty years before the bandwagons of community psychology or social ecology were underway.

Over the intervening years this view has been articulated repeatedly in the counseling literature. Wrenn (1962), Mok (1960), and Shoben (1962) all pointed to the roles that counselors can and should play in shaping educational systems to the needs of learners. Danskin, Kennedy, and Friesen (1965) conceptualized counselors as involved with the "ecology of student life." Stewart and Warnath (1965) described the role of the counselor as that of a social engineer. Blocher (1974b) pointed to an integration of theoretical models to provide the foundation for an ecology of human development. Banning and Kaiser (1974) proposed an ecological model for the design of campus environments. Conyne and Clack (1981) further developed ecological formulations as applied to college campuses and communities. Unfortunately, much of the impetus given to counseling psychology by these ideas appears to have been ignored, or at least not carefully nurtured.

We continue to hear today that counseling psychology is still seeking an identity, still struggling to define its uniqueness as compared to clinical psychology, for example. Some of this adolescent-like identity crisis stems from our inability or unwillingness to build upon our own foundations, rather than worrying about what ideas are currently being espoused by our more numerous and more highly visible colleagues in applied psychology. Some of the confusion arises genuinely from the fact, as we have seen, that these other groups have moved closer to the perspectives and approaches long espoused in counseling psychology.

It seems clear that counseling psychology must move in an articulate and forthright way to define itself in terms of the ideas, commitments, and competences that are part of its heritage, and that can clarify its role and contributions in the mainstream of the human services professions. We offer the following attempt at definition as a beginning step in that process. It is one that will guide our discussion of the counseling psychologist in community practice in the pages to follow.

Counseling Psychology Defined

Counseling psychology is a subdiscipline of the science of psychology and a specialty in the practice of professional psychology. As a discipline, counseling psychology draws upon and contributes to psychological knowledge, particularly in the following domains:

1. Vocational behavior, including the development of vocational interests, attitudes, values, and aptitudes and their relationship to vocational satisfaction and effectiveness.
2. Human cognition and cognitive development and their relationships to problem-solving, decision-making and judgment.
3. Human learning and behavior change particularly in their relationships to the acquisition, transfer, and maintenance of coping and mastery behaviors through the life span.
4. Human communication and interpersonal behavior especially within family and other primary group settings that influence developmental processes.
5. The nature of optimal person—environment fit, especially in family, educational, work, and other community settings as these impinge upon the health, happiness, and continuing growth of members.

As a professional practitioner, the counseling psychologist draws upon the science of human behavior to help people in a variety of settings and situations. The counseling psychologist engages in individual and small-group counseling around a variety of concerns involving educational and vocational planning, personal problem-solving and decision-making, family problems, and other activities related to the enhancement of personal growth and effectiveness. Such counseling also focuses on the prevention, removal, or remediation of obstacles to personal growth as these exist in the interaction between the individual and the environment.

The counseling psychologist also engages in consultation with individuals, organizations, and institutions in the society to help enhance the quality of physical, social, and psychological environments as these affect the growth of those who work, study, or live within them.

The counseling psychologist often engages in training a variety of people in basic interpersonal and life skills that can improve their functioning in significant social roles. The counseling psychologist also functions at times as a psychological educator who shares with a variety of others important psychological skills and knowledge needed to help them function more effectively in helping situations and to move to higher levels of personal and social development.

The definition above embraces a broad but finite set of roles, functions, responsibilities, and competencies. It represents a challenging but not impossible set of goals for the discipline and its professional practitioners as they seek to demonstrate both worth and uniqueness within the communities that they seek to serve.

The Training and Competence of Counseling Psychologists

The definition of counseling psychology presented above implies a set of competencies and a level of preparation that merit careful discussion. First, it implies that the counseling psychologist will understand the complexities of person–environment interactions within a variety of social contexts across the full life span. This means that the counseling psychologists must be able to assess, intervene in, and evaluate the dynamics involved in family, neighborhood, school, social agencies, and community institutions as these dynamics impact on the members of client systems.

This role definition also implies that the counseling psychologist will master a number of modes of psychological intervention. While the traditional treatment modes involving individual and group counseling are still major tools in the counseling psychologist's professional repertoire, they are no longer sufficient in themselves. Consultation, training, and organizational development are equally important interventions for the counseling psychologist to utilize.

The availability of multiple modes of intervention and alternative social systems within which they may be employed puts an even greater burden upon the assessment skills of the counseling psychologists. Assessment strategies must be developed and mastered that permit an understanding of individuals as they interact in natural environments. When social systems are the targets of intervention, environmental assessment strategies are at least as important as those that address primarily the psychological functioning of individuals.

Finally, counseling psychologists must understand processes of human development as these apply to both individuals and social organizations. As professionals, we must be able to conceptualize and facilitate growth processes as these arise out of optimal interactions between individuals and environments. We must go beyond the relatively static concept of person–environment "fit" to examine the notion of person–environment "flow," the growth-enhancing engagement between the individual and a learning environment.

To some extent the kind of preparation that is necessary to equip counseling psychologists for the kind of community practice that has been described here represents a departure from the traditional. Intrapsychic theories of personality functioning and the approaches spawned by them, as well as catalogue compilations of symptoms and syndromes in psychopathology and elaborate techniques for intrapsychic assessment may have to be relegated to positions of lesser priority. Strategies for assessing the impact of environments on individual behavior, supervised experiences in consultation, training, and organizational development, and research in family functioning and life span development may need to be given "prime time" exposure in the always hectic and congested curricula of our counseling psychology training programs.

In the subsequent pages of this book we attempt to introduce the reader to a set of topics, principles, and research findings that we think are central to the preparation of a counseling psychologist for community practice.

Scientific Concerns and Commitments in Counseling Psychology

One of the fundamental and distinctive characteristics of the counseling psychologist is his or her commitment to the science of psychology. In this sense there is, or ought to be, a basic unity across the various sectors of experimental and applied psychology.

The professional psychologist in applied practice is no less a scientist than is his colleague in the laboratory. What distinguishes science is adherence to method and a dedication to the pursuit of an understanding of the natural world and the human beings who live in it. The method of science is the method of observation and inference. The scientist observes phenomena in the natural world. These observations supply the raw material out of which empirical reality may be understood. From this basic understanding flows the ability of human beings to predict and control their natural world.

Human beings themselves are, of course, part of the natural world and so are very much within the domain of scientific investigation. Indeed, understanding our own existence and behavior within the natural world is perhaps the ultimate challenge for science.

Interestingly, but unfortunately, the science of psychology has tended to dichotomize itself in terms of a pure science versus applied practice distinction that has limited and to some extent distorted and inhibited both of the branches of the discipline. Clearly, the basic tools of the applied or professional psychologist are similar to those of the experimental psychologist. As Pepinsky and Pepinsky (1954) pointed out long ago, observation and inference are the basic processes out of which counseling develops. As counselors, we have access to clients only through our observation of their actions and reports. We can never really see inside them or even directly see any of the wealth of presumed entities that are inferred out of our myriad personality theories. All of the constructs of aptitudes, anxiety, ego-strength, interest, and insights that we use to understand and assist our clients are in reality merely inferences drawn from our limited and imperfect observations of them.

We are thus in exactly the same situation as other scientists engaged in a quest for understanding of any other aspect of the natural world. Our intent to help unfortunately does not buy us any degree of omniscience or any special powers that render our inferences infallible. Like other scientists we must obey the canons of the philosophy of science or be prepared to wade through the swamps of mysticism and pseudoscientific soothsaying. Two basic rules of evidence govern the conduct of all scientific inquiry: Observations must be intersubjectively testable, that is, objective or available to more than one observer, and they must be replicable, or repeatable over time.

The professional practices of counseling psychologists are based upon scientific knowledge and must follow the basic methods of psychology. We observe as carefully and as precisely as possible, taking care to share and compare our basic observations with appropriate others, including the client. We draw inferences cautiously and carefully, always seeking to remain aware of the extent to which they go beyond the data contained in our observations. We seek continuously to test our inferences against new observations. Our understandings are to be accepted and acted upon only until they are modified or refuted by later investigation.

As professional psychologists we intervene in human systems and human lives on the basis of our limited and tentative knowledge and understanding. It is of even greater importance for us to proceed cautiously and vigilantly in our practice than it is for the experimental psychologist, who has the luxury of the laboratory rather than a field setting.

As counseling psychologists we must think rigorously about human systems. We must distinguish between knowledge claims that are verifiable and those that are only presumed. We must think carefully and critically. We typically use the word *theory* in very sloppy and careless ways, for example. A scientific theory is not merely a set of untestable assumptions loosely strung together, nor is it a recipe or prescription to be used in a mechanistic way. A scientific theory is a way of organizing what is known about a phenomenon to generate a set of interrelated, plausible, and *refutable* propositions about what is unknown. As we work with human systems we are constantly engaged in building, testing, and modifying our theories. This process is the science of professional practice. In the next chapter we will look at a set of basic conceptual tools for scientific practice drawn from general systems theory.

References

Albee, G. W. The uncertain future of clinical psychology. *American Psychologist*, 1970, *25*, 1071–1080.

Allport, G. W. *Pattern and growth in personality*. New York: Holt, Rinehart & Winston, 1963.

Bandura, A. Self-efficacy: Toward a unifying theory of behavior change. *Psychological Review*, 1977, *84*, 191–215.

Banning, J. H., & Kaiser, L. An ecological perspective and model for campus design. *Personnel and Guidance Journal*, 1974, *52* 370–375.

Barker, R.G. Wanted: An eco-behavioral science. In E.P. Willems & L. P. Raush (Eds.), *Naturalistic viewpoints in psychological research*. New York: Holt, Rinehart & Winston, 1973.

Blocher, D. H. *Developmental counseling*. New York: Ronald Press, 1974. (a)

Blocher, D. H. Toward an ecology of student development. *Personnel and Guidance Journal*, 1974, *52*, 360–365. (b)

Bloom, B. L. Prevention of mental health disorders: Recent advances in theory and practice. *Community Mental Health Journal*, 1979, *75*, 179–191.

Bradshaw, C. E. The poverty culture. *Childhood Education*, 1969, *46* (2), 79–84.

Bronfenbrenner, U. *The ecology of human development*. Cambridge, Mass.: Harvard University Press, 1979.

Caplan, N. & Nelson, S. D. On being useful: The nature and consequence of research on social problems. *American Psychologist*, 1973, *28* (3), 199–363.

Conyne, R.K., & Clack, R.J. *Environmental assessment and design*. New York: Praeger, 1981.

Danskin, D., Kennedy, C. E., & Friesen, W. S. Guidance—the ecology of students. *The Personnel and Guidance Journal*, 1965, *45*, 130–135.

Dohrenwend, B. P., & Dohrenwend, B. S. *Social status and psychological disorder*. New York: Wiley, 1969.

Eysenck, H. J. *Behavior therapy and the neuroses*. New York: Pergamon Press, 1960.

Frank, L. Society as the patient. *American Journal of Sociology*, 1936, *42*, 335–344.

Greenblatt, M., Emery, P.E., & Glueck, B. *Psychiatric research report: Poverty and mental health*, No. 1. Washington: American Psychiatric Association, 1967.

Gibbs, J. C. The meaning of ecologically oriented inquiry in contemporary psychology. *American Psychologist*, 1979, *34*, 127–140.

Halleck, S. L. *Politics of therapy*. New York: Science House, 1971.

Hersch, C. The discontent explosion in mental health. *American Psychologist*, 1968, *23*, 497–506.

Hinkle, L E., Jr. Relating biochemical, physiological, and psychological disorders to the social environment. *Archives of Environmental Health*, 1968, *16*, 77–82.

Hobbs, N. Helping disturbed children: Psychological and ecological strategies. *American Psychologist*, 1966, *21*, 1105–1115.

Iscoe, I. Community psychology and the competent community. *American Psychologist*, 1974, *29*, 611–613.

Jahoda, M. Toward a social psychology of mental health. In M. J. E. Senn (Ed.), *Symposium on the healthy personality*. Josiah Macy Jr. Foundation, 1950.

Kelly, J. G. Ecological constraints on mental health services. *American Psychologist*, 1966, *21*, 535–539.

Lehman, S. Community and community psychology. *American Psychologist*, 1971, *26*, 544–560.

Maier, S. F., & Seligmann, M. E. P. Learned helplessness: Theory and evidence. *Journal of Experimental Psychology: General*, 1976, *105*, 3–46.

Maslow, A. H. *Toward a psychology of being*. Princeton, N. J.: Van Nostrand, 1968.

Masterpasqua, F. Toward a synergism of developmental and community psychology. *American Psychologist*, 1981, *36*, 782–786.

Menninger, K. *The vital balance*. New York: Viking, 1964.

Mischel, W. Toward a cognitive social learning reconceptualization of personality. *Psychological Review*, 1973, *80*, 252–283.

Mok, P. *A view from within*. New York: Garden Press, 1960.

Overton, W. Environmental ontogeny: A cognitive view. In K. F. Riegel & J. A. Meacham (Eds.), *The developing individual in a changing world*. Chicago: Aldine, 1976.

Pepinsky, H., & Pepinsky, P. *Counseling: Theory and practice*. New York: Ronald Press, 1954.

Piaget, J. *The origins of intelligence in children*. New York: International Press, 1952.

Ripley, S. D., & Beuchner, H. K. Ecosystem science as a point of synthesis. *Daedalus*, 1967, *96*, 1192–1199.

Rockwell, P., & Rothney, J. Some social ideas of pioneers in the guidance movement. *The Personnel and Guidance Journal*, 1961, *40*, 349–354.

Roe, A. Community resources centers. *American Psychologist*, 1970, *25*, 1033–1040.

Rogers, C. Toward becoming a fully functioning person. In A. W. Combs (Ed.), *Perceiving, behaving, becoming*. Washington: Yearbook, Association for Supervision and Curriculum Development, 1962.

Sarason, S. An asocial psychology and a misdirected clinical psychology. *American Psychologist*, 1981, *36* (8), 827–835.

Sarason, S. B. Community psychology, networks and Mr. Everyman. *American Psychologist*, 1976, *31*, 317–328.

Schulberg, A. C. Challenge of human services programs for psychologists. *American Psychologist*, 1972, *27*, 566–572.

Sharma, S. L. A historical background of the development of nosology in psychiatry and psychology. *American Psychologist*, 1970, *25*, 248–253.

Shoben, E.J. Toward a concept of the normal personality, *American Psychologist*, 1957, *12*, 183–190.

Shoben, E. J., Jr. Guidance: Remedial function or social reconstruction? *Harvard Educational Review*, 1962, *32*, 430–443.

Smith, M. B. "Mental health" reconsidered: A special case of the problem of values in psychology. *American Psychologist*, 1961, *16*, 299–306.

Stewart, L., & Warnath, C. *The counselor and society*. Boston: Houghton-Mifflin, 1965.

Suinn, R.M. Behavior pathology. In M.E. Meur (Ed.), *Foundations of contemporary psychology*. New York: Oxford University Press, 1979, pp. 651–679.

Sundberg, N. A., Snowden, L. R., & Reynolds, W. M. Toward assessment of personal competence and incompetence in life situations. *Annual Re-*

view of Psychology, 1978, Palo Alto: Annual Reviews, 1978, *29*, 179–221.

Szasz, T. S. *The myth of mental illness*. New York: Haber, 1961.

Tharp, R. G., & Wetzel, R. J. *Behavior modification in the natural environment*. New York and London: Academic Press, 1969.

Warren, S. F. A useful ecobehavioral perspective for applied behavior analysis. In A. Rogers-Warren, & S. F. Warren (Eds.). *Ecological perspectives in behavioral analysis*. Baltimore: University Park Press, 1977, pp. 173–196.

White, R. Motivation reconsidered: The concept of competence. *Psychological Review*, 1959, *66*, 297–333.

White, R. The concept of healthy personality: What do we really mean? *The Counseling Psychologist*, 1973, *4*, 3–12.

Williamson, E. G. *How to counsel students*. New York: McGraw-Hill, 1939.

Wrenn, C. G. *The counselor in a changing world*. Washington: American Personnel and Guidance Association. 1962.

Zax, M. History and background of the community mental health movement. In M. S. Gibbs, J. R. Lachenmeyer, & J. Sigel, *Community Psychology*. New York: Gardner Press, 1980, pp. 1–28.

2

The Community as Client

As we saw in chapter 1, both the historical roots from which counseling psychology emerged and the ideas posed by modern approaches to community psychology and social ecology have posed a challenge to us. This challenge involves helping individuals, as well as the organizations they create, to cope more effectively with the problems, opportunities, and stresses of everyday life in their natural environments.

Much of the psychological theory and research upon which we have focused in the past is less than adequate to meet the present challenge. We need ways to construe and conceptualize the behavior of human beings as they interact in the context of the groups and institutions that define their identities and largely control their destinies.

As O'Neill (1981) has pointed out, community psychology has been largely unable to define the domain of knowledge with which it is most concerned. He makes the case that while an individual psychology that fixates primarily upon individual differences, particularly *pathological* individual differences, may be of limited utility for community practice, other aspects of individual functioning may be of major significance.

Specifically, O'Neill proposes that community psychology be involved with cognitive social psychology, that is, with the study of social behavior based on knowledge of the processes of human thinking. Such a cognitive social psychology focuses upon the ways in which people gather, interpret, and use information (Taylor, 1976).

Goodstein and Sandler (1978) conceptualized community psychology as concerned with systems analysis, organizational development and restructuring, creation of settings, and evaluation research. Cognitive social psychology is concerned precisely with how people think about problems and issues involved in such processes.

As counseling psychologists intervene in the wide variety of human systems situations and problems encountered in community practice, they actually engage primarily in changing the ways in which individual human beings think about and act in those social organizations. One of the dangers in family counseling, group work, consultation, or organizational development is that we come to think of a social group as possessing some kind of mystique, or life of its own. All social organizations are composed of individuals. There is no "group personality," nor do organizations possess any of the actual properties of organisms.

In working with social organizations we are really concerned with how individual human beings behave in interaction with other human beings. In intervening we actually deal with processes that differ primarily only in complexity from those that we work with in individual counseling. The fundamental tools that we use in consultation, or group work, or organizational development are based upon sensitivity and understanding of human needs, values, and characteristics.

General Systems Theory

Unfortunately, many of the concepts drawn from traditional personality theory have only limited usefulness in more complex social situations. The problem with many of these constructs is that they tend to obscure or ignore the person–environment transactions that are at the root of social behavior. We need conceptual approaches that focus on the linkages and relationships that connect people with each other and with larger social environments.

One approach that seems able to deal with the complexities of these problems is called general systems theory. A systems analysis approach has been described as one that enables the observer to understand the overall picture in an organization. Thoreson (1968) pointed out that a systems approach is particularly useful in counseling because it recognizes the fact that counseling deals with behavior change, and that the behavior of a client is inextricably linked to the forces at work in the social environment.

A systems approach is a way of organizing information and developing concepts about any complex phenomenon. One of the major features of the systems approach is that it focuses upon the realization of specific goals. That is, in a systems analysis, we look first and foremost at the purposes and outcomes of a given activity or pattern of performance.

Systems theory is concerned with developing coherent and con-

cise theoretical frameworks for understanding complex sets of relationships in the empirical world. Many advantages accrue to the achievement of unifying theoretical models with which to study our complex world. With such frameworks, scholars and professionals from different disciplines can communicate more clearly about the interrelationships that govern the functioning of communities and other complicated social organizations. The effects of interventions on the operation of interrelated units can be traced, and the impact of the interventions can be more fully evaluated.

A system is a device, procedure, or scheme that behaves according to some pattern. Its function is to operate on some quantity that may consist of information, energy, or matter, or any combination of the three (Ellis & Ludwig, 1962). For example, a jet airplane engine converts certain chemical fuels into thrust. In any system there is some *input*, an operating *process*, and an *output* that is a product or consequence of the process.

Open and Closed Systems

Systems can be classified into two general categories, *open* and *closed*. Closed systems are those that admit no matter from outside themselves. They are subject to entropy, or a general running down or disorganization. A closed system has no restorative properties. A candle burning in a bell jar, or an automobile battery without a generator, are examples of closed systems. When their supply of energy is exhausted, they fail to function.

Open systems, on the other hand have certain characteristics that distinguish them (Griffiths, 1964). They *exchange* matter, energy, or information with their environments. Our burning candle inside the bell jar flickers and starts to die as its oxygen is exhausted. When we remove the bell jar, however, and allow the candle to exchange oxygen and carbon dioxide with the atmosphere, its environment, we have created an open system. The flame grows again to normal size and maintains a *steady-state* as long as it can transact with its environment. Such open systems are *self-regulating*. A sudden draft may cause our candle to flicker, but when the draft ends, the flame regains its normal characteristics.

Open systems also tend to display equifinality, that is, identical results can be obtained from different sets of beginning conditions. Two babies (open systems), one born prematurely, the other born at full term, illustrate this point. The babies may look very different at birth and may be in different stages of development. However, given adequate care and nutrition, the differences tend to disappear over time. Even though the initial states may differ, human beings generally attain similar states of physical development.

Another property of open systems is that they maintain their steady states through the interplay of their component parts, or subsystems, which operate together in dependable ways as functional processes. In the jet engine, for example, pumps deliver fuel to a burner, induction fans bring air into the engine to be heated, exhaust pipes discharge the air creating thrust. The engine operates in a steady state *only* as long as its component parts continue to function in their intended ways.

Open systems also maintain their steady states through *feedback* processes. The concept of feedback is of major importance in general systems approaches. Feedback refers to that portion of the output of a system that is put back into inputs to affect succeeding outputs. Feedback makes it possible for the system to adjust its future conduct by reference to past performance. The automatic pilot of an aircraft, for example, responds to changes in the aircraft's position or attitude and makes new inputs to the control surfaces.

As we can see, then, open systems achieve remarkable properties through their ability to interact with their environments. General systems theory enables us to identify and understand these properties and, eventually, to conserve or enhance them.

Cybernetics and Systems

Systems approaches have made considerable use of concepts taken from the field of cybernetics, or simulation of human cognitive processes. The term *cybernetics* was coined by Norbert Wiener (1948) to describe the processes involved in the study of control and communications problems between human beings and computers. The word *cybernetics* is taken from the Greek word for steersman and is indicative of the problems that arise in maintaining full human control over very complex processes. In a real sense this is the problem involved in modern community life. The basic concepts of cybernetics are very relevant to us, then, as we attempt to maintain or restore human control to complex community processes. Wiener (1948) specified three primary concepts in cybernetics that are crucial in a systems analysis approach. These are *control, entropy*, and *feedback*. We have briefly mentioned the latter two in the above discussion of the general systems model.

Of the three concepts, however, control is the most fundamental. It focuses upon the procedures and devices used to regulate the various processes at work within a system. In social systems such as communities, control is attempted or exercised through *planning*. Planning allows human beings to maintain the system at a desirable level and kind of output, or to induce positive changes in the system as these are required to satisfy emerging human needs and goals. In community life, planning is, as someone once said, merely intelligent cooperation with the inevitable. Human control of the physical and social world arises out of successful planning.

Entropy denotes the tendency of any system to "run down" or stagnate. It is the process by which systems tend to experience progressive deterioration and progressive failure to function in goal-directed ways. The concept of entropy is of major importance to the counseling psychologist in community practice because it centers on the causes of disorder or malfunctions within systems. When we see chaotic, disorganized communities in which human needs are chronically unmet, we are face to face with the images of entropy, and those images are never pretty ones.

The point of view taken in this book is that a fundamental goal of the counseling psychologist in community practice is to help reduce entropy within community systems. This is accomplished, not by some masterpiece of centralized planning, but through involving community members in *self-directed* changes toward what John Gardner (1962) has called "self-renewal."

The third key cybernetics concept that is of major importance in systems analysis is *feedback*. As we noted earlier, feedback denotes the mutual exchange of information that occurs within a system. Feedback becomes possible when "loops" that connect one component of a system with another are closed or joined so that part of the outputs of one component becomes available in the form of information as an input for another. Thus, mutual regulation can occur.

Feedback can operate in two ways: It can function to counteract deviation from preset standards and so maintain the steady-state operation of the system. The household furnace thermostat is a simple example of this kind of feedback loop. Feedback can also, however, lead to *deviation amplification*. In this type of feedback situation, reciprocal relationships and elements are simultaneously influencing each other to increase deviation. A delinquent gang of juveniles, or a group of convicts within a prison system, may function to amplify deviation from social norms and to escalate the frequency and severity of offenses. Not all deviation amplification may be bad, however. Information about deplorable social conditions or corruption disseminated by a crusading newspaper editor may arouse and awaken the public to change conditions through innovative and concerted changes.

Applying Systems Theory

In most of the examples cited above we dealt with relatively simple, natural or mechanical processes. General systems theory, however, allows us to use the same structure to examine complex social patterns, processes, and problems that define a community.

Systems theory allows us to understand that a change in one part of a community can have important and perhaps unforeseen consequences in another part of the community. It shows that changes in community functioning can be accomplished by *indirect* as well as *direct* interventions and that these interventions may be aimed at a variety of targets or subsystems. It thus creates multiple possibilities or strategies for our helping processes. The term *system*, then, emphasizes that an overall functional process, rather than a mere piecemeal collection of isolated events, is being considered.

Since many systems are related to other systems, and may in fact operate as part of them, a systems approach may be expanded or contracted to focus upon a desired process without obscuring or ignoring the essential relationships that tie it to larger or smaller systems. This is, then, a box within a box within a box way of viewing the world. For example, in the physical world, a systems approach could encompass the study of the nature of the universe at one extreme, and yet could be contracted to deal in the same format with the nuclear structure of a single atom.

Systems theory highlights the interrelationships and interconnectedness among different aspects of a phenomenon. It is this property that makes it such a powerful tool for understanding and intervening in communities.

The essence of a community is interdependence. The very concept of community arises out of the consideration of those things that people share or hold in common. These may include a geographical area or a culture with attendant customs and mores, or may arise out of commitment to a specific set of values, beliefs, or goals. An inevitable consequence of community membership is, however, interdependence with other members. Communities vary enormously, of course, in size and complexity. Large, modern, urban communities represent vastly complex systems, yet relatively simple system failures such as power blackouts, damage from floods or storms, or the impact of strikes and riots remind its members quickly and vividly of how fragile is the fabric of interdependence that sustains the steady-state outputs of the overall system.

Systems theory gives us a way of understanding how these complex, highly interdependent human inventions that we call communities operate. It allows us to identify key variables, causes, or components that enhance or inhibit the functioning of the overall community and the consequent satisfaction or frustration of human needs and purposes.

The Community as Social System

A basic premise that is taken in this book is the view that community characteristics can be understood and managed in the interests of those human beings who live in that system and that one of the prime goals of the counseling psychologist in community practice is to help to turn that possibility into a reality.

A community is a social system that exists to achieve objectives through collective effort; it is, among other things, an organization, or perhaps more accurately, an organization of organizations. Obviously, the patterns of organization through which people combine to meet their needs are myriad. Organizations take forms and shapes that reflect their size, composition, longevity, cohesiveness, and, not least, the nature of the culture from which they draw their existence. A basic thesis of modern behavioral science is that the forms and patterns of groups, organizations, and communities are among the basic determinants of the behaviors of their members. Following from this assumption, then, is the thesis that to understand fully the behavior of individuals, one must also understand the operation of those social systems within which they work, live, and interact.

Most of us, unfortunately, take social system dynamics pretty much for granted. At least partly, this is because one of the basic ingredients in any community is *mutuality*. Without some degree of mutuality of purposes, beliefs, and needs, communities would never come into being, let alone endure.

Mutuality, as well as the cohesiveness that is generated from it, is the adhesive that holds our communities together. That same mutuality, however, tends to obscure the questions, doubts, and uncertainties that are needed to move the community forward.

Precisely because most communities have a relatively high degree of consensus about fundamental premises and assumptions, they are difficult to change, even when the need for planned change is painfully apparent. Communities tend to be engines with heavy flywheels, that is, most of their energy goes into the *maintenance* of activity rather than into self-examination or evaluation. Within the common consensual space that defines a community, *one* way of doing and perceiving all too quickly becomes *the* way and finally the *only* way. This consensual bond often inhibits the capacity of the community to respond in planned and rational ways to new problems or opportunities. In systems terms, little output is made available for feedback.

Changing Social Systems

Someone once said that the best way to understand a social system is to try to change it. Certainly, this view seems to have considerable validity when applied to communities. The concept of change represents the most pervasive and universal phenomenon in our world. We live in a social and physical world that is kaleidoscopic in nature. Human existence is always dynamic, never static.

Despite its universality or perhaps because of it, change is often frightening. The very word connotes movement into the unknown with all of the fear that attaches to that which is uncertain and unpredictable.

From a systems view change is not something that we induce or avoid. It is a natural property of the system. Just as mountains erode, rivers deepen, and people grow older, we all encounter new roles and situations whether we will it or not. The one freedom that we can never hope to exercise is the freedom to stay the same, or to have our world remain the same. Not all things change at the same rate, however. Our ability to harness the power of nature, for example, has far outstripped our ability to use that power constructively and for humane purposes.

From a systems standpoint in our communities, we are interested not merely in inducing change. As we noted all systems change all of the time. The new suburban community of twenty-five or thirty years ago, busy constructing elementary schools, swimming pools, and parks to keep pace with the output of its maternity hospitals, is now a kind of ghost town of empty bedrooms, closing schools, deserted playgrounds, and outmoded shopping centers. It and its citizens have changed through the inexorable processes of time.

We are interested in *controlling* change, then, and in shaping ongoing and inevitable change processes to suit our fundamental human goals and purposes. From a systems point of view, the *planning process* may be considered the primary vehicle for accomplishing orderly, goal-directed change.

Social systems, however, unlike many systems in the physical world, must take into account human resistance to change, or rather human resistance to planning for and rationally accommodating to inevitable change. In the past, human reluctance to deal actively and in a planned manner with problems of change often took the form of a comforting belief in what William Stanley (1964) termed the cult of "automatic adjustment." People were once able to look at the changes around them secure in the illusion that their world was protected from disaster by all sorts of mysterious, but omnipotent self-regulating mechanisms. Man had but to wait patiently for these principles to assert themselves, and above all refrain from interfering with them.

Prices would be regulated by supply and demand, population would be controlled by food supply, good genes would assure their own survival through the rigors of economic competition. These beliefs that now seem so naive and self-deceptive were acted upon with devastating consequences. Millions of Irish were allowed to starve to avoid interfering with the Malthusian Theorem. Precious, non-renewable natural resources were pillaged and wasted while we waited for economic principles to assert themselves.

Twentieth-century men and women, shocked and disillusioned by wars, famines, depressions, genocide, and atomic devastation, have finally awakened to the awesome possibilities inherent in their *own* power. It *is* possible for us to poison our own atmosphere, to annihilate our own species, and to sabotage our own heredity.

We are now also in the process of being deprived of another comforting if naive illusion. We are awakening to the fact that we cannot rely blindly upon either the wisdom or good intentions of giant formal organizations, whether private or public, to protect and defend our individual or local interests. Great bureaucracies, either corporate or governmental, can grind our freedoms and aspirations under their ponderous wheels.

With the collapse of theories of automatic adjustment and a loss of faith in the blessings of bureaucracies has come the recognition that people must participate in the planned transformation of their world or forfeit their right to live in it as free men and women.

Values and Planned Change

One of the reasons for the relatively slow progress of our capacity to design and manage effective communities is, of course, the difficulty in a pluralistic society of obtaining reasonable levels of consensus about desired and valued directions for planned change in social systems. As we have seen, social planning does not produce change, it merely attempts to insure that change represents *improvement*. Improvement, however, is very much a value-laden concept that is sure to be variously defined by those whose value orientations differ.

Interestingly enough, people seem to mobilize around their value structures much more readily when changes in social systems are being considered than when much more profound or devastating changes in other areas of life occur. Human beings seem relatively complacent when a new and deadlier nuclear bomb is built that can incinerate them, they seem relatively unconcerned while their atmosphere and drinking water are slowly but surely poisoned, and they remain accepting when the noise levels around them reach almost diabolical levels from sonic booms and jet airplanes. These same people may, however, react with great emotional intensity to the merger of school districts, to changes in zoning regulations, or to efforts to reduce discrimination in housing or employment.

Despite such vast and often seemingly irrational differences in sensitivity to social change, obviously real value questions exist around all efforts to control social change through planning. Counseling psychologists and other professionals in community practice can be assured that their own personal and professional values are neither timeless nor universal. As professionals, their role is not to attempt to impose arbitrarily their own values on the communities they serve, although, like all citizens, they have a right to be advocates for their beliefs and values through the regular political processes of the community.

The community oriented counseling psychologist cannot expect to find that his or her own values are always shared completely by those agencies, groups, or individuals who become clients for counseling or consultation. Neither can a professional ever be sure that the final outcomes of a social change process will optimally reflect his or her own priorities and preferences. The consultant can, however, consistently reflect in his or her own professional behavior a set of values about the nature of social change processes in a democratic society that can provide an ethical and value structure around which to orient professional responsibilities and obligations.

Several general principles about the nature of planned change are discussed below.

Collaborative Planning

The first general organizing principle relevant to social change processes in a democratic society is that they should be *collaborative*. A democratic change process is collaborative in at least two ways. First, it is built around the common interests of the individuals and groups involved. Democratic change is not imposed from on high by either politicians or well-meaning but fallible do-gooders. The planned change process should provide discussions and interactions aimed at helping all those whose lives the proposed change will affect develop mutual confidence that their own legitimate needs and values will be considered in the process and be reflected in the ultimate outcome. When needs, interests, and values conflict, as they are certain to do at times, the differences should be dealt with directly and openly and be resolved through democratic processes.

A second vital aspect of collaborative change involves basic cooperation between professionals and community members. The facilitation of planned community change often requires the skills, knowledge, and expertise possessed by well-prepared professionals. Knowledge of social behavior, developmental needs, and specialized resources may be very important. Equally important, however, is that professionals are able to communicate genuine respect, understanding, and appreciation for community members as they share in the collaborative planning process. There is, as Kelly (1971) notes, a special kind of humility needed for successful community consultation that is often missing in the behavior of professional psychologists. As he puts it, community consultation is an antidote for arrogance.

Educational Participation

A second basic principle of the democratic change process is that it should be genuinely *educational* in nature—that is, the process should optimally be a growth-producing experience for those who participate. A successful community planning venture should enrich the human resources available to the community and prepare it to work more effectively in meeting the needs of its members in the future. The ultimate goal of the community consultant is the development of what Iscoe (1974) called "the competent community."

As individuals, community members need to learn skills in making contributions to group planning and decision making. In many situations community members need to develop positive attitudes about the nature of community planning. They need to experience as a reality the opportunity to participate in a successful and genuinely democratic process through which they can control their own lives and contribute to a better quality of life for their neighbors. Broad involvement and participation in community planning is based upon educational as well as democratic values.

The success of a community planning operation should be assessed on several process as well as outcome criteria. Consultants should be concerned that the planning process has broadened the base of leadership in the community, helping people to perform in new and more responsible roles and thus making greater contributions than before. The process should optimally promote greater mutual trust and respect across various segments or groups in the community. Increased openness of communication among groups should also result.

Experimental Change

A third principle of democratic change processes is that they are *experimental*. Any planned innovation represents an experiment, not a panacea. Changes that are viewed within a rigidly structured or ideological frame of reference as ultimate solutions to long-standing problems are likely merely to engender disappointment and disillusionment among their advocates. Every social experiment should be approached with caution and a degree of tentativeness and the ability and willingness to evaluate the outcome and, when necessary, return to the drawing board.

One of the major contributions of the counseling psychologist in community practice is to help build in effective evaluation components to programs and projects with which he or she works. The experimental attitude toward innovations and a firm recognition of the necessity for careful evaluation are both a part of the ethical framework for democratic social change.

Task-Oriented Change

A final basic principle of the democratic process of planned social change is that it should be oriented toward and evaluated in terms of task relevance. The process of planned social change should be oriented around the nature of the problem to be solved, or the human needs to be met, rather than around the needs for power, prestige, or recognition of those who originate or attempt to manipulate the change process for their selfish rather than social purposes. At times psychologists in community practice will encounter determined and clever attempts to manipulate them to the purposes of power-hungry groups or individuals.

The psychologist must be mature enough and secure enough to

recognize continuously the social-psychological fact that strong emotional identification with ideas and proposals may be either an asset or a liability in given situations. Such identifications are, of course, an asset in that they may mobilize powerful motivations to work for the adoption of a plan or program. On the other hand, they may also trigger self-serving and blindly rigid resistance to accepting compromises or modifications that have merit. One of the functions of professionals in the planning process is to help planning and advocacy groups to recognize and deal with their own motivations out of awareness rather than self-deception.

Resistance to Change

Facilitating planned change in social systems using the democratic principles described above is rather clearly analogous to the counseling processes that are utilized with individual clients. In both kinds of processes we avoid imposing arbitrary values on clients or attempting to coerce them into attempting new behaviors. Even when we have individual community members as clients, however, we recognize the possibility of various forms of resistance and opposition to counseling goals becoming part of the change process.

When we work with the community or, more typically, community groups and agencies as client, it should not be surprising that the resistance phenomenon is no less a problem than in individual counseling. In one sense working with a community clientele involves helping such groups and organizations improve their skills and resources for solving problems. Essentially, this means equipping the client system with an improved set of coping behaviors with which to deal with the continual disequilibrium that is an inevitable part of the operation of any dynamic human system. For a social system this kind of self-renewal process may be defined as the progressive institutionalization of a problem-solving approach that is optimally adaptive, flexible, and effective.

Viewed in this way, from the standpoint of the consultant, our goals seem so honorable, desirable, and rational that the magnitude of the resistance that we encounter may be difficult to understand and accept. Many times we as consultants become profoundly discouraged and even personally insulted when we feel the intensity of that resistance.

Actually, resistance from human systems stems from a variety of sources. As we noted earlier, social systems are composed of individual human beings. As Watson (1967) pointed out, human behavior is naturally and fundamentally resistant to attempts at influence or imposed changes. The central individual characteristics in human beings that we call personality are often the product of homeostatic mechanisms, habit acquisition, selective perception and retention, and other psychological processes that very properly provide stability and continuity to human behavior and experience.

Individuals resist attempts at influence for many reasons, some which are essentially irrational. Personal security is often built up more from the repetition of behavior patterns than from their adaptive value. We generally understand and accept the irrationality and resistive qualities of individual human beings at least when we engage in counseling with them. Strangely enough, however, when we work with people in social groups and organizations, we seem less able to appreciate and accept resistance and irrationality. We may be hurt or discouraged by behavior from an organization that we would see as an acceptable and predictable dynamic of individual behavior in a counseling situation.

Actually, individual resistance phenomena often tend to be compounded and magnified in social systems. Social systems, whether families, agencies, or other institutions, tend to be anchor points around which individuals organize and orient their personal identities and security. Conformity to the norms of social systems, no matter how pathological or self-defeating they may be, may become a source of personal security and so be zealously protected.

By meeting needs for security and continuity in people's lives, social systems build up strong cohesive forces and vested interests that are certain to resist efforts to alter them, even for clear and rational reasons and purposes. In fact, as we noted earlier, change is a frightening word that is often clothed in the safer-seeming terms of education, training, reorientation, or therapy.

Resistance and Opposition

In any influence attempt with a human system, whether group or individual, it is clear that some basic negative reactions will occur. Some of these will be rational and some will be irrational. Since coping and responding to rational versus irrational responses represent quite different problems for the consultant, a basic distinction between the two kinds of counterinfluencing forces is helpful.

For this reason we call those responses to suggestion or influence attempts that are rational and rooted in practical and reality-oriented objections and considerations *opposition*. Those forces that are essentially irrational and rooted in the relationship dynamics between the change agent and the individual or group responding to the influence attempt, we call *resistance*. Both are natural and expected properties of human systems, and neither are totally destructive nor undesirable.

All efforts at planned change have costs attached to them. At the very least they require the expenditure of time, energy, money, and other precious resources. In some instances they are, unavoidably, the sources of considerable discomfort, inconvenience, and anxiety for system members.

In situations where the outcomes of planning may be unclear, or the directions and objectives for changes appear uncertain, rational, practical, and well-founded sources of opposition to a plan or proposal almost always exist and are usually voiced. The dialogue set in motion by these sources of opposition is actually a necessary and productive component in the planning process. It helps make certain that attention will be directed to errors or shortcomings in the proposals under consideration, that cost–benefit relationships will be carefully weighed, and that practical solutions to difficulties will be worked through.

Part of the role of a community consultant is to insure a full airing and consideration of opposition views and to prevent an overly enthusiastic group of advocates from steamrolling over any opposition. Opposition is best dealt with in careful, open, and thoughtful consideration allowing ample time for serious discussion and debate.

Resistance, as we noted, is a separate and somewhat different phenomenon. Resistance is a product of the relationship dynamics operating in a group. When members feel their autonomy threatened by either overt domination or subtle manipulation, resistance is triggered. Resistance is often an indirect and irrational response. It may take the form of direct hostility, but it is often masked in passive and indirectly expressed negative reactions. Resistance is difficult to deal with directly because it is essentially a hydraulic phenomenon—that is, the harder one party pushes an influence attempt, the stronger is the resisting force elicited.

Generally, when resistance is clearly identified, the appropriate approach is a reduction in the immediate influence attempt and an invitation for a frank discussion of both the content and feeling aspects of the overall situation. A renegotiation of roles and relationships as well as of objectives may be needed to reduce resistance.

The Developmentally Responsive Community

We observed in chapter 1 that the unique contribution of the counseling psychologist in community practice arose from the fact that communities are social inventions that exert powerful influences upon the course of the individual's development. Communities provide the all-important context in which people grow. As such, communities vary widely in their capacity to nurture and sustain that growth.

If we take the goal of optimal opportunity for human growth and development seriously as a value for social organization, then we become vitally interested in the nature of those kinds of learning environments within the community that are responsive and potent in initiating and sustaining growth-producing interactions between individuals and the social systems within which they learn, live, and work.

Masterpasqua (1981) pointed out that community psychology has had difficulty in defining clearly the nature of conditions which can be articulated as goals for social advocacy. In a sense the question is this: What is the nature of the person–community interactions which can provide each member with a reasonable chance to develop his or her full human potentials and thereby realize an optimally fulfilling, satisfying, and productive life?

It would be pretentious to suppose that we have all of the needed knowledge with which to answer this question fully and unequivocally. Yet our knowledge of human development has given us at least a set of partial answers. We can specify several basic patterns of person–environment interaction which, when they occur at optimal levels, define the operation of a developmentally potent environment. Obviously, these characteristics of potent developmental environments must be superimposed on a set of basic conditions that enable people simply to maintain reasonable human life and dignity. The latter conditions, of course, include adequate housing, safety, nutrition, health care, and freedom within law.

Beyond these common decencies, what should our communities aspire to provide? We can begin by describing the kinds of person–environment interactions that have been found to be associated with personal growth and development (Blocher, 1977). These may be viewed as somewhat similar to the well-known necessary and sufficient conditions for therapeutic change that Carl Rogers (1957) articulated twenty-five years ago. These conditions for developmental change together constitute the prototypical elements for an ecology of human development.

1. *Challenge*. A developmentally responsive environment provides an optimal mismatch between the past or chronic level of stimulation for its members and the immediate or acute level represented in tasks and opportunities with which its members are confronted. Levels of stimulation in an environment are determined by the amount of novelty, complexity, ambiguity, abstraction, and emotional intensity that are experienced by the individual. When levels of stimulation are very high, as in highly disorganized, dangerous, or very rapidly changing situations, the individual may disengage physically or psychologically, or even react with panic. When, on the other hand, all situations are rigidly controlled or stereotyped, as in prisons or mental hospitals or even some school situations, the individual has little incentive or opportunity to use his or her talents and capacities or to experiment with new behaviors. Sometimes extremely restrictive or impoverished physical surroundings reduce challenge and result in a kind of stimulus deprivation. Special programs like Head Start and some of the camping, travel, or physical achievement programs have been used to increase challenge for children and adolescents from deprived environments.

2. *Involvement*. By involvement we refer to the degree to which individuals are allowed to participate actively in responsible social roles and invest self-esteem and other psychological or material values in the outcome of their own performances. In a sense, involvement means being allowed to take responsibility for one's own life and being able to make positive contributions to the lives of others. In some communities many members are prejudged as incompetent, inadequate, and unable to take responsibility for themselves or their families. These kinds of prejudgments have tremendous potential for becoming self-fulfilling prophecies. On the other hand, involvement can sometimes be too high and produce defeat and discouragement.

3. *Support*. Human beings, particularly as they encounter challenging or stress-producing situations, need to experience optimal levels of support. Support can be defined as a network of positive, empathic, and caring relationships, along with reasonably adequate physical or material resources that allow the community member to cope successfully with stress-producing situations. Optimal levels of support help people to cope with the stress involved in challenging and involving situations that can lead to growth in coping skills, confidence, and self-esteem.

4. *Structure*. Structure refers to the presence of clear, consistent, and rational expectations, strategies, or consequences for behavior within a community setting. The presence of structure allows community members to plan, organize, and build rational strategies for

meeting their needs and aspirations. When rules, expectations, or consequences are inconsistent, arbitrary or unreasonable, and unjust, planning, achievement, gratification-deferral, or self-regulating strategies for living have little meaning or utility. Systematic discrimination, corruption, or breakdowns in the justice system, unsafe and violent neighborhoods, or untreated chronic diseases all lead to a breakdown in the structures through which people are able to plan and take responsibility for their lives and their actions. Such conditions breed apathy, fatalism, alienation, and other essentially passive defenses against pain, disappointment, and frustration.

5. *Feedback.* The final pattern of person–environment interaction to be discussed concerns the ways in which individuals obtain information about the consequences of their behavior. When such information is clear and unambiguous, but not so emotionally intense as to generate denial or distortion, the individual is able to use the information to make alternative choices and to enhance desirable outcomes. When no feedback is available, or when it comes attached to emotionally devastating outcomes, it provides little help with subsequent control or planning processes.

To be most effective, feedback should be clear, be attached to specific behaviors, be delivered in relatively emotionally neutral terms, and have the possibility of further explanation and elaboration as requested by the recipient. Feedback is most effective when delivered in the context of supportive relationships, where the possibility of both positive and negative messages exists.

In many communities significant numbers of people are almost entirely cut off from positive feedback and often receive negative feedback in the context of violent or destructive interventions by community agencies, institutions, or individuals. Often programs such as police–community relations, parent–teachers, or youth club or neighborhood assistance projects are valuable in increasing the quality and effectiveness of feedback to individuals.

These five elements of growth-producing person–environment interaction are likely to occur optimally only when they are planned for in the design and operation of community systems. In every behavior setting in the community, three crucial system components exist that heavily determine the nature of person–environment interaction and hence of the developmental consequences of that system.

First is the *opportunity subsystem.* When a broad, just, and consistent opportunity subsystem exists, community members will be able to experience optimal levels of challenge, involvement, and structure.

The second system component or characteristic is the *support subsystem*. When a supportive network of relationships and resources is available, people will be able to cope with reasonable levels of tension and stress that are inevitably associated with achievement and development.

Finally, the third component is the *reward subsystem*. When developmentally relevant and prosocial behaviors are consistently and fairly rewarded, community members will be more able to behave in planned and rational ways in meeting their legitimate goals and aspirations. Rewards have both incentive and informational properties. Their effects are powerful in determining the long-term consequences of person–environment interactions.

We have discussed five patterns of person–environment interaction and three related community subsystem components that bear heavily on the consequences of community life for human development. In a sense they may be considered values or goal structures around which the counseling psychologist organizes interventions and brings into perspective his or her relationship with the community as the ultimate consumer or client in professional practice.

In succeeding chapters we will discuss a variety of psychological interventions addressed both to individuals and families and to community institutions and agencies. In a very broad sense, the ultimate goals of these interventions are to restore a growth-producing, dynamic equilibrium and interaction between the environments represented by various community subsystems and the behaviors of individual community members.

When communities are able to function as developmentally responsive environments attuned to the needs of all their members, they fulfill the goals of the counseling psychologists engaged in community practice. Whether psychological interventions take the form of individual counseling and psychotherapy, group work, consultation, training, or organizational development, the ultimate payoff resides in the improved fit between human needs and community resources.

References

Blocher, D. H. The counselor's impact on learning environments. *Personnel and Guidance Journal*, 1977, *55*, 356–358.

Ellis, D. O., & Ludwig, F. J. *Systems philosophy*. Englewood Cliffs, N. J.: Prentice-Hall, 1962.

Gardner, J. *Annual report of the Carnegie Corporation of America.* New York: Carnegie Corp., 1962.

Goodstein, L. D., & Sandler, I. Using psychology to promote human welfare: A conceptual analysis of the role of community psychology. *American Psychologist,* 1978, *33,* 882–892.

Griffiths, D. E. Administrative theory and change in organizations. In M.B. Miles (Ed.), *Innovation in education.* New York: Teachers College Press, Columbia University, Bureau of Publications, 1964.

Iscoe, I. Community psychology and the competent community. *American Psychologist,* 1974, *29,* 607–613.

Kelly, J. G. Qualities for community psychologists. *American Psychologist,* 1971, *26,* 897–903.

Masterpasqua, F. Toward a synergism of developmental and community psychology. *American Psychologist,* 1981, *36,* 782–786.

O'Neill, P. Community cognitive psychology. *American Psychologist,* 1981, *36,* 457–469.

Rogers, C.R. The necessary and sufficient conditions for therapeutic personality change. *Journal of Consulting Psychology,* 1957, *22,* 95–102.

Stanley, W.O. The collapse of automatic adjustment. In Bennis, W.C., Benne, K.D., & Chin, R. (Eds.), *The Planning of Change.* New York: Holt, Rinehart and Winston, 1964.

Taylor, S.E. Developing a cognitive social psychology. In J. S. Carroll & J. W. Payne (Eds.), *Cognition and social behavior.* Hillsdale, N.J.: Erlbaum, 1976.

Thoreson, C. E. The "systems approach" and counselor training: Basic features and implications. Paper read at A.E.R.A. meeting, Chicago, 1968.

Watson, G. Resistance to change. In G. Watson (Ed.), *Concepts for social change.* Washington, D.C.: National Training Laboratories, National Education Association, 1967.

Wiener, N. *Cybernetics.* New York: Wiley, 1948.

PART II
COMMUNITY INTERVENTIONS

3

Individual Clinical Interventions: Theories and Techniques

In the past, far too many counseling psychologists have acted as though they had an almost religious faith in one or another theory of counseling and psychotherapy. Theories were defended or attacked with emotional zeal. Shamans and gurus surrounded themselves with followers. Goldfried (1980) observed,

> We have all "taken up sides" and placed far too much emphasis on who is correct and not what is correct. There appears to be a slight but clearly growing trend toward questioning whether or not all answers may be found within any given school of psychotherapy. We seem to be entering a period of self examination, with therapists beginning to ask themselves such questions as, where does our approach fail? What are the limits of our paradigm? Do other approaches have something useful to offer? [p. 991]

Too much has been said about the rightness or wrongness of various approaches to counseling and therapy. As a result, various proponents may have misled the public about the merits of one school of psychotherapy over another. Far too many followers of different schools of psychotherapy have reported "miracle cures," yet there is very little empirical data to support even modest claims.

On one hand, it is difficult if not impossible to make clear-cut distinctions between counseling and psychotherapy. Rather than trying to maintain distinctions which fail to hold up under logical analysis, perhaps the terms should be used interchangeably. Although this argument has merit, counseling psychologists should be somewhat cautious about overgeneralizing from the psychotherapy literature. In some cases, particular theories or clinical practices in psychotherapy are based on unique populations of chronic patients

45

who may be quite different from the range of clients seen by many counseling psychologists.

Another viewpoint is that counseling and psychotherapy should be distinguished only on the basis of the "depth of the relationship." Kovel (1976) describes good counseling as providing emotional support, intellectual clarification, and some attention to concrete environmental problems. In contrast, he believes that therapy is more ambitious as it attempts to go beyond the limits of counseling into the area of the unconscious, and that it becomes more problematic, more liable to bog down or even to harm. However, even for Kovel, therapy always retains some of its basis in counseling.

In contrast, Schofield (1964) argues that psychotherapy is a conversation with therapeutic intent. Regardless of theoretical allegiance, the therapist is an expert conversationalist whose skills include sensitivity to the emotional nuances of the client's communication, an ability to listen selectively, facility in encouraging the client to start and continue conversations, deftness in leading the client to particular topics, and the capacity both to tolerate the client's silences and to use his own silence in communicating. Schofield observed that it was remarkable that so many have found so much to say about a variety of apparent diversities in psychotherapy theories and practice. He then makes the following point, which we would like to second.

> ... in our culture, it is far more acceptable to present oneself as an expert in some moderately occult and complex professionalized technique than to suggest the more modest claim to being generally perceptive and intelligent about personal problems. Certainly, the average counselor can much sooner be confident that he is technically proficient than he can be assured that he is wise [p.111].

We, like Schofield, encourage counseling psychologists not to differentiate superficially between counseling and psychotherapy and other forms of "helping" relationships found in society. For the professional working in community mental health settings, Schofield (1964) describes an important resource: a host of "invisible" psychotherapists who exist in society and who, by virtue of their roles and status as examples of stability, wisdom, and devotion to social service, are regularly turned to for help. Clergy and teachers are among the invisible therapists. Other sources of psychotherapy even more invisible as far as social recognition is concerned are work supervisors, respected colleagues, "good neighbors," and close friends. The counseling psychologist in a community setting should not underestimate the potential contributions of these "untrained" therapists. In one study, Strupp (1977) compared experienced psychotherapists and college professors who had no training in psychotherapy but had local reputations as individuals sought out by students for advice and counsel. Also included in the comparison were a minimal treatment group and a "silent control." The results showed that the college professors did as well as the trained and experienced professional psychotherapists, and both slightly exceeded the control condition in producing "improvement" in those treated.

Given these kinds of results, it is not surprising that the field is being called upon to become more accountable regarding the benefits of psychotherapy. Even though there have been a large number of studies of the effectiveness of counseling and psychotherapy, the results are not clear-cut. Eysenck's studies (1952; 1965) raised important questions about the efficacy of psychotherapy and spurred a serious reexamination of this research literature. Frank (1973) reported that statistical studies of psychotherapy consistently show that about two-thirds of neurotic clients are improved immediately after treatment, regardless of the type of psychotherapy they have received, and the same improvement rate has been found for clients who have not received any treatment that was deliberately psychotherapeutic.

In an extensive review of therapeutic outcome studies, Bergin (1971) concluded "It now seems apparent that psychotherapy as practiced over the last forty years has had an average effect that is modestly positive." However, he warns that the average group data on which this conclusion is based obscure the existence of a multiplicity of processes occurring in therapy, some of which are known to be unproductive or actually harmful. In another review (Bergin & Lambert, 1971) of outcome data, the results looked more favorable. The findings generally yielded clearly positive results when compared to no-treatment wait list, and placebo or pseudo-therapies. Still, the researchers caution that it is very disappointing to find that too often persons are not helped or are even hurt by inept applications of treatments.

The Office of Technology Assessment, a small research advisory arm of Congress (Foltz, 1980), released an eighteen-month study of psychotherapy intended to convince senators and congressmen that psychotherapy is safe and effective. Although psychotherapy was shown to be effective in some cases, they argued that more research is needed about the conditions under which therapy works and which aspects of mental health treatment can be linked with improved health conditions. More research is also needed on cost effectiveness and cost-benefit considerations.

Similar findings were reported from a meta-analysis or collation of nearly 400 controlled evaluations of psychotherapy by Smith and Glass (1977), who concluded: "On the average, the typical therapy client is better off than 75% of untreated individuals." However, in all of the studies reviewed, the average age was 22 and the typical dependent measures (taken on an average of 3½ months following completion of therapy) were fear, anxiety, and adjustment. Still, Smith and Glass concluded that in the aggregate, psychotherapies do apparently work and that overall various psychotherapies appear equally effective.

A word of caution! Horan (1980) argued that there were serious problems in the experimental methods used in the meta-analysis and that we really have proven far less than we purport to know. Before questions can be answered by meta-analysis studies, we must improve our experimental literature. Three major problems in this literature are: (1) experimental subjects often do not receive treatment appropriate to their clinical problems; (2) treatments are often not standardized and they often do not correspond to the theoretical principles upon which they are supposed to be based; and (3) control groups do not generate equivalent subject expectations for improvement.

Another way of discussing the effectiveness of counseling and psychotherapy is to ask the question, What is the effect of adding psychological services to an existing system of care? People undergoing psychological stress are extremely high users of medical services. Cummings and Follette (1976) report that one session of brief psychotherapy with no repeat psychological visits reduced medical utilization by 50 percent over a five-year period. Two to eight visits resulted in 75 percent reduction of medical utilization. Similar reductions were found in absenteeism from work. Keisler (1980) summarized this research as follows: "The major practical question is not the effectiveness of psychotherapy taken in isolation, but rather its marginal utility as an addition to existing systems. Psychotherapy can be shown to be very effective in reducing the total cost of care and in independently decreasing the number of inappropriate professional contacts."

Taking a humanistic tack, Kovel (1976) makes the following

"commonsense" argument. Therapy properly conducted can always be of benefit, because it can apply a needed cushion at times of emotional crises. Therapy can also provide a client with someone who pays attention to and accepts him or her without responding in the ways that others close to him or her have always responded. Thus, therapy can give virtually everyone some clarification and understanding of his or her position. A self-defeating sense of confusion can usually be alleviated to some extent by skilled therapy. Finally, each person is always at a given phase of development when some issues are critical. Therapy can address itself to these issues and by resolving them in a progressive way, help to restore the overall state of equilibrium of the client.

In this chapter, we will review some of the major theories and interventions in counseling psychotherapy. These will not be exhaustive systematic reviews. In evaluating the various psychotherapeutic interventions, the reader should keep in mind Kovel's (1976) advice that each therapy tends to address itself to the presumed basic dialectic among mind, body, and society by emphasizing one or another as the main causal factor in psychological dysfunctioning and consequently as the main area to be addressed. He recommends that we do not focus solely on the therapy's areas of ultimate intended influence, but rather learn to recognize its main area of concern: mind, body, or society! The limitations of each approach will then become more apparent.

The reader should also look for commonalities among the theoretical orientations. Goldfried (1980) gives two examples of clinical strategies that may be common to all theoretical orientations. The first is to provide the client with new corrective experiences. This idea is that concurrent life experiences can change client's lives even without necessarily producing insight into the origins of their problems. A second clinical strategy that may be common to all therapeutic approaches consists of direct feedback. Clients can be helped to become aware of what they are doing and not doing, thinking and not thinking, and feeling and not feeling in various situations. Clients may sometimes change merely as a result of observing their own behavior.

Behavioral Paradigms

Most techniques in behavioral therapy are based on operant or instrumental conditioning or on classical conditioning. Emotional behaviors, including autonomic activities, are classified as respondents and are seen to be controlled by immediate stimulus conditions. Behaviors involving the skeletal system, motor movements, and verbal responses are called operants and believed controlled by consequent situations. Responses can be covert processes or overt behaviors and may be treated as dependent or independent variables.

Operant Model

The operant model involves three phases:

1. An initial state of affairs in which a neutral stimulus precedes a response but no consequence occurs.
2. The learning condition, in which the antecedent cue occurs, a response is emitted, and a positive or a negative consequence is experienced.
3. The resultant condition, in which a response is either strengthened or weakened and the antecedent cue becomes informative in predicting the consequences of the response. The consequence may then precede other responses and neutral stimuli.

Therapeutic interventions based on the operant model primarily rearrange contingent behavioral consequences, including rewards and punishments, in order to eliminate undesired behaviors or to strengthen desired behaviors.

Reinforcement basically involves an environmental event or stimulus consequence that is contingent upon a particular response and whose occurrence increases the probability that the response will occur. Reinforcement operations are of four kinds. Positive stimuli can be presented (positive reinforcement) or removed (response cost) contingently, or negative stimuli can be presented (punishment) or removed (negative reinforcement). Positive stimuli can be withheld after a period of presentation (extinction) and negative stimuli can be similarly withheld (avoidance).

Some stimuli are called primary reinforcers because they are reinforcing to most members of a species regardless of prior conditioning history. These include food, water, stimuli that reduce pain or discomfort, and sexual stimuli. Conditioned reinforcers acquire their value from repeated association with other reinforcing events. Complex response chains in which component responses are discriminative stimuli for subsequent responses may be seen as a single operant in which all the components are related to the final reinforcing event. The analysis of such chains may be necessary in therapy when the clinician needs to build up appropriate response chains by positive reinforcement.

Reinforcement can be given continuously or intermittently on various schedules. In some cases, a given time interval elapses before reinforcement, while in other cases the delivery of reinforcement is based on the number of responses that occur. Time intervals and/or response rate schedules may be either fixed or variable. Behavior established by intermittent reinforcement tends to be more resistant to extinction.

Positive reinforcement is useful when there is a behavioral deficit. Extinction or withholding positive reinforcement is most useful with behavioral excesses. Extinction of undesirable behaviors may be preliminary to positive reinforcement of desired behaviors.

When there are undesirable behaviors, treatment may focus on strengthening desirable behaviors which are competitive with the undesirable behavior. If new, complex behavior is desired, shaping or the use of successive approximations can be used. Shaping combines reinforcement and extinction to build a complex chain of behaviors. An example of skill-shaping involves learning a complex task by learning a series of approximate skills.

In the operant model, aversive stimuli are contingent upon the behavior of the client. Aversion relief or negative reinforcement involves the removal of aversive stimuli following certain behaviors.

Classical Conditioning

The other model which is the basis for some forms of behavioral therapy is classical or respondent conditioning. Respondents are modified by variations in prior stimulus situations.

Classical conditioning involves three phases:

1. An initial state of affairs in which an unconditioned stimulus such as a loud noise elicits a reflexive fear response or unconditioned response.
2. A learning condition, in which a formerly neutral stimulus that produces neither intensely positive nor intensely negative reactions is paired with an unconditioned stimulus.

3. The resultant condition in which a formerly neutral stimulus has now become a conditioned stimulus and can by itself elicit the reflexive fear response. This fear is associated with the new stimulus and is referred to as a conditioned response.

The classical conditioning paradigm controls undesirable behaviors by controlling the stimuli that elicit them. Aversive therapy is often used as an example of a clinical intervention based on the classical conditioning paradigm. In aversive therapy, a noxious unconditioned stimulus (producing an undesirable event) is paired with a stimulus associated with the undesirable behavior. The conditioned stimulus evokes an unpleasant response, which is incompatible with the original pleasurable consequence. The new response interrupts the undesirable behavioral sequence. For instance, to eliminate the desire for alcohol, the cues associated with alcohol, that is the sight, smell, taste, and thoughts of alcohol, are the conditioned stimuli which are paired with unconditioned stimuli for pain or unpleasant reactions until the conditioned stimuli take on a similar stimulus function. Cautela's (1967) research suggests that vicarious stimuli are also effective in aversive therapy.

When a symptom is used as a conditioned stimulus, and the behaviors are followed by aversive stimuli, these may serve as punishing consequences for the symptom. It also may be true that the unconditioned stimulus has aversive reinforcing characteristics for behaviors, such as raising a glass, taking a sip, and tasting.

Aversive therapy includes three practices: (1) punishment or the use of an aversive stimulus to suppress undesirable behavior; (2) avoidance learning, which establishes new responses that prevent or terminate the noxious stimulation; (3) classical conditioning, in which an aversive stimulus leads to unpleasant results that become associated with and inhibit the undesirable behavior.

In classical conditioning, extinction of a conditioned response usually occurs, if a conditioned stimulus is repetitively presented without the unconditioned stimulus. When a positively reinforced response is being extinguished, such as in punishment procedures, there is often at first a burst of emotional behavior.

An important concept in the classical conditioning model is generalization. When a response has been conditioned to a particular conditioned stimulus, stimuli similar to the conditioned stimulus also will evoke the conditioned response. The response varies in strength depending upon the similarities of the generalized stimulus to the conditioned stimulus. The response becomes weaker when the stimulus is less similar. When an extinction procedure is applied to a generalized stimulus, extinction occurs more rapidly than extinction to the conditioned stimulus.

Based on Hull's theory, Dollard and Miller (1950) argued that the acquisition of particular stimulus–response patterns has to be preceded by a given motivational state. A stimulus–response pattern was reinforcing if there was a drive reduction. In their model, there are four fundamentals in learning: (1) Drive or a strong stimulus which impels action. The primary drives are sex, thirst, hunger, fatigue, cold, and pain. The secondary drives are elaborations of the primary drives. (2) Cues are distinctive stimuli that determine when and where a person will respond and which response he will make. (3) Responses to drives are channeled by distinctive cues. Cue-producing responses function to produce a cue, and cues can be either to self or to others. For instance, labeling a stimulus hot can produce a response. An example of an anticipatory response is anxiety. Responses near in time to the point of reinforcement will tend to occur before their original time in the response series. (4) Reinforcement is reduction in the strength of a drive. Verbal and motoric responses are also reinforced.

Another learning paradigm used in behavioral therapy is based on social learning through observation, imitation, and modeling (Kanfer & Phillips, 1970). There are five classes of observational learning:

1. Matched dependent learning. The subject follows the example of a leader with reward for success.
2. Identification. The subject acquires the style of the model by observation and is rewarded for imitation of style.
3. No-trial learning. The subject observes a model and is given opportunity to perform the same tasks without practice or contingent reinforcement.
4. Co-learning. The model and observer are engaged in the same learning task with alternate opportunities for watching and doing.
5. Vicarious classical conditioning. The subject witnesses the administration of an unconditioned stimulus for an emotional response, or the response itself and the observer's vicariously elicited response becomes associated to a formerly neutral stimuli.

Modeling of approach responses may reduce the arousal potential of an aversive stimulus to a point which does not activate avoidance responses, allowing the observer to make approach responses that do not result in aversive consequences (Bandura, 1969). Modeling procedures can be used to transmit new patterns of behavior, eliminate fears, and facilitate expression of responses.

Behavioral Treatments

Behavior therapy has been described as the application of three kinds of conditioning (Wolpe, 1969). In *counterconditioning,* responses inhibitory to anxiety are made to occur in the presence of anxiety-evoking stimuli. This process attempts to weaken the bond between particular stimuli and anxiety. In *positive reconditioning,* new behaviors are elicited in a relevant situation by rewarding desired behaviors and punishing or not rewarding undesirable behaviors. In *experimental extinction,* habits are extinguished through the repeated nonreinforcement of the responses that manifest them.

Systematic Desensitization

Systematic desensitization involves: (1) training in deep muscle relaxation, (2) determination of hierarchies of anxiety-producing stimulus situations, (3) paired presentations of anxiety situations and relaxation procedures. The sequence is relax, imagine, relax, stop imagining, and relax.

A behavioral analysis of the problem situation is completed and then the anxiety hierarchy or hierarchies are determined using a scaling procedure in terms of intensity of anxiety produced by the offending stimulus. Relaxation techniques may involve tension–relaxation procedures. In this case the client is instructed to tighten each muscle group, count to five, let go, and then notice the difference. A modified cognitive approach involves visualization and imagery. For instance, clients might be told to close their eyes, notice their body and feelings, notice their breath and the feeling of the chair. Instructions might include: "Think about a scene where you felt comfortable and happy, notice as much as possible. Enjoy the scene."

Traditional desensitization focuses on scenes while self-control desensitization focuses on monitoring proprioceptive stimuli associated with anxiety. The emphasis is on awareness of physical reactions to various anxiety-provoking situations. As the client is able to work through the hierarchy of anxiety-producing situations while maintaining a relaxed state, the old stimulus–response connections are broken down.

Social Modeling/Behavioral Rehearsal

Social modeling is a behavioral technique used to help a client acquire desired responses or to extinguish fears. Models may be live, on film, or covert. When using models, a rationale and instructions about the features of the modeled behavior are first presented. A complex pattern of behavior is usually presented in modeled sequences. It is important to maximize the similarity between the client and the model; coping rather than mastery models are particularly effective. Exposure to appropriate models has been found to be effective regardless of whether the model or the observer receives visible reinforcement.

The self-as-a-model procedure has been described by Hosford (1980). During the first phase of this procedure, clients are taught self-observation and self-monitoring skills to apply in those situations in which the problem behavior occurs. The objective is to help the client gain an awareness of how his or her behavior is controlled and shaped and what behaviors need to be acquired. In the second phase, the client identifies those specific behaviors that he or she would most like to change. A base rate audio- or videotape is then made to gain some objective idea of present level of performance on each of the goal behaviors. During the fourth step, the counselor and client construct the self-model often using a videotape. Only instances in which the client performs the target behaviors in the desired ways are included in the model. The client sees himself or herself successfully performing the target behavior. In the fifth step, the client observes the model tapes and covertly practices performing the behaviors in the same way as shown on the tapes. After the client views himself or herself consistently performing the target behaviors, he or she practices the responses with the counselor prior to trying them out in real-life situations.

Behavioral rehearsal or role-playing can be used in three situations: (1) to acquire responses or learn skills to handle a situation; (2) to facilitate use of certain responses; and (3)to discriminate between positive and negative applications or appropriate and inappropriate times to enact responses. Role-playing or behavioral rehearsal can be used for changing attitudes, for increasing self-awareness, and for changing behaviors.

In behavioral rehearsal, the counselor and client specify the target behaviors, determine situations in which skills need to be used or fear reduced, and arrange the situations in a hierarchy. A sequence is established with covert rehearsal, analysis, role-playing, rehearsal, and feedback.

Covert Treatments

Covert conditioning is based on three assumptions: (1) covert processes are subject to laws of reinforcement; (2) individuals can differentiate between the occurrence or nonoccurrence of covert events; (3) individuals can control covert reinforcements.

Covert sensitization involves having the client imagine an aversive stimulus at the same time he or she is about to engage in an undesirable behavior. With repeated exposures, the response to the aversive stimulus becomes associated with the undesirable response. For example, following a behavioral analysis, and after the client has achieved a relaxed state, the psychologist instructs the client to visualize a scene depicting the maladaptive behavior, then visualize an experience which has a very unpleasant affect connected to it.

In covert positive reinforcement, an individual enacts a desirable behavior and then shifts to an image that is positively reinforcing. With covert negative reinforcement, the client imagines a negative situation that terminates when a desirable response occurs.

Self-Management Techniques

Self-control involves the specification of behavior, the identification of antecedent cues and environmental consequences, and the implementation of an action plan that alters some of the antecedents and/or consequences. The client administers the change strategy and directs the efforts.

Self-observation or self-monitoring is a strategy that interferes with stimulus–response associations. Desired behaviors may increase simply as a result of being monitored. Another strategy is environmental planning. The idea is to change the environment so that either the cues that precede the behavior or the consequences that follow it are changed. Behavioral programming is a strategy aimed at altering the consequences of behavior. Self-reward, self-punishment, and self-treatment are used to effect behavioral changes.

Behavioral approaches are often criticized for their mechanistic approaches and dehumanizing methods. Kovel (1976) argues that the real complication is not that behavioral therapy is the wrong therapy, but that unless it is scrupulously controlled and limited, it is just wrong. For him, behavior therapy emphasizes proclivities for being passively manipulated and minimizes the realm of fantasy, spontaneity, and imagination. According to Kovel, behavior therapy shows contempt for people and blends too well with political authoritarianism. We believe that this kind of rhetoric confuses goals and methods of treatments and is grossly oversimplified. According to Mahoney and Thoreson (1974) and Thoreson and Mahoney (1974) behavioral techniques can be directed toward humanistic ends. Many humanistic concerns can be translated into behavioristic terms. For instance, a humanistic phrase, such as, "Self-disclose, be assertive when necessary; empathize with others," can be translated as follows: "increase the frequency and variety of positive verbal responses." Thoreson argues for a therapeutic synthesis called behavioral humanism in which behavioral techniques are merged with a humanistic philosophy.

Cathartic Theories and Interventions

Psychoanalysis

Sigmund Freud was born in Moravia on May 6, 1856, and died in London on September 23, 1939. Although he studied with Jean Charcot, the famed French psychiatrist who used hypnosis in the treatment of hysteria, he was more influenced by Joseph Breuer, a Viennese physician who effectively cured symptoms by having patients talk about them.

The development and the acceptance of psychoanalysis has been attributed to the experience of alienation that was associated with modern urbanizaton (Bakan, 1968). Psychoanalysis deals with man in a state of conflict between self and society. The neurotic personality is one in whom control over self has balked in the face of social demands, creating a condition of alienation in which the person is not functioning effectively in relationship to the outside world.

In the traditional psychoanalytic model, personality consists of three systems: id, ego, and superego. Behavior is nearly always the product of the interaction of these three systems. The id consists of everything psychological that is inherited and present at birth. The id is viewed as the reservoir of psychic energy and represents the inner world of subjective experience. The ego comes into existence because the needs of the organism require appropriate transactions with the "objective" world of reality. The ego distinguishes between things in the mind and things in the external world. The ego is said to obey the "reality principle" and operate by means of the secondary process. The aim is to prevent discharge of tension until an object that is appropriate for satisfaction is discovered. The superego is the internal representative of the traditional values and ideals of society as interpreted to children by their parents. The superego is the moral arm of personality and strives for perfection. What is said to be improper and for which a child is punished is incorporated into the conscience, while the ego ideal is composed of those things which are called "good" and which are rewarded. The pyschological mechanism by which this incorporation is accomplished is called introjection.

The id, ego, and superego are not merely manikins that operate the personality. Instead, they are names for various presumed psychological processes that obey different system principles. Freud regarded the human organism as a complex system that derives engery from food it consumes and expends it for such purposes as circulation, respiration, muscular exercise, perceiving, thinking, and remembering. The point of contact or bridge between biological energy and that of personality is the id.

Freud's early approach to therapy involved recovering a patient's prior memories and feelings regarding traumatic events. He saw hysterical symptoms as due to the existence outside of consciousness of such memories and feelings (strangulated affects). The goal of treatment was to effect a catharsis or abreaction of the repressed feelings and thus alleviate the source of symptoms.

Freud did not discover the unconscious but he did bring together two major regions of the unmanifest (Bakan, 1968). Freud pointed out that there is a region of the psyche which is not manifest and which is important, and there is a relationship between this region and the region of regularities with which science was concerned.

Transference is a major concept in the psychoanalytic approach. Transference is the tendency in the patient for attitudes and impulses experienced in past relationships to repeat themselves in relation to the analyst. The patient interprets and misinterprets the present in terms of the past and strives to relive the past in a more satisfactory way. Psychoanalysis is the method of creating conditions for the development of a transference neurosis. The past is recreated in the present and, through a systematic interpretative attack on resistances, the neurosis is resolved, and this brings about structural changes in thinking which make for optimal adaptations. The clinician uses interpretations to show the client how misidentifications and distortions in present relationships have their origins in early life experiences.

The analyst attempts to represent a blank screen or a "mirror" in order that the transference neurosis can develop uninfluenced by the analyst's own personality. However, countertransferences may develop that involve the analyst's reacting to the client in terms of his or her past experiences.

The psychoanalyst uses three primary techniques:

1. **Confrontation.** Telling the client what he or she is revealing at the moment.
2. **Interpretation.** Explaining the client's behavior in a new way that reflects unconscious elements.
3. **Reconstruction.** Providing hypothetical historical statements regarding repressed fragments of the client's past. Through these techniques, the therapist attempts to make patients more aware of the unconscious elements in their lives. Psychoanalytic therapy devotes so much attention to the unconscious because under normal circumstances in everyday life it receives very little attention (Kovel, 1976).

An interpretation can be related to a treatment goal. The following quotation gives an example of psychoanalytic thinking.

This tentative formulation came to mind: The patient right after her marriage, being called upon to muster her feminine identifications, had as a result a great intensification of her symptoms. It is not unlikely, therefore, that something about femininity was dangerous to her. Moreover, since her mother's superstitions were frightening and her father's rationalism comforting, the latter might be used in treatment, if it could be divorced from the violence that accompanied his anticlerical attacks. With this in mind, I purposefully developed the aim of aiding her identifications with the more intellectual father [Reider, 1955, p. 224].

A psychodynamic view of counseling psychology proposes that counseling and therapy are best understood as the building and repairing of strong working alliances (Bordin, 1980). The treatment resides in the alliance. Three features of these alliances are: mutuality of goals, agreement regarding tasks and responsibilities, and the kinds of bonds and attachments formed.

In order to develop a working alliance, a therapist and a client must negotiate a set of mutual goals. Both must first air their hidden agenda and resolve any incompatibility in goals. Next, the therapist and client must reach some agreement regarding tasks and responsibilities.

Strong working alliances occur when the personal characteristics of the client fit the goals to which he or she is ready to be committed and fit the requirements of the associated tasks and bonds. All of these also should fit the personal characteristics and commitments of the therapist.

A concept of brief psychoanalytic psychotherapy has been developed around the role of time and the development of maturity (Mann, 1973). The client is confronted with a time-limited, finite relationship which provides an opportunity to come to terms with these elements in the growth process. The Mann format specifies the time limit as twelve interviews. The number of interviews may be shortened for clients presenting transitory problems. Although counselors may find it difficult to enforce these time limits, the limits must be firm and they should communicate the counselor's commitment to the limit.

Another aspect of Mann's model of brief psychotherapy is a statement of focus which defines the change goals for treatment. The statement of focus is stated for the client and is the basis for negotiation of the contract. The statement should reflect the client's current pain and should relate to his or her life situation. Therapy may focus on four conflicts: independence versus dependence; activity versus passivity; adequate versus diminished self-esteem; and unresolved or delayed grief.

The first four sessions are characterized by a strong sense of cohesion and purposeful work. In the next four sessions, the client attends to the limited goals and time limits in the relationship, which can result in the reappearance of ambivalence and discussion of concerns that brought the person to counseling in the first place. In the final sessions, the client comes to terms with, acknowledges, and accepts his or her anger and frustration. Finally, the client learns how to terminate a relationship.

There are numerous stereotypes about the psychoanalytic approach in therapy. In many cases, the therapist is viewed as an exaggerated authority figure who continually spouts analytic insights. However, Reider (1955) negates many of these stereotypes when he describes a meaningful clinical experience as one that recognizes the relative strength and weakness of various drives and defenses and that is developed through numerous errors and occasional successes. The clinician learns to gauge when one individual can tolerate the investigation of his hostile impulses while another cannot. The therapist learns to recognize when an hysterical patient may tolerate a considerable amount of ventilation about his anxiety; and when a schizophrenic may need a great deal of reassurance and strengthening before etiological factors in regard to his anxiety can be touched. Reider (1955) concludes that any formula for the indications and contraindications of use of specific therapeutic devices is too mechanical.

Several notable individuals (Dollard & Miller, 1950; Wachtel, 1977) have called for an integration of psychoanalytic and behavioral therapy. Still, Messer and Winokur (1980) warn that there are some significant differences between the two orientations. Differences between the behavioral and psychoanalytic approach have to do with the form of empathy and the type interpretations used. Behavior therapists attempt to be empathetic in the sense of establishing a facilitative emotional climate, but they do not use empathy to understand the nuances of a client's subjective sense of things. In contrast, psychoanalytic therapists try to convey an understanding of the individual's subjective experience. For the behavioral therapist, interpretations are of a rather general kind and usually involve a relatively restricted number of standard constructions. A psychoanalytic interpretation relies on theoretical schemata and attends to the specifics of an individual's thoughts, memories, fantasies, and feelings.

The behavioral and psychoanalytic approaches also differ in regard to their perspective on reality. They disagree about (1) realism versus idealism, (2) objectivism versus subjectivism, and (3) extrospection versus introspection. The realist thinks the world has an existence of its own independent of the observer. The idealist claims that there is no external world of reality independent of the perception and cognition of the perceiver. Objectivity implies a shared frame of reference, a common understanding of events or experiences that is open to being checked and that can be generalized. Subjectivity implies that experience is unique, private, and not generalized beyond the individual. In the extrospective frame of reference, the individual constructs a hypothesis about a client from one's own vantage point as an observer, regardless of the subject's viewpoint. With the introspective frame of reference, the formulation of constructs takes the subject's point of view seriously. These different perspectives about reality lead to different emphases in conducting therapy and assessing outcomes.

Gestalt Therapy

Freidrich S. Perls is considered to be the foremost proponent of gestalt therapy. Although Perls borrowed heavily from psychoanalytic theory, he was also influenced by gestalt psychology. The basic premise of gestalt psychology is that human reality is organized into patterns or wholes that are experienced by the individual in these terms, and human reality can be understood only as a function of the patterns or wholes of which it is made (Van deReit, Korb, & Gorrell, 1980; Perls, 1969).

Personality is essentially structured out of the interactions within the individual and interactions between the individual and the environment. Each person experiences perceptions, needs, thoughts, and emotions through a process of gestalt formation and destruction. Figure/ground relationships emerge for the individual and are satisfied or "put aside" unfinished. The organism is the totality of a given person and operates according to gestalt formation and destruction principles. The primary functions of personality are to be aware of and regulate internal needs and to interact with the environment to meet these needs. The organism has a powerful need to gain completeness and a sense of wholeness in its activities. Many times, individuals are prevented from dealing with their present needs because they carry unfinished past experiences, feelings, and thoughts into the present.

The organism makes numerous contacts with the environment, and the awareness of these contact points is a significant aspect of the self. The distinctions between the organism and the environment are sharpened (Van deReit et al., 1980). In times of great stress or heightened emotions, persons experience contact with surroundings in sharply defined terms and experience their evaluations of them with clarity and immediacy. In other words, the self organizes perceptions of an event around an immediate need and causes one to evaluate the events. This is organismic responding. Another aspect of self involves the process of evaluating the appropriateness of perceptions for the organism or of knowing what is true for the organism. The major activity of the self is forming figure/ground relationships.

The ego is a system of identification with the needs, desires, and experiences that are clearly figural or predominant. Like the self, the ego is a functional process of the organism and mobilizes energy and resources for the satisfaction of needs and wants. Ego activities involve abstraction and labeling of events. When the ego functions, activities result. When the client identifies with certain experiences and is alienated from other experiences, ego boundaries can prevent the individual from perceiving reality fruitfully and using that reality as a source of growth.

Gestalt therapy identifies three zones of experience: interior, exterior, and intermediate. The interior zone is the experience of everything that occurs within the body. The exterior experience is gained through the senses and personal association with phenomena being experienced. The psychological contact between external and internal regions occurs in the middle zone of experience. When an individual gives a label or meaning to an internal or external experience, he is dealing with the middle zone of experience. All interpretations, labels, and images are associated with the middle or intermediate zone; contact through the senses with things outside the individual occurs in the outer zone; feelings from the inside occur within the inner zone.

The assumption is that a major dynamic process in the personality is the ability to symbolize all aspects of personal experience. In this process undifferentiated impressions are transformed into recognizable patterns which are then related to the whole of a person's synthesized experience. In the healthy personality, organismic experiences are brought to conscious awareness through appropriate symbolization. Symbolic functions enable individuals to experience existence in a self-reflective manner. People learn how they respond to their constructions of reality rather than to reality directly. The capacity to abstract appropriately is a function of an individual's perceptual styles, such as an overintellectualized orientation. Self-perception is possible because of an individual's capacity for symbolization. The subjective feeling of having experiential processes that arise from within oneself is an important aspect of a healthy personality. Perls (1969) emphasized the importance of the ability of persons to respond totally to their personal experiences. This means that a person's voice quality and words should be connected to his or her personal experiences. The polar opposite of environmental contact is the withdrawal or transferring of good contact from the environment to largely internal processes.

In optimal functioning, there are clear and distinct contacts with the environment and clear and distinct withdrawals. The withdrawal process may be associated with such things as mixed emotions, conflicting desires, and painful responses. In therapy, individuals are encouraged to become aware of and clarify the diffuse and confused parts of themselves.

Another example of polarization is identification-alienation. For most people, there is partial identification with and partial alienation from other persons, experiences, and aspects of their own characters.

When an individual's expectations are not met, he may develop resentments, which he then tries to repress. Holding back an expression of resentment can lead to difficulties in communicating with others. The individual may feel guilty about this resentment and what he really wants to do to someone else. Guilt is a demand that people be different than they are. Resentment toward others may build up when they do not live up to one's unexpressed expectations. The individual learns to reown personal responsibility through identification with personal expectations.

Perls used the term *growth disorders* rather than *neuroses* when referring to most personality disorders (Prochaska, 1979). In his model, there are five different layers or levels of psychopathology: (1) the phony, (2) the phobic, (3) the impasse, (4) the implosive, and (5) the explosive.

The phony layer involves playing games and roles. At the phobic layer, individuals avoid and run from emotional pain, which indicates that something is wrong and needs to be changed. The most critical level of pathology is the impasse or the point at which individuals are fixated in their maturation. Individuals become convinced that they have no chance of survival because they cannot find the means within themselves to move ahead in the face of withdrawal of emotional support. Individuals may pretend to be helpless, stupid, or crazy in order to get others to take care of them.

The implosive layer of pathology involves an individual experiencing the deadness of certain parts of themselves which they have disowned. To go through the implosive layer, an individual must be willing to shed the very character that has served as a sense of identity. The explosive layer of pathology can involve a tremendous release of energies depending on how much energy is bound up in the implosive layer. There is explosion into orgasm, anger, grief, and joy.

In gestalt therapy, consciousness raising is the major technique used to liberate the client from "maya," the phony, fantasy layer of existence. Maya is a world of concepts, ideals, fantasies, and intellectual rehearsals. This process involves "getting back to your senses." The client's task is to stay in the "here and now." This allows the client to work on the healthy gestalt principle that the most important unfinished situation will emerge into consciousness and can be dealt with.

At the onset of therapy, clients act out the phony layer of their neurosis. Gestalt exercises can be used to make them more aware of the phony roles and games they play. One consequence of gestalt exercises is that clients become more aware of their phobic layer, that is, the things that they run away from because of their catastrophic expectations and that are used as excuses. During such exercises clients may be asked to express their conscious experiences in action by taking the chair that symbolically represents their parents and then expressing what they, the parents, would say.

The therapist's goal is to frustrate the client and not to assume responsibility for the client's well-being. Clients must take responsibility for themselves. Gestalt therapists are present-centered and do not use any predetermined pattern of exercises in therapy. The purpose of exercises is to increase clients' awareness of what is keeping them from remaining in the here and now.

The gestalt client is usually involved in acting out different aspects of conflicts. The empty chair is the best known and most widely used gestalt technique. The client is usually asked to move back and forth between two seats or positions which represent two aspects of himself or the relationship between himself and another person. In this context, the client engages in a dialogue. Any number of splits, polarities, or conflicts can be adapted to the empty chair technique.

Gestalt therapy, as we have seen, involves exercises for developing awareness. Examples of such exercises are: (1) contacting the environment through becoming aware of present feelings, sensing opposing forces, attending and concentrating, and differentiating and unifying; (2) developing awareness of self through remembering, sharpening the body sense, and listening to one's verbalizing; and (3) directing awareness by converting confluence into contact and changing anxiety into excitement.

Specific exercises include:

1. Games of dialogue. Clients carry on dialogue between polarities of the personality.

2. I take responsibility. Clients end every statement about themselves with "and I take responsibility for it."
3. Playing the projection. Clients play the role of people involved in their projections.
4. Reversals. Clients act out the opposite of what they are in order to experience a hidden polarity.
5. Rehearsals. Clients reveal what they most commonly do in preparation for playing social roles.
6 Marriage counseling games. Spouses take turns revealing their most positive and negative feelings toward each other.
7. May I feed you a sentence? The client repeats and tries on for size a statement about himself or herself that the therapist thinks is particularly significant for the client.

Gestalt therapists do not generally make interpretations. However, the exercise "may I feed you a sentence" borders on interpretation. Gestalt therapists do not reflect on the client's words. However, they may reflect on the nonverbal expressions of the clients.

Clients are helped to become aware of their phony games and roles and their phobic avoidance of the "here and now." Clients learn to express emotions which they have held back because of catastrophic expectations.

Catharsis is a very important aspect of gestalt therapy and usually involves clients expressing their inner experiences. These cathartic experiences are corrective emotional experiences. Dream work is an exercise in which a client may choose a dream to act out. In the process, the gestalt therapist may use theatrical techniques to intensify the situation. Gestalt therapy is often done in group settings. The client, through gestalt exercises, achieves increasing awareness and cathartic release of disowned parts of the personality.

Anxiety is considered to be one of the incomplete emotions. Whenever we leave the reality of the here and now and become preoccupied with the future, we experience anxiety. By living in the present, clients transform anxiety into excitement. The major problem is that people avoid contact with the "here and now" by using defensive maneuvers. They may use projection to attribute disowned parts of themselves to others in the environment. Introjection, retroflection, deflection, and confluence are other defensive maneuvers. Thinking may also be used to avoid the "here and now."

Gestalt therapists view growth as an important goal of the counseling process (Harman, 1975). Growth is the ability to assimilate novelty in the environment, the willingness to experience new things in the environment, and experience old things differently. For growth to occur, the individual must attend to that which is novel in the organism/environment field and be open to experiencing familiar items in a new way.

Through skillful dealing with frustrations, clients can learn to solve their own problems. Because of their style of therapy, gestalt therapists have the potential to do more than their share of psychological damage. Kovel (1976) warns that Gestalt therapy offers a tempting opportunity for therapists who want to exploit the infantile attitudes of transference and set themselves up as a seer or shaman. We wish to second the warning.

Cognitive Theories and Interventions

Reality Therapy

The major proponent of Reality Therapy is Dr. William Glasser, a psychiatrist who thinks that therapy and guidance differ only in their intensity. Reality Therapy teaches a client how to meet two basic psychological needs: (1) the need to love and to be loved and (2) the need to feel worthwhile or maintain a satisfactory standard of behavior (Glasser, 1969). Later he merged these two needs into one basic need: the need for identity (Glasser & Zunin, 1979). An individual must find some identity even if it is a "negative" or "failure" identity. Fulfilling the two basic needs will contribute to a positive or "success" identity. From time to time in life, the world and situations change, requiring people to learn and relearn how to fulfill needs under different conditions and stresses. Individuals must stay involved with other people if they are going to learn to fulfill needs effectively. If at any time in one's life this involvement is broken, he will very quickly be unable to satisfy basic needs. Glasser concluded "that all people who have any kind of serious psychiatric problems are at that time lacking the proper involvement with someone, and lacking that involvement, are unable to satisfy their needs."

Reality Therapy emphasizes social behaviors as important to good mental health. Glasser (1969) believes, "We must be involved with other people, one at the very minimum, but hopefully many more than one. At all times in our lives, we must have at least one person who cares about us and whom we care for ourselves. If we do not have this essential person, we will not be able to fulfill our basic needs" (p. 7).

For clients to meet their needs, they must be involved with others whom they love, and who love them. They must also maintain a satisfactory standard of behavior that will enable them to feel worthwhile to themselves and others. If they do not fulfill their basic needs, clients will feel pain or discomfort and then try to use unrealistic methods to fulfill their needs.

The goal of therapy is to help clients to become more responsible persons. Responsibility is the ability to fulfill needs in such a way that others are not deprived of the ability to fulfill their needs. According to this view, there are not mentally ill people, but only irresponsible people. Neurotic or delinquent people are simply not *living responsibly*.

Reality Therapy involves three steps: (1) personal involvement, (2) rejection of unrealistic behavior, and (3) teaching responsible behavior. Glasser (1969) says that therapy is a special kind of teaching or training which attempts to accomplish in a relatively short, intense period what should have been established earlier during normal development. Reality Therapy involves a particular kind of teaching. The first step is to become so involved with clients that the unrealistic aspects of the behavior are recognized. The therapist must convince the clients that he or she will stay with the clients until they are successful.

The qualities of the therapist are a major factor in developing proper involvement. The therapist must be: (1) a very responsible person who is tough, interested, human, and sensitive; (2) a strong and not expedient person who has the strength to resist inappropriate client demands; (3) a person who has knowledge and understanding about people who are isolated or different because they cannot properly fulfill their needs; (4) a person who has the ability to become emotionally involved with clients.

In Reality Therapy, the second step in the process occurs when the therapist insists that the clients face the reality of their behavior. In order to accomplish this second step, they must achieve a sufficiently deep involvement with the client. This involvement makes it possible for the therapist to ask clients why they remain in therapy if they are not dissatisfied with their behavior and are willing to stop defending their irresponsible actions. Clients must face the truth: they are responsible for their behaviors. The therapist accepts no explanations or excuses for irresponsible behavior. The therapist gives praise when clients act responsibly and shows disapproval when they do not. However, clients must ultimately decide for themselves that their behavior is irresponsible and they must decide to change.

The third step in Reality Therapy is to teach responsible behavior. Actually this relearning phase tends to permeate the whole treatment. The therapist will focus on the present and directly encourage a client to try new patterns of behavior, regardless of whether or not the client thinks the new behavior will work. In this way, clients can learn how changed behavior can lead to changed attitudes. The therapist must deal with clients' behaviors and not be misled by emotions. Emotions often result from behaviors. When behaviors change, better feelings will often follow. Glasser (1969) recounts how he told a female client to move from a shabby furnished room into a nice apartment and buy a few decent pieces of furniture. He told her, "Even if you feel bad, you don't have to live so badly." When the client mentioned a possible promotion, he told her to work for it rather than look around constantly for excuses.

Eight basic principles of Reality Therapy are as follows:

1. In reality therapy, the therapist communicates that he cares. He or she is obviously warm and self-disclosing when appropriate. However, the therapist is also clear about the limits of the "caring" relationship. Entanglement is avoided.
2. The therapist focuses on present behaviors rather than feelings. The emphasis is on the behavior of the client which contributes to the problem feelings.
3. The therapist deals with what is going on currently in the client's life. The past is seen as related to current behaviors. The case history assesses personality strengths and successes.
4. The client must judge his own behavior and evaluate what he is doing to contribute to his problems. This involves a judgment about whether his behavior is responsible and good for himself and those with whom he is involved. The main task is for the patient to face the morality of his behavior.
5. The client is helped to make specific plans to change failure behavior to success behavior. A client may be referred to an expert in a specific area in which help is needed. Simple plans with a good chance of success are formulated. The plan is put into writing in the form of a contract.
6. The client is assisted to make a commitment to carry out his plans. The emphasis is on making a commitment to someone else and not just to oneself.
7. The reality therapist makes it clear that excuses for plans

that fail are not accepted. Things fail ordinarily when individuals do not do what they said they were going to do. The
therapist's job is to help make a new plan or to modify the old
one.
8. The therapist does not punish the client with critical statements. Punishment is seen as working poorly with clients
having a failure identity. The focus in Reality Therapy is on
the client's strengths, attributes, and potentials as related to
his current attempts to achieve his goals. However, the patient and therapist will hear things that are both very agree-
able and disagreeable. Constructive arguing and intelligent
heated discussions can be a part of Reality Therapy. Verbal
shock or extreme confrontation is also effective in some therapeutic conditions. Obviously, timing is very important if a
therapist decides to use shock techniques.

Reality Therapy has been used in working with delinquent teenage girls, private outpatients with a variety of problems, severely
psychotic individuals, couples with marital problems, and students
with school-related disciplinary problems. Overall, the research suggests that Reality Therapy may be particularly effective with clients
in correctional settings or with other problems involving control of
behavior.

Rational-Emotive Therapy

The basic premise of Rational-Emotive Therapy (RET) is that irrational ideas cause emotional disturbances. Neuroses are seen to originate and be perpetuated by unsound ideas. Anxiety is viewed as an
inappropriate feeling that stems largely from irrational ideas.
    In this view, neurotics have what may be called a cultural or
philosophic rather than a psychiatric disturbance. We live in a generally *neuroticizing* civilization in which most people are more or less
emotionally disturbed, partly because they are brought up to believe
nonsense which leads them to become ineffective, self-defeating, and
unhappy (Ellis, 1969). The task of psychotherapy is to get clients to
disbelieve their irrational ideas and to change their self-sabotaging
attitudes. The rational-emotive psychotherapist makes a forthright,
unequivocal attack on irrational ideas and tries to induce more
rational views.
    Rational-Emotive Therapy is an active cognitive approach based
on the assumption that the labels we give our "emotional" reactions

are a result of conscious and unconscious evaluations, interpretations, and philosophies (Ellis, 1969). There are virtually no legitimate reasons for people to make themselves terribly upset, hysterical, or emotionally disturbed. The therapeutic core of Rational-Emotive Therapy involves an A-B-C format (See Figure 3.1).

At Point A there is an activity, action, or agent that the individual becomes disturbed about. For example, the client goes for an important job interview. At Point rB, the client has a rational belief about the activity, action, or agent that occurs at Point A. At Point iB, the client has an irrational belief about the activity, action, or agent. Rational beliefs can be supported by empirical data and are appropriate to the reality of Point A. Irrational beliefs state or imply a should, ought, or must—an absolutistic demand or dictate that the client obtain what he wants. At Point rC, the client experiences or feels rational consequences. Actions and feelings are appropriate to the situation at Point A and tend to help the client in reaching goals, or the client feels suitably regretful for not achieving these goals. At Point iC, the client experiences irrational consequences. The individual tends to feel anxious, self-hating, self-pitying, depressed, and enraged. Sometimes the client gets dysfunctional psychosomatic symptoms. The client's actions are based on magical demands regarding the way he and the universe ought to be.

The cognitive core of Rational-Emotive Therapy is described by a D-E model. At Point D, the client can be taught (or can teach himself) to dispute his irrational beliefs. If a person disputes irrational beliefs which are creating inappropriate consequences, he will see that the beliefs are unverifiable and superstitious. As a result, he will be able to change and reject them. At Point cE, the individual is likely to obtain the cognitive benefits of disputing irrational beliefs. He will change his way of thinking about his irrational beliefs. At Point bE, the individual will most likely obtain the behavioral effects of disputing irrational beliefs. An individual may become much less anxious about a forthcoming job interview.

The major theoretical contribution of Rational-Emotive Therapy concerns the influence of cognitions and beliefs on emotional arousal. Ellis' (1979) major point is that thinking creates emotion and cognition is a mediating operation between stimuli and responses. People talk to themselves (and others) and the kinds of things they say to themselves, as well as the form in which they say these things, significantly affect their emotions and behaviors. Individuals also think about what happens to them in nonverbal ways, including images, fantasies, and dreams.

Humans have very strong innate as well as acquired tendencies

FIGURE 3.1 RET model of therapy.

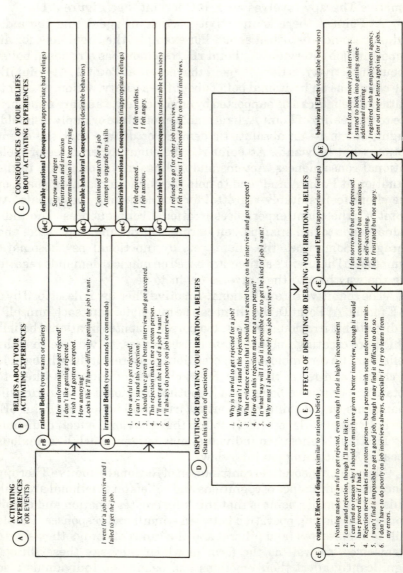

A) ACTIVATING EXPERIENCES (OR EVENTS)

I went for a job interview and I failed to get the job.

B) BELIEFS ABOUT YOUR ACTIVATING EXPERIENCES

rB) rational Beliefs (your wants or desires)

How unfortunate to get rejected!
I don't like getting rejected.
I wish I had gotten accepted.
How annoying!
Looks like I'll have difficulty getting the job I want.

iB) irrational Beliefs (your demands or commands)

1. How awful to get rejected!
2. I can't stand this rejection!
3. I should have given a better interview and got accepted.
4. This rejection makes me a rotten person.
5. I'll never get the kind of a job I want!
6. I'll always do poorly on job interviews.

C) CONSEQUENCES OF YOUR BELIEFS ABOUT ACTIVATING EXPERIENCES

deC) desirable emotional Consequences (appropriate bad feelings)

Sorrow and regret
Frustration and irritation
Determination to keep trying

dbC) desirable behavioral Consequences (desirable behaviors)

Continued search for a job
Attempt to upgrade my skills

ueC) undesirable emotional Consequences (inappropriate feelings)

I felt depressed.
I felt anxious.

I felt worthless.
I felt angry.

ubC) undesirable behavioral consequences (undesirable behaviors)

I refused to go for other job interviews.
I felt so anxious I functioned badly on other interviews.

D) DISPUTING OR DEBATING YOUR IRRATIONAL BELIEFS
(State this in form of questions)

1. Why is it awful to get rejected for a job?
2. Why can't I stand this rejection?
3. What evidence exists that I should have acted better on the interview and got accepted?
4. How does this rejection make me a rotten person?
5. In what way will I find it impossible ever to get the kind of job I want?
6. Why must I always do poorly on job interviews?

E) EFFECTS OF DISPUTING OR DEBATING YOUR IRRATIONAL BELIEFS

cE) cognitive Effects of disputing (similar to rational beliefs)

1. Nothing makes it awful to get rejected, even though I find it highly inconvenient
2. I can stand rejection, though I'll never like it.
3. I can find no reason why I should or must have given a better interview, though it would have proved nice if I had.
4. Rejection never makes me a rotten person—but a person with some unfortunate traits.
5. I won't find it impossible to get a good job, though I may find it difficult to do so.
6. I don't have to do poorly on job interviews always, especially if I try to learn from my errors.

eE) emotional Effects (appropriate feelings)

I felt sorrowful but not depressed.
I felt concerned but not anxious.
I felt self-accepting.
I felt frustrated but not angry.

bF) behavioral Effects (desirable behaviors)

I went for some more job interviews.
I started to look into getting some additional training.
I registered with an employment agency.
I sent out more letters applying for jobs.

to think, emote, and behave in certain ways, although virtually none of our behavior stems solely from instinct and just about all of it has powerful environmental and learning factors that contribute to its "causation." There are powerful organic and biological factors that exist in human disturbance. Still, social and therapeutic relearning can greatly help disturbed individuals even when they clearly appear to have innately predisposed handicaps.

Since people act differently depending on their expectations, therapists can use client expectations to help them overcome their disturbances. Individuals will change their thoughts, feelings, and behaviors when they expect that others want them to do so. Clients improve their dysfunctional emoting and behaving if a therapist helps them see how they react to external sources and instead see how they can learn, to a large degree, to take control of their own thoughts, feelings, and actions.

Individuals significantly influence their own emotions and behaviors by their attributions of motives, reasons, and causes. Clients can be helped to understand and change misattributions which contribute to emotional disturbances. Virtually all individuals frequently have several important irrational ideas or absolutistic and anti-empirical modes of thinking that interfere with their healthy thoughts, emotions, and behaviors, and when they change these ideas their dysfunctional behavior tends to change.

Individuals tend to evaluate or rate themselves and they influence their emotions and behaviors by the kind of self-ratings they choose. People who rate themselves usually or frequently end up with low self-esteem and would better learn to rate themselves unconditionally as good or refuse to rate themselves or their essences at all while they continue to rate their specific behaviors.

People use various kinds of cognitive defenses to obscure or deny their perceived "wrong" or "shameful" acts. Cognitive defensiveness tends to be minimized or to disappear when people change their irrational ideas about self-rating and self-damning. People have both an innate and acquired tendency to have low frustration tolerance— to do things that seem easier in the short run. Effective therapy leads to higher frustration tolerance or a philosophic outlook that accepts the fact that personal gains usually involve pain.

Anticipation of threat is an important cognitive mediating process in emotional disturbance. Therapists must deal with it in effective therapy. Because people have very powerful innate and acquired tendencies to disturb themselves emotionally and act dysfunctionally, they will benefit most from a highly active, directive psychotherapeutic approach. Effective psychotherapy demands a therapist who actively and directly disputes, challenges, and questions clients' irrational philosophies and persuades them to adopt less self-defeating beliefs. Effective psychotherapy will include a considerable amount of active-directive homework assignments, especially through in vivo practice that interrupts or contradicts dysfunctional behavior. Efficient therapy often consists of helping clients not to take others' insults too seriously and of helping them to accept others without condemning those who act against them even when these others intentionally do so. People distinctly upset themselves or make significant changes in their behavior when they feel insulted.

Catharsis of dysfunctional emotions, particularly anger, may have palliative effects on relieving these emotions, but catharsis may also reinforce irrational beliefs and thereby help them *feel* better instead of *get* better. Catharsis can lead to increases in anger and punitiveness. People to a large extent choose their emotional disturbances and therefore can choose to surrender them. Clients can choose significantly to change most of their natural and long-practiced disturbances and choose to actualize potential for personality growth.

When people feel emotionally disturbed, they have considerable ability to determine to change and to follow various kinds of self-control or self-management procedures. Self-control procedures have clear-cut and important cognitive elements. Persons' ability to cope with distress and threat seems significantly affected by their conceptions of how well they think they can cope. Teaching coping skills and helping clients to believe strongly that they can cope with distress and threat constitute effective methods of psychotherapy.

A good deal of psychotherapy consists of cognitive diversion or distraction. When people distract themselves from various kinds of disturbed thoughts, feelings, and actions, they significantly change their behavior. Effective psychotherapy consists of education and reeducation—of providing clients with salient information and instruction that will help them understand what they have done to disturb themselves and what they can do to make themselves less disturbed. Effective psychotherapy includes some elements of suggestion. At the same time, therapy can help clients to achieve less suggestibility and make themselves more influenced by their own empirically and experimentally based thinking and less influenced by the absolutistic suggestions of others.

Effective therapy often includes the therapist's using modeling procedures and sometimes helping clients gain specific awareness of how they can employ RET techniques to help themselves overcome their disturbances. Modeling involving distinct cognitive mediating processes and modeling with specific informational awareness elements proves more helpful than modeling without such elements. Showing clients how to increase their problem-solving skills is an effective cognitive form of psychotherapy. Individuals with problem-solving deficiencies tend to behave in more disturbed ways. Role-playing that includes a clear-cut cognitive analysis of the feelings involved during role enactment and that includes cognitive restructuring of the attitudes revealed by the role-playing is more effective than nonreflective role-playing without cognitive analysis or cognitive restructuring. Effective therapy often includes some amount of skill training and helping of clients to perceive their abilities and capacities as they acquire new skills.

Rational-Emotive Therapy largely employs direct philosophic confrontation. The therapist demonstrates to clients how dysfunctional emotions or behaviors only indirectly stem from such activities or agents. These symptoms more directly result from their beliefs. The therapist then teaches the client to dispute irrational beliefs until the client thinks differently about a situation and behaves more appropriately.

Rational-emotive therapists may use behavioral techniques such as activity homework assignments which are assigned during various sessions. Assignments are to help the student take risks, gain new experiences, interrupt dysfunctional habits, and change philosophies regarding certain activities.

Another technique of rational-emotive therapists is emotive release. The therapist may persuade the client to express himself openly, no matter how painful it may be to do so. The therapist expresses unconditional positive regard at the same time he reveals and attacks defenses.

The main philosophic ideologies that are the underpinnings of most disturbed behavior are the irrational ideas that (1) clients must totally condemn themselves and others for wrong or inefficient conduct; (2) clients must be absolutely sure that certain undesirable events will not occur; (3) clients are utter heroes when they follow a proper line of conduct and complete villains when they do not. The rational-emotive therapist shows clients that only by accepting reality, uncertainty, and tolerance are they likely to overcome emotional disturbances.

RET therapists show clients how (1) to rid themselves of anxiety, guilt, and depression by accepting themselves whether or not they succeed at important tasks and whether or not people approve of or love them; (2) to minimize anger, hostility, and violence by becoming tolerant of other people even when they find others' opinions or performances unfair; and (3) to reduce their low frustration tolerance by working hard to change unpleasant reality, but learning to accept adversity when it is truly inevitable (Ellis, 1979).

The setting for RET is similar to other forms of therapy. However, the relationship between the client and the therapist is somewhat different. Rational-emotive therapists are highly active, give their own views without hesitation, usually answer direct questions, and do a good deal of speaking.

A review of the outcome studies of the effectiveness of Rational-Emotive Therapy shows that a course based on the principles of Rational-Emotive Therapy can be used effectively as a preventive mental health educational model with "normal" populations (DiGiuseppe, Miller, & Trexler, 1977). A few studies indicate that a modification of a child's self-verbalizations or irrational self-statements can have a positive effect on emotional adjustment and behavior. Other findings suggest that systematic desensitization is a more effective treatment of persons with monosymptomatic or classical phobias, while a cognitive approach such as Rational-Emotive Therapy works better with those who demonstrate more general anxiety or social phobias. Finally, Glass and colleagues (Glass & Smith, 1976; Smith and Glass, 1977; Glass, 1978) examined 375 psychotherapy outcome studies, thirty-five of which involved Rational-Emotive Therapy. They reported that Rational-Emotive Therapy ranked second among ten types of therapy examined in terms of a mean effect compared with the control group outcomes. Only systematic desensitization fared better.

Cognitive Therapy

Beck (1976) argues that common psychological disturbances center around aberrations in thinking and that psychological skills such as integrating, labeling, and interpreting can be applied to correcting these aberrations. Treatment identifies misconceptions, tests their validity, and substitutes more appropriate concepts. The patient may also be exposed to experiences that are in themselves powerful enough to change misconceptions. These corrective emotional experiences will help a person to perceive others more realistically and modify inappropriate maladaptive responses. Finally, treatment may involve the development of specific forms of client behaviors that lead to more general changes in the way the client views himself and the real world. The strategies may involve practicing techniques for dealing with people who frighten the client, such as in assertiveness training.

Cognitive therapy is most appropriate for clients who have the capacity for introspection and for reflecting about their thoughts and feelings. Such clients can increase their awareness of what they are thinking, recognize what thoughts are off-base, substitute accurate for inaccurate judgments, and receive feedback about the changes they have made.

The kinds of thinking that underlie most client problems involve distress, difficulty in expressing behaviors, or a deficiency in behaviors. Client thinking may reflect direct, tangible distortions of reality or illogical thinking in which the system of making inferences or drawing conclusions from observations is at fault.

Beck's approach to cognitive therapy posits the existence of so-called automatic thoughts. These thoughts do not arise as a result of deliberation, reasoning, or reflection about an event or topic; they "just happen," as by reflex. Automatic thoughts are specific and discrete, occurring in a kind of shorthand. The thoughts are regarded by the client as plausible, or reasonable. The wording of the thoughts varies according to the situation, but generally there is the same theme. The automatic thoughts are often repetitive and idiosyncratic, being peculiar to an individual patient or to other patients with the same diagnosis. The particular way a person monitors and instructs himself, praises and criticizes himself, interprets events, and makes predictions, influences most normal behavior as well as emotionally disordered behavior. The sequence of scanning the situation, debating, and making decisions leads to self-instruction or verbal messages directing behavior.

Individuals have general cognitive rules that guide how they react to specific situations. These rules channel overt actions, form the basis for specific interpretations, and provide standards for judgment. The content of rules for coding experiences revolves around two axes: (1) danger versus safety and (2) pain versus pleasure. The ratio between potential harm and coping mechanisms is the risk factor. Many interpersonal situations involve an assessment of risks.

The primary component of cognitive therapy is collaboration between the client and the therapist. Cognitive therapy is relatively short-term, structured, and focused on present events. There is usually an agenda determined by the client and the therapist. Therapy has a problem-solving orientation; problems with similar causes are grouped together and then the therapist selects appropriate techniques for each group of problems. The therapist may identify either a constellation of symptoms or the first link in a chain of symptoms.

In cognitive therapy, the client focuses on those thoughts or images that produce unnecessary discomfort or suffering or lead to self-defeating behavior. A basic procedure for helping a client to identify his automatic thoughts is to train him to observe the sequence of external events and his reactions to them. The process of regarding thoughts objectively is called *distancing*. When a client can regard a thought as a hypothesis or inference, rather than fact, he is distancing well. The technique of teaching the client not to regard himself as the focal point of all events is called *decentering*.

In Beck's model, there are maladaptive underlying assumptions that give rise to automatic thoughts. Events will trigger an assumption that leads to automatic thoughts or symptoms. Cognitive distortions that can be observed in individuals who exhibit maladaptive behavior are selective abstraction, arbitrary inference, overgeneralization, magnification, minimization, and inexact labeling.

The cognitive approach to depression separates the syndrome into specific components. A cognitive therapist could start with any of the symptom clusters—emotional, motivational, cognitive, behavioral, or physiological—and concentrate on changing the symptom cluster. Each symptom cluster is a problem which can be viewed first as observable abnormal behavior or symptoms, second as an underlying motivational disturbance, and third as a cluster of cognitions. The assessment of improvement in depression will require an evaluation of changes in affect, motivation, cognition, and physiological functions as well as overt behaviors.

Meichenbaum's Cognitive Behavioral Therapy

Another important cognitive therapist is Meichenbaum (1978), who has described the clinical potential in modifying what clients say to themselves. Moreover, he has described how behavior therapy techniques can be used to modify client "self-talk." His cognitive *self-guidance training* technique has been used with impulsive children. First the therapist performs a task while a client observes; then the client performs the same task while the therapist instructs the subject aloud. Next the client performs the task while instructing himself aloud, the client performs the task while whispering, and finally the client performs the task while self-instructing covertly. Verbalizations include questions about the nature of the task, answers to the questions in the form of cognitive rehearsal and planning, self-instruction in the form of self-guidance, and self-reinforcement. Impulsive children were exposed to a self-instructing model and also had opportunities to try out the "self-instructions." Self-instruction packages have also been used with schizophrenics and neurotics. Highly test anxious clients are another population whose self-statements evidently contribute to maladaptive behavior. In the latter case, the desensitization component of the treatment was modified to include coping rather than mastery imagery. In treating phobics, a coping model that uses verbalization throughout the treatment was found to facilitate the most self-report affective change.

A major intervention used in cognitive therapy is called *stress inoculation training*. Adaptive defenses allow a client to deal with threatening material in small doses. Adaptive defenses or coping skills will allow paced mastery to occur, which provides inoculation to greater intensities of threat. Inadequate coping skills either shut out the awareness of threat or expose the individual to the threat in full intensity. Stress inoculation training involves three phases. The first provides the client with a conceptual framework for understanding the nature of his stressful reactions. In the second phase, a number of behavioral and cognitive coping skills are offered for the client to rehearse. Third, the client is given an opportunity to practice his coping skills during exposure to a variety of stressors.

During the first part of stress inoculation, the psychologist provides a conceptual framework in lay terms for understanding the nature of the client's response to stressful events. The logic of the training is related to the conceptualization. For instance, the therapist might describe client fear as involving two major elements: (1) heightened arousal and (2) anxiety-engendering avoidant thoughts. Logically, then, treatment should help the client control his physiological arousal and change the self-statements that occupy his mind under stressful conditions. Four phases in a stress reaction are also described: (1) preparing for a stressor, (2) confronting or handling a stressor, (3) possibly being overwhelmed by a stessor, and (4) reinforcing oneself for having coped with a stressor. The client is introduced to a conceptualization of stress which has two components and progresses through four stages.

In the second phase of stress inoculation, the client is introduced to a variety of coping techniques that can be employed at each stage of the coping process. These techniques involve direct actions and cognitive coping strategies. Direct action such as physical relaxation exercises can provide a basis for reducing physiological arousal. This kind of activity could also eliminate negative self-statements. A cognitive coping strategy could include increasing awareness of negative self-statements in phobic situations, which then provide the occasion for producing incompatible coping self-statements. The client is helped to develop examples of self-statements that could be used during each phase of a stressful event.

The third part of stress inoculation involves the client testing and practicing coping skills under stressful conditions. For instance, unpredictable electric shock can be used to induce anxiety and a client could experiment with a variety of different coping techniques. Stress inoculation training packages have also been used for control of anger and control of pain.

Relationship Theories and Interventions

Rogerian or client-centered therapy has its roots in phenomenologic-al psychology. This approach to understanding and predicting be-havior assumes that things are what they appear to be and that the significant determinants of behavior are the individual's perception of himself and his environment. Phenomenology is concerned with the self-reports of sensations and feelings as well as perceptions of the external world and persons themselves (Rogers, 1951). This theory is basically phenomenological in character and relies heavily upon the concept of self. The end-point of personality development is a basic congruence between the phenomenal field of experience and the conceptual structure of the self. This situation represents the max-imum in realistically oriented adaptation, which means the estab-lishment of an individualized value system having considerable identity with the value system of any other equally well-adjusted member of the human race.

As can be seen, the self-concept is a major construct in client-centered therapy. Rogers' earliest formulation of the self-concept emphasized the role of the self as the basic factor in the formation of personality and the determination of behavior (Patterson, 1961). The self-concept was defined as the self as seen by the experiencing person. In 1959, Rogers defined the self-concept as the "the organized, consistent conceptual Gestalt composed of characteristics of the 'I' or 'me' and the perceptions of the relationships of the 'I' or 'me' to others and to various aspects of life, together with the value attached to these perceptions." At that time, Rogers also discussed the concept of an ideal self and the concept of self-actualization. The self-concept is an important determiner of behavior but is not an executive or doer.

Self is a central factor in the healthy development of the personality. The self-concept becomes disturbed when the maintenance or enhancement of the self is frustrated or threatened. Emotional or personality disturbances have, then, a common characteristic, which is a loss of self-esteem. Stress results from threat to the preservation and enhancement of self.

Rogers postulates a unitary concept of motivation. The basic actualizing tendency is the only significant motive, and the self is only one expression of the general tendency of the organism to behave in those ways that maintain and enhance itself. Rogers (1951) said, "The organism has one basic tendency and striving—to actualize, maintain, and enhance the experiencing organism." The general tendency toward actualization expresses itself also in the actualization of that portion of the experience of the organism which is symbolized in the self. If self and experience are incongruent, then the general tendency to actualize the organism may work at cross-purposes with the tendency to actualize self.

Rogers' theory of psychopathology emphasizes the role of the parents and whether their love has been conditional or not. Children may begin to perceive experiences selectively based on the conditions of worth as defined by their parents. Experiences and behaviors that are not consistent with parental conditions of worth are not perceived accurately, and they may be distorted or excluded from awareness. If experiences are distorted and denied access into consciousness, the situation arises where there is an incongruence between what is experienced and what is symbolized as part of a person's self-concept. Maladjustment is the incongruity between the organism's total experience and what is actually symbolized as part of the self-concept. For the sake of being liked by others, individuals may deny or distort their experiences. Symptoms can function to prevent threatening experiences from being accurately represented in awareness.

The Rogerian model of successful psychotherapy has six basic conditions.

1. Two persons are in contact or have the minimum essential of a relationship when each makes a perceived or subceived difference in the experiental field of the other.
2. The person who is called the client is in a state of incongruence, being vulnerable or anxious. Therapy is more likely to

get underway if the client is anxious rather than merely vulnerable. Incongruence is a discrepancy between the self as perceived and the actual experience of the organism. Anxiety is the response of an organism to the "subception" that the discrepancy between self-concept and experience may enter awareness, thus forcing a change in self-concept.

3. The person who is called the therapist is congruent in the relationship. When self-experiences are accurately symbolized and included in the self-concept, then the state is one of congruence of self and experience. The therapist should be "himself" or "herself" in the relationship. For therapy to occur, the wholeness of the therapist is primary, but a part of this congruence must be the experience of unconditional positive regard and the experience of empathic understanding.

4. The therapist is experiencing unconditional positive regard toward the client. Unconditional positive regard means that the self-experience of another is perceived in such a way that no self-experience can be discriminated as more or less worthy of positive regard than any other.

5. The therapist is experiencing an empathic understanding of the client's internal frame of reference. To be empathic, the therapist must perceive the internal frame of reference of another with accuracy and with the emotional components and meanings which pertain thereto, as if one were the other person, but without ever losing the "as if" condition.

6. The client perceives, at least to a minimal degree, the unconditional positive regard of the therapist for him or her and the empathic understanding of the therapist.

These therapeutic conditions exist continuously and are not meant to be all-or-none statements. However, Rogers does believe that these six conditions are sufficient for therapy regardless of the particular characteristics of the client or the client's problem.

Empathy is a critical aspect of Rogerian therapy. Rogers' concepts of empathy have changed over the years. At first empathy was considered the reflection by the therapist of the client's feelings. Later, empathy involved the therapist going beyond what the client has overtly communicated. Rogers (1959) said, "This is not to say, however, that the client-centered therapist responds only to the obvious in the phenomenal world of the client." If that were so, it would cast doubt upon evidence that seems to indicate that therapists work through empathic responses to introduce their clients to slightly new points of view.

Client-centered therapy has been criticized from a number of vantage points. Ellis (1969) described Patterson's (1969) account of client-centered therapy as parochial, definitional, and impractical. Moreover, Ellis says that although client-centered therapy purports to establish a monistic view of the nature of man and psychotherapy, it never escapes from pluralism. A behavioral therapist, Phillips (1969) also criticized client-centered therapy and in particular the concept of self-actualization and the assumption that man is free and can actualize himself when he has already argued that self-actualization has to occur in a social context. Phillips maintained that therapy implies causality and determinism. "We cannot talk about self-actualization as meaningful socially in a deterministic way and also argue that somehow the individual has this self-actualizing power in a free sense." The definition of freedom and determinism in counseling and psychotherapy is still to be resolved.

Conclusion

The variety of helping models that we have discussed seems imposing and even confusing to the student who comes to the field looking for ways to simplify problems and reduce ambiguity. Unfortunately, we have little empirical evidence upon which to base claims that any single approach to treatment is superior to any other across all types of clients and situations.

Indeed, the search for panaceas and patented prescriptions has not been very fruitful. At this point in the history of psychology it may be more worthwhile to ask of our theories very specific questions. These crucial questions concern which treatments with which clients in what situations produce which specific outcomes. Hopefully our research efforts in the future will begin to answer these questions.

References

Bakan, D. *On method*. San Francisco: Jossey Bass, 1968.

Bandura, A. *Principles of behavior modification*. New York: Holt, Rinehart & Winston, 1969.

Beck, A. *Cognitive therapy and emotional disorders*. New York: International Universities Press, 1976.

Bergin, A. E. The evaluation of therapeutic outcomes. In A. E. Bergin & S. L. Garfield (Eds.), *Handbook of psychotherapy and behavior change*. New York: Wiley, 1971.

Bergin, A. E., & Lambert, M. J. The evaluation of therapeutic outcomes. In S. L. Garfield & A. E. Bergin (Eds.), *Handbook of psychotherapy and behavior change*. New York: Wiley, 1971.

Bordin, E. S. A psychodynamic view of counseling psychology. *The Counseling Psychologist*, 1980, *9*, 62–69.

Cautela, J. R. Covert sensitization. *Psychological Reports*, 1967, *20*, 459–468.

Cummings, N. A., & Follette, W. J. Brief psychotherapy and medical utilization. In H. Dorken & Associates (Eds.), *The professional psychologist today*. San Francisco: Jossey Bass, 1976.

DiGiuseppe, R., Miller, N., & Trexler, L. A review of rational-emotive psychotherapy outcome studies. *The Counseling Psychologist*, 1977, 7, 64–72.

Dollard, J., & Miller, N. E. *Personality and psychotherapy*. New York: McGraw-Hill, 1950.

Ellis, A. Comments on C. H. Patterson's current view of client-centered or relationship therapy. *The Counseling Psychologist*, 1969, *1*, 37–42.

Ellis, A. The practice of rational emotive therapy. In A. Ellis & Whiteley, J. M. (Eds.), *Theoretical and empirical foundations of a rational emotive therapy*. Monterey, Calif.: Brooks/Cole, 1979.

Ellis, A., & Abrams, E. *Brief psychotherapy in medical and health practice*. New York: Springer Publishing Company, 1978.

Eysenck, H. J. The effects of psychotherapy: An evaluation. *Journal of Consulting Psychology*, 1952, *16*, 319–324.

Eysenck, H. J. The effects of psychotherapy. *International Journal of Psychiatry*, 1965, *1*, 97–178.

Foltz, D. OTA Report says "hard facts" possible on psychotherapy. *APA Monitor*, December, 1980, *11*, 186.

Frank, J. D. *Persuasion and healing* (2nd ed.). Baltimore: Johns Hopkins University Press, 1973.

Glass, B. V. Primary, secondary and meta analysis of research. *Educational Researcher*, 1978, *5*, 3–8.

Glass, G. V., & Smith, M. L. Meta-analysis of psychotherapy outcome studies. Paper presented at the Society for Psychotherapy Research, San Diego, 1976.

Glasser, W. *Reality therapy*. New York: Harper & Row, 1969.

Glasser, W. & Zunin, L. *Reality therapy*. In R. Corsini (Ed.), *Current psychotherapies* (2nd ed.). Itasca, Ill.: Peacock Publishers, 1979.

Goldfried, M. Toward the delineation of therapeutic change principles. *American Psychologist*, 1980, *35*, 991–995.

Harman, R. A gestalt point of view on facilitating growth in counseling. *The Personnel and Guidance Journal*, 1975, *53*, 363–366.

Hosford, R. E. Self-as-a-model: A cognitive social learning technique. *The Counseling Psychologist*, 1980, *9* (1), 45–61.

Horan, J. J. Experimentation in counseling and psychotherapy, part 1: New myths about old realities. *Educational Research*, 1980, *9* (11), 5–10.

Kanfer, F. H., & Phillips, J. S. *Learning foundations of behavior therapy*. New York: Wiley, 1970.

Keisler, C. A. Mental health policy as a field of inquiry for psychology. *American Psychologist,* 1980, *35,* 1066–1080.

Kovel, J. *A complete guide to therapy.* New York: Pantheon Books, 1976.

Mahoney, M. J., & Thoresen, C. E. *Self control: Power to the person.* Monterey, Calif.: Brooks/Cole, 1974.

Mann, J. *Time-limited psychotherapy.* Cambridge: Harvard University Press, 1973.

Meichenbaum, D. Teaching children self-control. In B. Lahey & A. Kazdin (Eds.), *Advances in child clinical psychology* (Vol. 2). New York: Plenum Press, 1978.

Messer, S. B., & Winokur, M. Some limits to the integration of psychoanalytic and behavior therapy. *The American Psychologist,* 1980, *35,* 818–827.

Patterson, C. H. The self in recent Rogerian theory. *Journal of Individual Psychology,* 1961, *17,* 5–11.

Patterson, C. H. A current view of client centered or relationship therapy. *The Counseling Psychologist,* 1969, *1,* 2–24.

Perls, F. *Gestalt therapy verbatim.* Layfayette, Calif.: Real People Press, 1969.

Phillips, E. L. Review of Cecil H. Patterson's "A current view of client centered or relationship therapy." *The Counseling Psychologist,* 1969, *1,* 57–61.

Prochaska, J. *Systems of psychotherapy: A transtheoretical analysis.* Homewood, Ill.: The Dorsey Press, 1979.

Reider, N. Psychotherapy based on psychoanalytic principles. In J. L. McCary (Ed.), *Six approaches to psychotherapy.* New York: Dryden, 1955.

Rogers, C. R. *Client centered therapy.* Boston: Houghton-Mifflin, 1951.

Rogers, C. R. A theory of therapy, personality and interpersonal relationships, as developed in the client-centered framework. In S. Koch (Ed.), *Psychology, a study of a science* (Vol. 3). New York: McGraw-Hill, 1959, pp. 184–256.

Schofield, W. *Psychotherapy: The purchase of friendship.* Englewood Cliffs, N.J.: Prentice Hall, 1964.

Smith, M. L., & Glass, G. V. Meta-analysis of psychotherapy outcome studies. *American Psychologist,* 1977, *32,* 752–760.

Strupp, H. H. The Vanderbilt psychotherapy process-outcome project. Paper presented at the 8th Annual Meeting, Society of Psychotherapy Research, Madison, Wisconsin, June 1977.

Thoresen, C., & Mahoney, M. *Behavioral self-control.* New York: Holt, Rhinehart & Winston, 1974.

Van deRiet, V., Korb, M., & Gorrell, J. *Gestalt therapy—An introduction.* New York: Pergamon Press, 1980.

Wachtel, P. L. *Psychoanalysis and behavior therapy.* New York: Basic Books, 1977.

Wolpe, J. *The practice of behavior therapy.* New York: Pergamon Press, 1969.

4

Group Work in Community Practice

Counseling psychologists in community practice have a long-standing and vital interest in group dynamics and group interventions. In a real sense the life of the community is a group life. Almost all of the vital processes of a community, in families, schools, churches, agencies, and political institutions, as well as in businesses, transpire in the context provided by groups and group interactions. Understanding, participating in, and contributing to these processes is possible only to the degree that the counseling psychologist is aware of and insightful about the nature and impact of group interaction.

Similarly, almost all of the interventions that constitute the professional armamentarium of the counseling psychologist can be delivered in groups as well as one-to-one modes. All of the major theoretical counseling and psychotherapy approaches have group applications. Similarly, interventions such as consultation, training, organizational development, and marriage and family counseling tend to be embedded in group settings and contexts. No aspect of human behavior is more fundamental to the practice of professional psychology than that which involves small group social interaction.

The Counseling Psychologist as an Observer of Groups

The counseling psychologist begins to develop group skills by becoming an observer of different groups. Most effective group techniques are based on careful observations of group characteristics and interactions.

Table 4.1 shows some of the major dimensions of groups which provide a model for use in structuring observations. These dimensions do not constitute an exhaustive list, but do suggest a frame of reference for observing group behavior. However, we caution that a clear single statement of *all* the relevant properties of groups simply does not exist (Hartman, 1979).

TABLE 4.1
Dimensions of Groups

Group Composition
    Level, homogeneity, and pattern of characteristics members bring to the group:
        Abilities
        Attitudes
        Background characteristics
        Personality characteristics
Group Structure
    Patterns of differentiation and interrelations among roles:
        Work structure
        Power structure
        Communications structure
        Affect structure
Task and Environment
    Effects of properties of the group's task and environmental conditions:
        Task type
        Reward conditions
        Environmental stress
Group Process
    Patterns of activity by and interaction among members:
        Task behavior
        Communication
        Influence
        Interpersonal behavior
Group Development
    Development of norms
    Changes in role patterns
Task Performance
    Quality and quantity of performance
    Alteration of group's relation to environment
Effects on Group Members
    Changes in skills
    Changes in attitudes
    Effects on adjustment

Adapted from Joseph E. McGrath, *Social Psychology: A Brief Introduction.* New York: Holt, Rinehart and Winston, 1964.

Group Composition

Group composition includes the level, homogeneity, and patten of characteristics members bring to a group. Group composition involves both the homogeneity or similarity of members and their compatibility. In some cases, groups need members with different kinds of characteristics. For instance, some group problems arise from not having members with an appropriate mix of skills and attitudes. Certain dimensions of a group, such as the communication structure or power structure, can impede the full utilization of members' abilities. This is one reason that the power or communication structure of groups sometimes needs to adapt as tasks and goals change.

It is possible to examine group composition from the standpoint of personality characteristics of members. Schutz (1961) talks about "compatibility" as a function of the needs to give and receive control, affection, and inclusion. He found that compatible pairs (i.e., one individual who needs to *give* affection, inclusion, or control paired with another individual who needs to *receive* these elements) tend to work more effectively in relatively complex group problem-solving tasks. The group worker should remember, however, that groups in which members are more similar in personality characteristics may communicate more easily, but still be less effective in some kinds of task performances.

Group composition includes the motivation that members bring to the group. Groups differ in terms of their motivation toward group goals. Group member motivation has to do with the balance between the strength of member motivation in regard to individual and group goals. Four possible patterns of rewards for group membership exist: (1) a member obtains rewards independently on the basis of personal performance, (2) a member obtains rewards through competition with others, (3) a member obtains rewards through cooperation or teamwork, and (4) a member obtains rewards from the interpersonal relationships in the group.

Role Structure

Groups can be viewed as systems of interrelated parts; but the parts tend to represent roles rather than simply individual members. Individuals are involved with many groups simultaneously, but they *participate in* rather than *belong to* a group. Group structure involves role systems that represent the total pattern of role relationships among occupants of various positions. Both personality characteristics and role expectations and conceptions will influence role behavior.

Task and Communication Structure

The work structure of a group is determined by the way tasks are divided and integrated. Work structure can be divided either horizontally, by special function, or vertically, by level of authority and responsibility. The power structure of a group involves group members' potential influence on each other in particular areas. A group is seen as having power over the behavior of members to the degree that those members are attracted to it.

The communication structure of a group will influence both members' morale and their satisfaction. However, the status or power hierarchy of a group can affect the communication structure. For example, high status members tend to both send and receive more messages in groups than do low status members.

The friendship or affect structure of a group involves relationships among group members as individuals. Proximity, similarity, and attraction are important factors which determine friendship patterns. Although group members will tend to influence and be influenced by members whom they like, there is little evidence that group members who like each other will necessarily perform tasks more effectively. Negative affect in a group may be disruptive, but positive affect is not *necessarily* facilitative for task performance. Task success may lead to positive affect even though positive interpersonal relations do not necessarily lead to task success.

Group structure is related to three kinds of group interaction processes: (1) flow of communication, (2) flow of influence, and (3) flow of affect. These three processes are interrelated. Communication is necessary if influence or positive and negative affect is to exist. Also, members are more likely to communicate with people toward whom they have positive feelings and with people who have high status in the group.

Group Interaction Analysis

A large number of theoretical systems exist for measuring group interaction processes. Such systems may deal with manifest content, functional meaning, or underlying meaning of interactions.

Bennis and Shephard (1956) described methods of systematic data collection regarding group activities. One basic method concentrates on frequency of group interaction and patterns of interaction. The observer is interested in the frequency of interaction, the specific participants engaged in interaction, the initiator of interaction, the ordering of interaction, and the duration, direction, and interruption of interactions.

Bales (1950) developed a system for categorizing behavior known as interaction process analysis. The system analyzes interaction and the sentiments accompanying them. There are twelve categories of interaction; the first three and the last three concern social-emotional units such as positive and negative reactions of the group members to one another and to the group's task. The middle six categories are task oriented and cover exchanges of information among the group members related to the job of solving some problem under discussion. An interaction graph can allow the psychologist to observe fluctuations of a group as they move from hostile to friendly reactions and from problems of communication to problems of evaluation.

In small discussion groups where there is a problem to be solved, group process tends to follow a sequence of four phases. First is the adaptive phase of pooling information and other resources to see how they can be used to accomplish a task. Second is the goal attainment phase of actually working out the decisions and taking the action that completes the task. Third is an integrative phase of reestablishing group solidarity. And finally, fourth comes a tension-relieving phase which consists of joking, laughter, and expressions of relief that the job has been accomplished.

Bion (1961) conceptualized groups as essential to people's mental and emotional life. Group members have needs and desires and attempt to derive satisfactions from the group. The "group mentality" is a product of the individual needs of group members. Individual needs often contribute to the group mentality in ways of which members are unaware. The group mentality can affect members disagreeably when they are at variance with the prevailing emotional forces within a group. The group's "culture" is the structure which the group achieves at any given moment, the activities it pursues, and the organization it adopts. It should be noted that these are all characteristics attributed to the group by participants or observers.

Bion's ideas were formalized into a set of categories for recording group behavior (Thelen, 1954). The group mentality is divided into three emotional modalities or recurring patterns of expressive behavior: (1) fight-flight, (2) pairing, and (3) dependency.

Fight-flight represents the desires of the group to escape the task that faces the group either by fighting one another or running away from the task. Pairing represents the tendency of the group to seek security by establishing pair relationships within the group. Dependency represents the group's desire to be dependent on the leader. A fourth category called "work" represents the desire of the group to engage in problem-solving activity. Persons who support a modality are said to have high "valency" for the modality. Persons who lead the group from one modality to another are called "barometric."

The work modality is differentiated into four classes. Level One is personal-need oriented work which often involves expressions of personal needs. Level Two work maintains or follows through on a task. These are group oriented, routine expressions. Level Three work is group focused. These expressions are group-oriented, focused and energetic and tend to give direction and meaning to the group. Level Four work is creative, insightful, and integrative. These expressions integrate experiences and suggest meaning which is relevant to present problems.

In formally organized groups, members may hold special positions which have associated role expectations. In any group there are a number of roles which are not formally designated. For example, the habitual opposer is a role that exists within a group and is recognized rather than sanctioned.

In observing membership roles, a psychologist should be concerned with the interpersonal consequences of these roles. What needs of the individual does the role satisfy? Second, the psychologist should try to identify the consequences of these roles for other group members. What needs of others do they satisfy or arouse? Next, the psychologist should ascertain the consequences of different membership roles for the integration of a group. What is the effect of these roles on cohesiveness, solidarity, mutual respect? Finally, the psychologist should identify consequences of different membership roles for performance of group tasks. Gibb (1954) has developed a system for observing groups which has four types of roles: (1) task roles, (2) group maintenance roles, (3) task and group roles, and (4) individual roles.

Hemphill (1956) has developed a useful tool for observing group interaction. It utilizes a questionnaire consisting of 150 statements about group characteristics or attributes. The respondent indicates to what degree each of the 150 statements is true for a group. There are scores on thirteen group dimensions: (1) autonomy, (2) control, (3) flexibility, (4) hedonic tone, (5) homogeneity, (6) intimacy, (7) participation, (8) permeability, (9) polarization, (10) potency, (11) stability, (12) stratification, and (13) viscidity.

Scores provide a profile of group members' orientations toward a group. The profile is based on the responses of all members of a group or a random sample of them and gives a description of the group as it appears to the members.

Another multidimensional scaling procedure for studying groups is called Systematic, Multiple Level Observation of Groups (SYMLOG) (Bales, 1980). The method uses the observations of group members. They observe and describe not only the group's overt behavior but the values they felt they ought to realize in their behavior. A somewhat similar approach is the INDSCAL program developed by Gazda and Mobley (1980). These methods use complex scaling and factor analytic procedures to examine the relationships among members' perceptions of group processes and interpersonal relationships. They are sophisticated, but rather complex procedures that may go beyond the needs of many group leaders.

Another useful instrument is the Hill Interaction Matrix, which allows the observer to describe quantitatively leadership style, group composition, and group development (Hill, 1965). The two basic dimensions, both referring to styles of operations, are content/style and work/style. The content/style dimension describes *what* groups talk about and has four categories: *topic, group, personal,* and *relationship.* A group may talk about "here and now" relationships and reactions of members (relationship). A group may talk about personal problems of members in an historical fashion (personal). A group may talk about the group itself (group). A group may talk about topics external to the group (topic). (See Figure 4.1.)

Within the work/style dimension, there are two subdivisions: *Work* and *Pre-Work.* In pre-work, members are not trying to gain self-understanding. The lowest level is called *responsive,* where little or nothing is taking place except in response to leader probes. The *conventional* category is characterized by engagement in social amenities, stylized transactions, and chitchat. The *assertive* category is characterized by assertions of independence from group perceptions or pressures and a rejection of help from group members. Members are *acting out,* not *acting on,* their problems. The work subdivision has two categories: *speculative* and *confrontive.* A speculative interaction is characterized by cooperative two-way open communication. The key word is discuss. The confrontive category focuses on clarification. Confrontive statements are backed up with some form of documentation.

The matrix places content/style on the horizontal axis and work/

style on the vertical axis and has twenty cells which characterize typical behavior in therapy groups (see Figure 4.1). A HIM statement-by-statement rating assigns every member statement to one of the matrix cells. The HIM-G rating system can be completed by an observer after viewing of a group session, hearing a tape, or reading a

FIGURE 4.1. Content/style categories.

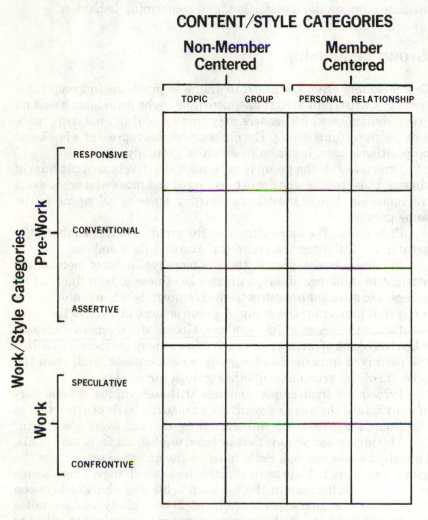

Adapted from: Hill, W. F., *Hill Interaction Matrix*. Los Angeles, Youth Study Center, University of Southern California, 1965.

typescript. It allows the rater to rate group performance on the same dimensions.

In observing groups, the counselor should first try to identify the relevant group outcomes. No single, all-encompassing system for group observation exists. Task performance is one kind of group outcome and is related to group efforts to reach goals. Group development is another kind of outcome and is related to changes in development of group norms and modifications in group structure. Effects on group members is another outcome having to do with changes in attitudes, individual satisfaction, and conforming behaviors.

Group Leadership

Group leaders often are asked to diagnose problems in group functioning. Cartwright (1951) has identified eight principles based on group dynamics which leaders may find helpful in analyzing problems in group functioning. The eight principles represent a few basic propositions emerging from research in group dynamics.

Principle 1. If the group is to be used effectively as a medium of change, those people who are to be changed and those who are to exert influence for change must have a strong sense of belonging to the same group.

Principle 2. The more attractive the group is to its members, the greater the influence the group can exert on its members.

In more cohesive groups, there is more readiness of members to attempt to influence others, a greater readiness to be influenced by others, and stronger pressures toward conformity when conformity is a relevant matter for the group. A group is more attractive the more it satisfies the needs of its members. Group cohesiveness increases when the liking of members for each other as persons increases, when the perceived importance of a group goal increases, and when the prestige of the group among other groups increases.

Principle 3. In attempts to change attitudes, values, or behaviors of individuals, the more relevant they are to the basis of attraction to the group, the greater the influence the group can exert upon them.

The important point is that isolated or abstract facts may not be enough to cause change. Facts must be the accepted property of the group if they are to become an effective basis for change. There seems to be all the difference in the world in achieving changes between those cases in which experts are hired to do a study and present a report and those in which experts are asked to collaborate with the group in doing their own study.

Principle 4. The greater the prestige of a group member in the eyes of the other members, the greater the influence he or she can exert.

From a practical point of view it must be emphasized that the factors giving prestige to a member may *not* be those characteristics most prized by the designated leadership of the group. The most prestigious member of a Sunday School class may not possess the characteristics most similar to the minister of the church. The teacher's pet may be a poor source of influence within a class. This principle is the basis for the common observation that the designated leader and the *actual* leader of a group are often not the same.

Principle 5. Efforts to change individuals which, if successful, would have the result of making them deviate from the norms of the group will encounter strong resistance.

A great deal of evidence has been accumulated showing the tremendous pressures which groups can exert upon members to conform to the group's norms. The price of deviation in most groups is rejection or even expulsion. This is the reason that efforts to change people by taking them from the group and giving them special training or indoctrination so often have disappointing results. This principle also accounts for the finding that people thus trained sometimes display increased tension and aggressiveness toward the group, or a tendency to form cults or cliques with others who have shared their experiences.

These five principles concerning the group as a medium of change would appear to have readiest application to groups created for the purpose of producing change in members. They provide certain specifications for building effective training or therapy groups. They also point, however, to a difficulty in producing change in people in that they show how resistant an individual is to changing in any way contrary to felt group pressures and expectations. In order to achieve many kinds of changes in people, therefore, it is necessary to deal with the total group as a target of change.

Principle 6. Strong pressure for changes in a group can be established by creating a shared perception by members of a need for change, thus making the source of pressure for change lie within the group.

Principle 7. Information relating to the need for change, plans for change, and consequences of change must be shared by all relevant people in a group.

Another way of stating this principle is to say that change in a group ordinarily requires the opening of communication channels. If we look closely at a pathological group (that is, one that has trouble making decisions or effecting coordinated efforts of its members), we are likely to find strong restraints in that group against sharing vital information among its members. Until these restraints are removed, there can be little hope for any real and lasting changes in the group's functioning. In passing it should be pointed out that the removal of barriers to communication may be accompanied by a sudden increase in the communication of hostility or anxiety. The group may appear to be falling apart, and it may afford a painful experience to many of the members. This pain and the fear that things are getting out of hand often stop the process of change once begun.

Principle 8. Changes in one part of a group can produce stress in other parts of a group which can be reduced only by eliminating the change or by bringing about readjustments in the related parts.

It is common practice, for example, to undertake improvements in group functioning by providing training programs for certain classes of people in an organization. A training program for foremen, for nurses, for teachers, or for group workers may be established. If the content of the training is relevant for organizational change, it must of necessity deal with the relationships these people have with other subgroups. If nurses in a hospital change their behavior significantly, it will affect their relations both with the patients and with the doctors. It is unrealistic to assume that both these groups will remain indifferent to any significant change in this respect. This is essentially the basis for studying human groups as interrelated systems, as we saw in chapter 2.

Group Effectiveness

Counseling psychologists can also be asked to assist in evaluating the effectiveness of various kinds of groups. A good beginning point on this task is the proposition that all interpersonal relationships are oriented toward some set of primary goals or functions whose presence is necessary for the relationship to continue and whose absence would seriously undermine it (Bennis, Schein, Berlew, & Steele, 1964). In other words, the goals of interpersonal relationships will influence the norms or criteria used by individuals to evaluate those relationships. Thus, the issue of defining effective interpersonal relationships "boils down" to how well an interpersonal relationship meets the perceived goals of the participants.

Bennis et al. (1964) identify four goals of interpersonal relationships. *Emotional-expressive* relationships are formed for the purpose of self-fulfillment of members, and the main transaction involves *sharing feelings*. An emotional-expressive relationship is good if it is mutually satisfying to the participants. Solidarity is the indicator of a good relationship; ambivalence, alienation, or chronic hostility are indicators of a bad relationship. Solidarity encompasses a wide range of complex attitudes as well as the capacity for the individual to risk the confrontation of their personal and emotional ups and downs.

Confirmatory relationships exist in order to establish two different types of social reality. In the first type of confirmatory relationship, the content of the transactions is information about the self or about the relationship, while in the second type, content includes information about the environment or definitions of situations. In the first type of confirmatory relationship, individuals begin to see each other as others see them and begin to take the perspectives of others. In the second type of confirmatory relationship, individuals are trying to make sense or develop "cognitive mastery" over some element in the environment. In either case, the outcomes of good confirmatory relationships are *consensus* and *confirmation* regarding perceptions of reality. A bad outcome of a confirmatory relationship could involve a situation in which people confirm their relationship but seriously distort some aspect of social reality.

Change or influence relationships involve one or both parties in a relationship coming together to create a change in each other or the relationship. The main transactions involve information about the desired state to be achieved and feedback concerning how the person to be changed is doing. In this kind of relationships, a major criterion is *"desired change."* These relationships are normally planned, almost always oriented toward eventual termination, and the interpersonal changes tend to be "slanted," "tilted," and less reciprocal than other types of relationships. A good *change* relationship leads to three outcomes: (1) consensus that the desired change has been achieved, (2) awareness that the relationship has reached a point wherein continuation will not lead to significant further progress, and (3) internalization of change by the recipient of the learning process so that learning continues.

An *instrumental* relationship is formed in order to achieve some goal or task, and productivity is the key criterion. Competence and output are two main indicators of a good instrumental relationship. Competence involves the way people manage their work, i.e., decision-making, problem solving, quality of collaboration.

Educational Groups

Laboratory Education

Counseling psychologists have become more and more interested in laboratory education, that is, in courses or workshops that combine lectures, focused exercises, and T-groups or sensitivity training techniques. In 1947, the National Training Laboratories pioneered in developing various approaches to human relations training. In some cases T-group or sensitivity training may not be used, and personal development of members may or may not be a major goal. In other cases, laboratories may be designed to improve organizational effectiveness. This aspect of laboratory education is discussed in chapter 6.

A major training activity in laboratory education has been the T-group. A T-group has no formal leader, preset agenda, or rules by which it must operate. The group decides what to do and how best to learn from its experience. Students often study their own reactions to this novel situation and compare their reactions to those of others. T-group experiences can contribute to (1) increased awareness of one's own feelings and the feelings of others, (2) increased awareness of the complexity of the communication process, (3) increased awareness and acceptance of genuine differences in people's needs, goals, and ways of approaching dilemmas, and (4) increased awareness of an individual's own impact on others.

The T-group had its beginnings in a workshop held on the campus of the State Teachers College in New Britain, Connecticut, in the summer of 1946. Over the years the content and operation of T-groups has evolved into a variety of forms. Two variations or types of T-groups are called Therapy for Normals and Instrumented T-groups. Therapy for Normals emphasizes the promotion of individual understanding of oneself and relations with others. In Therapy for Normals, the trainer helps the members to become more aware and to try to understand the nature of their feelings as they respond to the lack of structure in a T-group.

A second kind of T-group is called an Instrumented T-group. In this T-group the trainer is removed from direct participation in the group. In his or her place is a series of self-administered instruments or directions. The feedback provided by the analysis of the data from these instruments is the major mechanism in the development of the T-group. In the Instrumented T-group, emphasis is placed upon the early establishment of a feedback model in the group. Feedback is aided by a set of scales, checklists, and ratings which are used to plot on wall charts the characteristics of the group and personal reactions during each meeting.

A second kind of training activity in laboratory education has been theory sessions. A major assumption underlying laboratory education is that direct experience with a phenomenon should precede the introduction of theoretical concepts. A second equally important assumption is that direct experience *without* intellectual understanding is insufficient to produce learning that is useful and can be generalized to other groups and settings. Theory sessions may examine issues, the social roles played by members, problems of understanding authority, and general issues of social or organizational living.

The third major learning activity in laboratory education has been focused exercises. Exercises are designed to elicit some specific behaviors from group members so that a particular topic such as communication can be studied directly. The exercises may provide opportunities for students to practice some skill such as observing group interaction. Exercises may also be used as a means of simulating the realities of organizational and social life. For example, an exercise might highlight the positive and negative consequences of intergroup competition.

The fourth learning activity has to do with the informal contacts made between students and staff in individual or seminar sessions. Sometimes staff or students may schedule special seminars around topics selected by either. These informal times provide an opportunity to talk about there- and-then and back-home problems or general issues and concerns.

Two main value systems influence laboratory education. The first set of values evolves out of science. Laboratory education encourages students to adopt a hypothetical spirit or a feeling for tentativeness and caution and respect for probable error. Laboratory education thus places a high value on experimentalism or the willingness to expose ideas to empirical testing. A second set of values which affects the course of laboratory education is described as democratic. Collaborative relationships or joint planning efforts are encouraged among students and staff. Also, laboratory education emphasizes a rational or problem-solving approach to conflict resolution. The typical objectives for laboratory education are: (1) self-insight or increased self-knowledge, (2) understanding the conditions that inhibit or facilitate group functioning, (3) understanding interpersonal operations in groups, and (4) developing skills for diagnosing indi-

vidual, group, and organizational behavior. The following processes
are central to laboratory education:

1. *Here and Now Focus*. The focus of examination in laboratory
education is the immediately experienced behavior of students.

2. *Feedback*. Individuals obtain information about their performance and then determine how far their progress deviates from some
desired goal.

3. *Unfreezing*. There are periods of unlearning or "being shook
up" which take place before learning is initiated.

4. *Psychological Safety*. In order for unfreezing to lead to an
increased desire to learn, rather than to heightened anxiety where
the individual is immobilized or impervious to new inputs, an environment must be created with maximum psychological safety.

5. *Observant Participation*. Students learn to master the skill of
observation and analysis.

6. *Cognitive Maps*. Cognitive maps or frameworks for thinking
about experiences help to provide a mastery over phenomena that
previously perplexed students. These maps provide a linkage between laboratory experiences and concepts, and between laboratory
experiences and back-home responsibilities.

Campbell and Dunnette (1968), in a review of the research concerning the effectiveness of laboratory education, report that laboratory education has not been shown to bring about any marked change
in one's standing on general objective measures of attitudes, values,
outlooks, interpersonal perceptions, self-awareness, or interpersonal
sensitivity. However, research suggests that individuals who have
been trained by laboratory education methods are more likely to be
seen as changing their job behaviors than are individuals in similar
job settings who have not been trained. The reported changes are in
the direction of more openness, better self- and interpersonal understanding, and improved communication and leadership skills. Unfortunately, many of these reports may suffer from several sources of
bias. Since the time of the review by Dunnette and Campbell, a need
has existed for more well-designed experimental research about
laboratory education.

Theme-Centered Groups

Another group model that is particularly appropriate and useful in
community practice is one that is termed the "theme-centered"
approach (Cohn, 1969). Many times psychologists are called upon to

organize and lead community groups around particular concerns, issues, or problems that confront specific populations. These topics or "themes" may include such problems as school–community relationships, drug abuse, childrearing practices, police–community relationships, juvenile delinquency, or any of a host of other concerns. Themes may also be quite personal such as "learning to self-disclose," or "learning how to deal with sexual harassment," or any of a variety of self-help or growth concerns. These may have a strong educational flavor and may even be part of in-service training or adult education programs.

In any event, in the theme-centered model, the group leader utilizes the chosen theme both to provide needed information and open discussion in the topic area, and also to develop maximum opportunity for group members to express themselves, become involved in the theme, and relate the theme to their own lives in a deeply personal way (Cohn, 1972).

In this sense the theme-centered approach represents something of a bridge between therapeutically oriented group models that foster high levels of emotional involvement through the use of ambiguity, and traditional educational or academically oriented classes in which narrow discussions of intellectual material about the topic are the overriding rule or norm.

Although theme-centered group work is psychoanalytic in terms of origin, it has been used primarily with populations of "normals" in a variety of settings including business management situations, continuing education workshops, and a variety of community settings (Shaffer & Galinsky, 1974).

The theme-centered group approach is based upon two fundamental philosophic premises. First, it assumes that human beings experience life as separate and autonomous persons. Second, it also assumes that people are social organisms who crave and need social interaction and are fundamentally interdependent. In a sense the theme-centered group represents an effort to meet both of these somewhat disparate or contradictory sets of needs.

The functions of the group within this context are represented in what is called the "I-We-It" triangle. These three points represent aspects of social interaction that are considered crucial in the life of a group.

The "I" represents the individual psychological experience of each group member at a given time. The "We" represents the patterning of interrelationships within the group at any specific time. Finally, the "It" point of the symbolic triangle stands for the theme or task with which the group is jointly involved at a given moment.

The group leader is concerned with helping the group deal with all three of these legitimately significant aspects of their interaction in appropriate ways as they work together. All three aspects of interaction are considered important and necessary ingredients for a maximally beneficial group experience.

A fourth basic concept is called "The Globe." The globe represents the total environmental context within which the group is embedded. As such this environmental context cannot be ignored, nor can the group be expected to function as though it did not exist. For example, if a local community group devoted to discussing the theme or topic of school–community relationships meets on a day in which a near riot occurs between police and unemployed youths, that event is very much a part of the "globe" or environmental context, and is appropriate and legitimate for the group to discuss. Aspects of the "globe" may be external to the group or part of the immediate physical or social environment. For example, the death or serious illness of a group member might be a significant aspect of the "globe."

The theme-centered group approach establishes a specific procedural model for the group leader to follow.

1. *Theme Setting*. The initial step in establishing a group is that of theme setting. Sometimes this is done in a direct and simple way in advance of the establishment of the group. The theme may be advertised or be part of an existing program or curriculum. Many times, however, particularly in community settings, the theme arises out of the concerns of a loosely knit constellation of concerned community members. These people may have articulated only a common feeling of unease or concern with some aspect of community life.

Out of this often dimly articulated concern, a community organizer attempts to help the concerned individuals define a theme that they are committed to and are willing to address as part of a formal group.

The organizer may or may not be the eventual group leader, but the degree to which the chosen theme genuinely reflects the interests, commitments, and involvements of members is an important determinant of the eventual success or failure of the group.

2. *Introductory Procedures*. The theme-centered group leader proceeds in a relatively structured way to initiate the activity of the group. Two primary objectives are implicit in this phase. The group leader attempts first to get all members to focus on the theme topic in a total and open way that involves both their thinking and feeling responses. Second, the group leader attempts to reduce anxiety associated with a new and perhaps unfamiliar social situation

so that each member will be relaxed, safe, and comfortable in the group.

The group leader may begin by establishing a short period of silent reflection on the topic, giving members a chance to "shift gears" away from other concerns. This technique is sometimes called the "triple silence." Members are asked to concentrate on three silent tasks: (1) to think about the theme, (2) to try to be in contact with how it feels to be in the group, and (3) to connect a theme-oriented task with the present group.

After this silent period, if the group members are strangers or if some element of distrust may carry over from prior relationships, the members are asked to introduce themselves and describe briefly their thoughts and feelings. The group leader responds to these initial comments in a warm, accepting, and empathic way, using active listening techniques much as a client-centered counselor might respond in an initial interview. In this process the leader models a style of relating that hopefully becomes part of the developing group climate.

3. *Dynamic Balancing*. The next step in the group process involves the responsibility of the leader to help the group maintain an appropriate balance of attention and time to the three elements represented in the "I-We-It" triangle. The leader may accomplish this through selective responding to various elements of the group interaction or he or she may use techniques such as "snap-shotting." In this technique the leader stops the ongoing action and asks each member in turn to share briefly his or her inner thoughts at that specific moment. This very brief and focused sharing then provides the basis for attending to a neglected aspect of the triangle. Sometimes in working with the "We" element, the leader will focus on dyadic interactions between members or will encourage here and now confrontations much as in a basic encounter group situation. The key, however, for the leader's role is in maintaining a productive *balance* among the three aspects of the theme and the group interaction.

4. *Ground Rules*. As group interaction proceeds, the leader and the group begin to articulate a set of ground rules or norms that help to facilitate their discussion. The first of these is the "Be Your Own Chairman" rule. Essentially, this rule means that each member accepts responsibility for his or her own behavior during the sessions. It is based upon the "autonomy" principle discussed earlier and implies that each member will accept and exercise responsibility for obtaining benefits from the group discussion, rather than depending

upon others to obtain them for him. In practice this means that members will take responsibility for asking questions when clarification is needed, proposing shifts in discussions, or otherwise meeting their own legitimate needs as group members.

Other ground rules are established as they are needed. Typical of such rules are the following:

> *Speak per I.* This guideline means that members will state their own experiences and opinions as clearly as possible and accept ownership of them. They will avoid speaking for others or the group as a substitute for expressing their own views or needs.
>
> *Give the statement behind your question.* This rule involves honest and open sharing of information. For example, rather than merely asking another member if he or she is often nervous in the group, a member states what effect the appearance of such nervousness has on him.
>
> *Disturbance takes precedence.* This rule means that the group will address directly any agitation or emotional interference caused by the group process. The assumption is that such an event reduces concentration on the theme and should not be ignored or disguised.

These and other rules are efforts to facilitate open, honest, and responsible participation in the group. They make explicit the kinds of obligations to each other that are involved in positive group relationships.

The Role of the Leader. The role of the group leader in the theme-centered approach flows out of the process model described above. The group leader may or may not be expert in the content area represented by the theme. The leader's primary role, however, is to help insure that the total group process represents a fully involving and personally relevant experience for each member. That obligation transcends the leader's responsibility to provide specific information or technical assistance.

This model of group work is one that has the advantage of being a psychologically sophisticated and very adaptable approach that can be used in a great many situations. Although it represents a relatively involving experience for members, the high level of structure and well-defined leader responsibilities make it a rather low-risk and low-anxiety-arousing group intervention.

Personal Growth Groups

Personal growth groups were the "rage of the '60s." All kinds of unwarranted claims were made about their effectiveness. Since that time, however, growth group practitioners have been making more modest claims. Moreover, there has been a growing body of research which has helped us to learn more about the significant agents of change in "growth groups." Berman and Zimpfer (1980) reviewed the research on the impact of growth groups. They encourage growth group practitioners to reassess the potential benefits to participants from any particular or growth-oriented group intervention. Growth groups will differ in the way in which they fit into a person's life. For some people, all that is desired is an intensive, small-group interaction. For others, the expectation is that participation will leave a more permanent effect. They conclude that it is increasingly important that potential clients be able to distinguish treatment modalities and their intended effects from one another. The intended effects of particular personal growth group experiences need to be identified so that clients can make informed choices. We heartily second their recommendation!

Encounter Groups

Carl Rogers (1970) is a major proponent of a kind of personal growth model called the basic encounter group which he describes as a potent new force or culture. He presents a naturalistic, observational picture of the process patterns which take place in these groups.

1. *Milling around.* There tends to develop a period of initial confusion, awkward silence, polite surface interaction, or "cocktail party talk," together with frustration and great lack of continuity. Individuals come "face to face" with the fact that there is no structure here except that which they provide.

2. *Resistance to personal expression or exploration.* During the milling phase, individuals are likely to reveal some rather personal attitudes. This tends to foster a very ambivalent reaction among other members of the group.

3. *Description of past feelings.* The past feelings have a "there and then" flavor that is removed and detached from the present situation. They foster a somewhat remote and impersonal climate.

4. *Expression of negative feelings.* The first expressions of significant "here and now" feelings are apt to come out in negative attitudes toward other group members or toward the group leader.

5. *Expression and exploration of personally meaningful material.* Individuals begin to reveal themselves to the group in significant ways. They may let the group understand some deeper facet of themselves.

6. *The expression of immediate interpersonal feelings in the group.* There is the explicit bringing into the open of the feelings experienced in the immediate moment by one member about another. These are sometimes positive and sometimes negative.

7. *The development of a healing capacity in the group.* Group members show a natural and spontaneous capacity for dealing in a helpful, facilitative, and therapeutic fashion with the pain, confusion, and suffering of others.

8. *Self-acceptance and the beginning of change.* Individuals report feelings of greater realness and authenticity. They are closer to their own feelings and hence they are no longer so rigidly organized and are more open to change.

9. *The cracking of façades.* There is an increasing impatience with defenses, and group members are intolerant when any member tries to live behind a front or mask. The group demands that the individual be himself, that his current feelings not be hidden, that he remove the mask of ordinary social intercourse.

10. *The individual receives feedback.* Individuals rapidly acquire a great deal of data as to how they appear to others.

11. *Confrontation.* Individuals confront each other. These confrontations can be positive but they are frequently negative.

12. *The helping relationship outside the group sessions.* Group members provide assistance to one another outside of the regular sessions. They may provide important support for one another by listening and talking to each other about mutual problems.

13. *The basic encounter.* Individuals come into much closer and more direct contact with one another than is customary in ordinary life. I-Thou relationships occur with some frequency in group sessions.

14. *The expression of positive feelings and closeness.* Changes in behavior appear in the group itself. Individuals show an astonishing amount of thoughtfulness and helpfulness toward each other.

The most obvious deficiency of the basic encounter group experience is that frequently the behavior changes, if any, which occur are not lasting. A second hazard associated with intensive group experiences is that individuals may become deeply involved in revealing themselves and then still be left with problems which are not worked through. Another problem is that some individuals who have participated in previous encounter groups may exert a stultifying influence on new workshops that they attend. Finally, in mixed groups, there is sometimes a risk that the warm, positive feelings that develop will have a sexual component that is threatening to some members of the group.

Encountering has been described as "content-free" (Coulson, 1970). A basic encounter group has been described as an "empty occasion" or what happens when one has a lot of time to spend with people and no agenda. The content which emerges under these conditions often has similarities across groups. Some typical events in encounter groups are the following:

1. *Giving and receiving feedback*. An individual learns that he comes across differently than he or she thought.

2. *Explicating the implicit*. There is feedback about events and there are comments about matters which are usually implicit.

3. *Being personal*. Personal is considered to be an attitude, a way of running risks with people, not content. Being personal is reaching out to another not knowing what might happen next.

4. *Identification*. One of the things one brings away from encounter groups is an awareness that we are more alike than we had thought.

5. *On expressing intention*. Intention, if openly communicated and if believed by the recipient, can be sufficiently healing in itself.

6. *On moving the body*. On the whole, one will see more physical movement and more touching in encounter groups than on ordinary social occasions.

A primary learning in an encounter group is procedural learning; that is, an individual learning that he or she can call on others (Coulson, 1970). Surprisingly, one of the long-run effects of encounter groups tends to be that individuals often wind up behaving much as they did before the encounter. The major difference is that individuals choose to be the way they are and no longer feel *compelled* to present themselves in a particular way.

Not everyone agrees with Rogers and Coulson about the benefits of encounter groups. Corsini (1970) contends that encounter groups and "swinging parties" are essentially the same. He says, "Just as youth is rebelling with pot and burning down schools, so, too, adults are rebelling. The timid ones go to encounter groups; the bold ones to swinging parties." It seems clear that encounter groups are not without risk (Hartley, Roback, & Abramowitz, 1976).

Malliver (1971) asks whether the encounter movement provides a beneficial form of growth or whether it is just a lot of (occasionally dangerous) fun and games. He says that nothing approaching comprehensive statistics are being kept by growth centers, and most encounterists are wary of any close, formal evaluation of their work. Although Malliver states many criticisms of encounter groups, he also makes it clear that he does not think the encounter movement is all bad. It already has had an effect on many conventional therapists, giving them second thoughts about some of their long-cherished beliefs, particularly with respect to how the body expresses and interacts with personality. Therapists have long been concerned that their treatment techniques may be too heavily rooted in the verbal interchanges known as intellectualizing (". . . so he said he felt this, and then I said I felt that," etc.). Perhaps the most important result of the encounter movement is that many conventionally trained psychotherapists are selectively incorporating encounter techniques into all sorts of group work and even into individual practices.

Integrity Groups

Integrity groups are based on the idea that many forms of human difficulty can be attributed to a failure or deficiency in personal integrity, in the areas of honesty, responsibility, and involvement. However, Mowrer (1972), the leading exponent of integrity groups, does not believe that "personal integrity" is the sole determinant of effective living. Other factors are genetic, biochemical, and ecological in nature.

An important and unique part of integrity groups is the intake procedure. At first, an individual indicates a desire to be a member of an integrity group. Then the message is conveyed to the Total Integrity Group community (composed of several integrity groups). If there are glaring contraindications, an ad hoc intake committee is established for the applicant. The intake procedure attempts to help the new person change and tries to get him or her to "level" with the committee.

If the candidate is evasive, inconsistent, or defensive in certain areas, he or she may be specifically and very directly "challenged." If the applicant divulges the material he has been hiding, the "heat" subsides and approval and admiration will be expressed. If the individual is intoxicated, heavily medicated, supercilious, or stubbornly uncooperative, the applicant is then told the committee will not recommend admission to an integrity group.

If a person is recommended for admission to an integrity group, the integrity group contract is explained. The contract includes such rules as:

1. There is no physical violence or threat of physical violence.
2. No one leaves a group session when he is under challenge or "upset."
3. There is no "Red-Crossing" or "rat packing." When a person is being challenged, another person does not go to his or her aid until the nature of the challenge is clear and the merits of the case reviewed. Also, a group never "gangs up" on a member.
4. There is no restriction as to what language can be used in a group.
5. There are no "subgroupings."
6. All conversation and action that transpires in a group is confidential.
7. Each newcomer is asked to commit himself to the three principles of Honesty, Responsibility, and Involvement, and to be open to challenge in regard to his nonpractice of any of these.

Integrity groups emphasize honesty and consider dishonesty to be in the "long run" very dysfunctional and destructive. The major reason for the practice of deception is seen as the wish to avoid the work, sacrifice, or self-discipline involved in keeping a contract without losing the privileges associated therewith. Integrity groups may also press their members to make formal commitments with stipulated sanctions if the commitments are not kept. However, in some cases, confession is followed by acceptance, reassurance, forgiveness, and absolution, with little or no emphasis upon *punitive action*.

Four meanings for responsibility are identified. First, responsibility means confession and restitution. Responsibility also means to confess intentions, plans, and contemplated future actions, or "to seek counsel." A third meaning of responsibility is simply "keeping one's word," doing what one says one will do, or if for any reason that proves impossible or highly undesirable, going back to the party or parties to the agreement and "renegotiating the contract." A final meaning for responsibility is not to blame others.

Mowrer (1972) says, "In Integrity Groups, until it is proved otherwise, the assumption is made that even though a given individual in the beginning may truly not be able to 'control himself' in certain areas, he can acquire control if he will trust the group and let it teach him some of the 'facts of life' which up to this point he has successfully prevented himself from learning." A person is not likely to change without the concern and help of others, and they are unable to bring about such change unless the person who is the object of their efforts is willing and eager to be changed.

Integrity group members often ask a person to say how he or she has felt or feels now about incidents, other persons, or self. The group tries to get an individual to verbalize real feelings fully and in nonsanitized terms. Hopefully, a person may then "get in touch with his feelings" and establish more meaningful interactions with others. An example of an integrity group exercise involves asking an individual to move around a circle formed by the group and stop in front of each person in turn, call him or her by name, and say something that the group has reason to believe is emotionally charged for him. This may involve admitting to inordinate pride, ambition, vengefulness, or brutal domination of others, or the person may say, "I am in pain and need help" or "I am lonely and frightened and need your love."

Transactional Analysis Groups

The group method is often a preferred mode of operation in transactional analysis, in which the role of the therapist is more heavily weighted toward teaching than is true of most forms of group therapy (Dusay & Dusay, 1979). The therapist has to be particularly alert to verbal and nonverbal cues in the group. Group members learn about each others' Parent, Adult, and Child while focusing on the present problems of members. A blackboard is usually used for structural diagrams of various interactions.

Transactional analysis is a method of examining social transactions and determining what parts of an individual's "personality" are involved. The basic motivation for all human social behavior is seen as the need for "strokes."

Transactional Analysis assumes that when two people confront each other, there are six ego states involved, three in each person. The basic types of ego states are as follows:

1. The Parent ego state is derived from parental figures. In this

state, a person feels, thinks, acts, talks, and responds just as one of his parents did when he was young. This ego state may affect behavior as the "Parental Influence" performing the functions of a conscience.

2. The Adult ego state is the one in which a person appraises his or her environment objectively and calculates its possibilities and probabilities on the basis of past experience. The Adult functions almost like a computer.

3. The Child ego state is the one in which a person feels, thinks, talks, and responds just the way he or she did as a child. The Child ego state is considered the most valuable part of the personality.

The separation of feeling-and-behavior patterns in diagnosing ego states is called structural analysis. Transactional analysis proper is the second step after structural analysis and involves the analysis of single transactions. A transaction consisting of a single stimulus and a single response, verbal or nonverbal, is the unit of social action. In a transaction, each party gains something. Anything that happens between two or more people can be broken down into a series of single transactions, which can be analyzed on the basis of specifically defined ego states into a finite number of established types. Only about fifteen of these types commonly occur in ordinary interaction.

Three general types of transactions are: complementary, crossed, and ulterior (Dusay & Dusay, 1979). In transactional analysis, individuals are represented by their ego states, and stimulus and response are represented by arrows. Whenever the arrows between the ego states of two individuals are parallel, it is a complementary transaction and communication on the subject may proceed indefinitely. The second type of transaction occurs whenever the arrows are crossed, and in this situation, communication on the original subject will cease abruptly. An ulterior transaction occurs when two levels of transactions are occurring at the same time. Social-level transactions are readily observable and contain overt messages, while psychological-level transactions are hidden and contain ulterior messages. One cannot predict behavior by focusing on the social level of transactions alone.

"Games" are played by two or more people, and there is always an ulterior transaction, a "gimmick" and a "switch." For a "game" to develop and succeed, it must "hook" into a weakness of the respondent; a gimmick is the device which "hooks" the respondent.

Each person has a preconscious life plan or script by which he or she structures fairly long periods of time with ritual activities, pastimes, and games which further the script while giving him or her immediate satisfaction, usually interrupted by periods of withdrawal and sometimes by episodes of intimacy. Scripts are often based on childlike illusions which may persist throughout a whole lifetime. In more sensitive, perceptive, and intelligent people, these illusions dissolve one by one, leading to various life crises.

Harris (1969) describes four basic life positions held with respect to one's self and others:

1. I'm Not OK—You're OK.
2. I'm Not OK—You're Not OK.
3. I'm OK—You're Not OK.
4. I'm OK—You're OK.

By the end of the second year of life, or during the third year, the child has decided on one of the first three positions. Position one is the first year of life. By the end of the second year, it is either confirmed and settled or it gives way to position 2 or 3. Once finalized, the child stays in his chosen position and it governs everything he does. This position stays with a child the rest of his or her life unless he or she consciously changes to the fourth position. The first three positions represent nonverbal decisions.

When growth potential gets thwarted, a developing person may decide that he is not OK and may proceed to live an unproductive or tragic life. In transactional analysis, the therapist and the client form a distinct mutual treatment contract. The contract states the question, "How will you and I both know when you get what you are coming for?" Without the contract, the therapist might be viewed in a rescuing Parent position, and the client might be viewed as a victimized patient.

The ideal function of a group therapist, according to Berne (1972), whatever theoretical approach he is using, is to observe every movement of every muscle of every patient during every second of the group meeting. The size of groups should be limited to no more than eight patients. Script analysis is considered the major instrument in effective group treatment. The therapist looks and listens for specific signs which indicate the nature of the patient's script and its origins in past experience and parental programming.

Dusay and Dusay (1979) indicate that the therapist, using transactional analysis, may work at any one of three different levels:

1. **Script change.** The therapist works with the client so that the initial moment of decision regarding a script is rediscovered, and the person recognizes how and under what conditions his life-style deviated from growth and positive potential.
2. **Game interruption.** If a person's predominant game is interrupted or broken up, pathological behavior will desist.
3. **Ego state change.** If energies are shifted from an ineffective ego state to an effective one, this is an exhilarating and self-reinforcing experience. Relationship diagrams or "egograms" are used to illustrate the intensity of various ego states.

Finally, we close our discussion of transactional analysis by quoting Thomas Harris (1969).

It is my belief from long observation of this phenomenon, that game analysis must always be secondary to Structural and Transactional Analysis. Knowing what game you are playing does not *ipso facto* make it possible for you to change. There is a danger in stripping away defense without first helping a person to understand the position—and the situation in childhood in which it was established—which has made the defenses necessary [p. 120].

Group Interventions: A Brief Evaluation

Reviews of the literature on group counseling have consistently pointed out that no single body of theoretically related knowledge exists on which the practice of group counseling can be solidly grounded (Silver, Luben, Silver, & Dobson, 1980). Most research suggests that people who are affectively oriented, flexible, highly motivated to change, and sufficiently well adjusted to interact rationally with others function well in counseling or therapy groups (Anderson, 1969; Bednar and Kaul, 1978; Bednar and Lawlis, 1971).

Anderson (1969) suggested the following standards for evaluating outcome research on group counseling: (1) Measures on clients which broadly sample goal-related behavior should be explicitly determined and administered before and after the counseling experience. (2) Measured client changes during the time that counseling occurred should be compared with similar changes on control subjects. (3) Effects of completing evaluation instruments should be studied. (4) The nature of the treatment and the specific procedures used should be spelled out in operational terms.

Researchers in the area of group interaction should clearly specify treatment procedures and systematically identify the information contained in a unit of communication, the manner in which the information is given, and the effect it has on the relationship between the receiver and the sender of the message. The purpose of group interaction research should be to classify systematically and evaluate the communication occurring in a group. Group development appears to be one area of small group work in which theoretical models abound, yet a solid empirical base is lacking. It is likely that the patterns of interaction which develop in a counseling group depend on the group composition, leadership, style, and expected outcomes. However, the precise nature of these interactions in relation to those factors is yet to be clearly and comprehensively related to outcomes.

Group treatments in the community setting are used in a wide variety of situations with widely assorted populations. The counseling psychologist should move cautiously in the use of group treatments. Evidence is accumulating that group psychological treatments under some set of as yet unspecified conditions are associated with client improvement. As Bednar and Kaul (1978) explain: "Accumulated evidence indicates that group treatments have been more effective than no treatment, than placebo or even non-specific treatments. . . . Statements about why these treatments elicit therapeutic benefits from some participants are necessarily tentative. Causal statements regarding the curative factors operating in the group context, the circumstances under which they can be brought to bear or the form in which they can be expressed are hard to support on the basis of the available literature." Bednar and Moeschel (1981) suggest

> that just as group therapies began to enjoy their place in the sun, they attracted the attention of theorists in individual psychotherapy and psychopathology. Implicit in most of their theories were assumptions and vague axioms about individual behavior from which systems of group treatment would eventually develop. The result has been the development of a group discipline whose conceptual identity is clearly borrowed and for the most part impoverished.

Since theory guides observations and research, the present theories related to group interventions should be examined very critically. Group interventions used judiciously are useful tools. They are by no means panaceas or risk-free approaches (Reddy and Lepert, 1980). Careful attention must be given to screening clients and selecting outcomes for group interventions.

References

Anderson, A. R. Group counseling. *Review of Educational Research*, 1969, *39* (2), 209–226.

Bales, R. F. *Interaction process analysis: A method for the study of small groups*. Reading, Mass.: Addison-Wesley, 1950.

Bales, R. F. *SYMLOG: Case study kit*. New York: Free Press, 1980.

Bednar, R. L., & Kaul, T. J. Experimental group research: Current perspectives. In S. L. Garfield & A. E. Bergin (Eds.), *Handbook of psychotherapy and behavior change*. New York: Wiley, 1978.

Bednar, R. L., & Lawlis, G. F. Empirical research in group psychotherapy. In A. E. Bergin & S. L. Garfield (Eds.), *Handbook of psychotherapy and behavior change*. New York: Wiley, 1971.

Bednar, R. L., & Moeschl, M. J. Conceptual and methodological considerations in the evaluation of group psychotherapies. In Paul McReynolds (Ed.), *Advances in psychological assessment* (Vol. 5). San Francisco: Jossey Bass, 1981.

Bennis, W. G., Schein, E. M., Berlew, D. E., & Steele, F. I. *Interpersonal dynamics*. Homewood, Ill.: Dorsey Press, 1964.

Bennis, W. G., & Shephard, H. A. A theory of group development. *Human Relations*, 1956, *9*, 415–457.

Berman, J. J., & Zimpfer, D. Growth groups: Do the outcomes really last? *Review of Educational Research*, 1980, *50*, 505–524.

Berne, E. *What do you say after you say hello?* New York: Grove Press, 1972.

Bion, W. R. *Experience in groups*. London: Tavistock Press, 1961.

Cambell, J. P., & Dunnette, M. D. Effectiveness of T group experiences in managerial training and development. *Psychological Bulletin*, 1968, *70*, 73–104.

Cartwright, D. Achieving change in people: Some complications of group dynamics theory. *Human Relations*, 1951, *4*, 381–393.

Cohn, R. C. From couch to community: Beginnings of the theme-centered interactional method. In H. M. Ruitenbeck (Ed.), *Group therapy today*. New York: Atherton Press, 1969.

Cohn, R. C. Style and spirit of the theme-centered interactional method. In C. J. Sager & H. Kaplan (Eds.), *Progress in group and family therapy*. New York: Brunner-Mazel, 1972.

Corsini, R. J. Issues in encounter groups: Comments on Coulson's article. *The Counseling Psychologist*, 1970, *2*, 28–33.

Coulson, W. Inside a basic encounter group. *The Counseling Psychologist,* 1970, *2,* 1–27.

Dusay, J. M., & Dusay, K. M. Transactional analysis. In R. Corsini (Ed.), *Current Psychotherapies* (2nd ed.). Itasca, Ill.: F. E. Peacock Publishers, 1979.

Gazda, G. M., & Mobley, J. A. Indscal: A technological breakthrough for group therapy. Mimeographed report, University of Georgia, Athens, Ga., September, 1980.

Gibb, C. A. Leadership. In G. Lindzey (Ed.), *Handbook of social psychology.* Reading, Mass.: Addison-Wesley, 1954, Chapter 24.

Harris, T. A. *I'm O.K. You're O.K.* New York: Harper & Row, 1969.

Hartley, D., Roback, H. B., & Abramowitz, S. I. Deterioration effects in encounter groups. *American Psychologist,* 1976, *31,* 247–255.

Hartman, J. J. Small group methods of personal change. *Annual Review of Psychology, 1979.* Palo Alto, Calif.: Annual Reviews Inc., 1979, pp. 453–476.

Hemphill, J. K. *Group dimensions: A manual for their measurement.* Columbus: Ohio State University, 1956.

Hill, W. F. *Hill Interaction Matrix.* Los Angeles: Youth Study Center, University of Southern California, 1965.

Malliver, B. L. Encounter groups up against the wall. *New York Times Magazine,* January 3, 1971.

McGrath, J. E. *Social psychology: A brief introduction.* New York: Holt, Rinehart & Winston, 1964.

Mowrer, O. H. Integrity groups: Basic principles and objectives. *The Counseling Psychologist,* 1972, *3,* 4–6.

Reddy, W. B., & Lepert, K. M. Studies of the processes and dynamics within experiential groups. In P. Smith (Ed.), *Small groups and personal change:* London: Methuen, 1980, pp. 64–92.

Rogers, C. R. *Carl Rogers on encounter groups.* New York: Harper & Row, 1970.

Schutz, W. C. The ego, FIRO theory, and the leader as completer. In L. Petrullo & B. M. Bass (Eds.), *Leadership and interpersonal behavior.* New York: Holt, Rinehart & Winston, 1961.

Shaffer, J. B., & Galinsky, M. D. *Models of group therapy and sensitivity training.* Englewood Cliffs, N.J.: Prentice-Hall, 1974.

Silver, R. J., Luben, B., Silver, D. L., & Dobson, N. H. The group psychotherapy literature: 1979. *International Journal of Group Psychotherapy,* 1980, *30,* 491–538.

Thelen, H. *Dynamics of groups at work.* Chicago: University of Chicago Press, 1954.

5

Consultation and Training

Consultation is a term that is widely used and frequently poorly understood in the psychological literature. In chapter 1 we made the point that perhaps the most important single task of the counseling psychologist in community practice involves facilitating the work of the host of other professionals who constitute the real backbone of the human services delivery system. These people include teachers, social workers, family practice physicians, nurses, counselors, school psychologists, and welfare or corrections workers. They may also include people who are not strictly speaking members of helping professions. These may include foster parents, community volunteers, police, or others whose interests or work bring them into contact with those in need of help.

Types of Consultation

Obviously, the variety of people and situations involved in activities that are termed consulting is very great. Generally, the term *consultation* can be used accurately to describe two major types of professional helping activity.

Triadic Consultation

One of these categories can be termed "indirect helping," that is, the consultant works through a "mediator" who delivers help directly to the ultimate client. Consultation with teachers, parents, counselors, or case workers about their clients or offspring are typical cases in point. The consultant works with the mediator to help produce benefits for the ultimate consumer, the student, client, or child. The consultant does not engage in a direct relationship with the ultimate clients and indeed may never even meet them. He or she does, nevertheless, measure the effectiveness of the consultation process primarily in terms of the outcome to the ultimate client.

This tripartite arrangement of consultant–mediator–client is probably the most frequent and familiar situation in psychological

117

consulting. It encompasses most so-called mental health consultation and consultation in schools as well as much of the psychological assistance to troubled families. We will call it *triadic* consultation.

Process Consultation

A second major category of consulting activity is also important, however. This category of activity involves the situation in which the consultant works with a complex natural human system in its normal setting to improve its functioning, for the benefit either of members or of some public that the system is intended to serve.

The distinction here between what is often called "process consultation" and group counseling or therapy is that the natural client system, for example an organization or part of an organization, is seen together as a permanent system, and that the goals of intervention primarily involve the improved functioning of that system rather than fulfillment of the separate goals of individual members. In group counseling, for example, the reverse tends to be true. We form a temporary and artificial system, the counseling group, to facilitate the goals of individuals in the clear expectation that when those goals are met, the counseling group will self-destruct.

In process consultation, then, the consultant focuses primarily on the group processes that hinder or facilitate the functioning of the client system in performing its designated task or mission. Individual goals and dynamics are usually dealt with only as they relate rather clearly and specifically to system functioning and group task effectiveness. Obviously, these distinctions are not perfectly clear-cut and at times become differences in emphasis and degree rather than of absolutes.

The special relevance of process consultation to counseling psychologists in the community ties back to the interest in developmental human ecology discussed in chapters 1 and 2. Often the growth and well-being of community members is inextricably tied to the optimal functioning of community institutions and organizations such as schools, social agencies, criminal justice systems, or other subsystems. Intervening to help improve the functioning of these important components of the community is just as important as the facilitation of the work of individual helpers and healers, described in our discussion of the triadic model.

These two categories of consultation embrace most of the psychological consulting activity involved in community practice. An examination of the literature on consultation is sometimes confusing in that the term is used to cover activities that involve primarily direct training, supervision, or even salesmanship. In a sense, almost any activity between an expert or professional and a person in need of that expertise can be called consultation. In this general sense we have consulting engineers, physicians, lawyers, and so on. For the purposes of this chapter, however, we will separate consultation and training as distinct functions and utilize the two specific categories of psychological consultation defined above.

The Need for Consultation

The need for outreach or consultation services has been recognized in the counseling psychology literature for many years. Wrenn (1962), McCully (1965), and Danskin, Kennedy, and Friesen (1965) all recognized the need for counselors to intervene actively in the learning environments that were crucial to the growth and development of clients.

In the community mental health literature, Caplan (1970) pioneered much of the conceptual work on consultation in community services. Essentially, this approach utilized the triadic model described above. Caplan saw a need for the use of highly skilled mental health workers such as psychiatrists and psychologists to work heavily as backup or special resource people to those who were heavily involved in direct service delivery.

Caplan, then, saw consultation as a process through which two professionals (one of whom is more skilled or specialized) interact about the management or treatment of one or more patients. Obviously, this was a time-honored and traditional approach in medicine, by which the general practitioner utilized the resources of a specialist to help meet the needs of a particular patient.

In mental health services bound to the medical model, this approach had clear and immediate appeal. As explicated and advocated by Caplan, the approach went well beyond the general practitioner–specialist relationship of traditional medicine. At first the approach was termed crisis consultation (Caplan, 1970), but then as acceptance grew it has simply been termed mental health consultation.

Essentially, mental health consultation grew up around the view that the best way to prevent severe mental illness is to facilitate the work of first-line human services people and to utilize the most highly trained and specialized professionals for this purpose, rather than for the treatment of only the most severely disturbed or impaired people, many of whom may be beyond helping through psychotherapeutic approaches.

As this notion was elaborated, a recognition developed that front line human services workers are themselves exposed to great stress and tension arising out of the explosive and potentially tragic crisis situations to which they are exposed on a daily basis. The provision of consultation services was, thus, more a recognition of their legitimate needs than an aspersion upon their professional credibility.

In this model the purpose of consultation is to help the consultee find and implement the most effective way to treat a client. The consultant may or may not observe, interview, or test the client, but clearly the consultant does not usurp the basic therapeutic relationship between therapist and client.

The primary focus on mental health consultation is upon the interaction and relationship between consultant and consultee or therapist. The nature of the interaction and particularly the content of the consultant–consultee interaction depends heavily upon the theoretical orientation of the consultant.

The use of triadic consultation spread rapidly from community mental health settings to schools and even to consultation with parents. An impetus to this rapid growth was provided by the development of important new technologies for changing behavior, often labeled "behavior modification" (Tharp & Wetzel, 1969). As psychologists mastered this new technology, they sought to disseminate it, particularly to parents and teachers, through the triadic or third-party consultation model (Patterson, 1971).

At the same time that triadic consultation was becoming a major psychological intervention, the burgeoning interest in social and ecological psychology discussed in chapters 1 and 2 highlighted a need for another and somewhat broader outreach approach that we call "process consultation." It became clear that systematic social psychological interventions directed to improving the effectiveness of schools, community agencies, and other settings could significantly enhance the contributions of those agencies to the development and welfare of the people they serve.

Process consultation is the outgrowth of that need. Process consultation is based upon a number of assumptions about social interaction in task or work groups. These include the following:

1. An open and direct approach to examining work relationships is helpful to the performance of a work group.
2. Members of a work group should participate actively in diagnosing or identifying problems within the group.

3. Members of a work group have the major responsibility for developing solutions and action plans to resolve their organizational problems.
4. In the final analysis, members of a work group have more relevant knowledge about themselves and their own situation than any outside "efficiency expert."

Out of these kinds of assumptions, process consultation emerged as an activity or method for helping members of work groups identify, diagnose, and solve their own work-related or organizational problems. In this activity the consultant focuses upon such group process elements as communication patterns, leadership behavior, decision-making procedures, social influence strategies, and power or status relationships.

Consulting interventions include helping the work group members become aware of group process elements, examine the utility of their own patterns of communication in terms of group goals and purposes, and engage in problem-solving activities aimed at improving the quality of social interaction in the interests of improved effectiveness. Process consultation has points of tangency with another intervention—organizational development—which we will consider in a subsequent chapter. Ordinarily, a distinction between the two is that process consultation generally deals with a fairly narrow band of strata within an organization, primarily those who are routinely engaged in close personal and face-to-face interactions in the course of their daily work, whereas organizational development often deals with a wide range of levels within a large or complex system.

In a sense, then, both triadic and process consultation roles have developed out of the emergence of ecological views of human functioning and out of the "quiet revolution" in the human services field that was described in chapter 1.

They have become increasingly important with the recognition that traditional individual and group counseling modes, while important, are not sufficient to meet the varied needs of individuals and communities for human services.

Particularly when the counseling psychologist is committed to goals involving the prevention of barriers to development, as well as their remediation, it becomes important to reach out to work with people and organizations within natural settings such as schools, social agencies, political institutions, civic groups, and neighborhoods.

In these situations the counseling psychologist is often not dealing with an individual, identified client seeking specific help with specific problems but with a client system that represents a complex set of personal and social dynamics. The complexity of these dynamics sometimes makes consultation a difficult task. The fact that these natural social systems are often very powerful forces within the lives of their members and publics, however, makes the payoff in working with them very high indeed.

Reaching out to work with a variety of others within the psychological frameworks represented in their natural social environments represents a major shift in focus and orientation for psychological helpers. The traditional counseling relationship represents a temporary, and largely artificial, social system set up solely for the purpose of providing psychological assistance from an identified help-giver to an identified help-seeker.

From the standpoint of the help-giver, the counselor, it is a secure and comfortable arrangement. Role expectations, norms, and procedures are structured very largely by and for the professional. The help-seeker or client is, initially at least, cast in a passive and compliant role. The counselor, on his or her own geographical and psychological turf, is very much in control.

The consulting situation is sometimes a different kind of setting. The consultant often, of necessity, moves out of his or her own office into the domains of others. The assignment of roles into helper and helpee, professional and layman, host and visitor are quite differently delineated and articulated.

Many members of groups or organizations with whom the counseling psychologist consults do not see themselves at all as clients or patients. They may not be prepared either to self-disclose about their personal and professional lives or to accept unequivocally the perceptions or suggestions of a person who is seen as an outsider.

For these reasons the counseling psychologist operating in a consulting capacity must be aware of a number of issues that may be of relatively less concern in the typical counseling or psychotherapeutic situation.

Levels of Focus in Consultation

One of the first issues with which the consultant must be concerned involves the expectations that exist around his or her intervention. Three major levels of focus for consulting relationships can be identified, each with rather specific sets of attendant expectations. These foci are not necessarily mutually exclusive, but when the consultant moves from one to another precipitously, new dynamics may be brought into play that can change the levels of acceptance or resistance in the system.

The first level of focus for consultation can be termed *technical*. In many situations the consultant is brought in to provide expert opinion, direction or information about specific problems or situations. The consultant in the technical role may, for example, undertake to do diagnostic workups on a particular group of students for a school or to do a needs survey of the clientele of an agency or to provide specialized information on child development to a community group. In the technical mode the focus of consultation is specific and relatively narrow. It is generally defined by the client system in terms of its own perceived needs and its view of the perceived competence of the consultant. A second somewhat broader level of focus for consultation is termed *collaborative*. In this mode the emphasis is on the pattern of interaction or cooperation between systems. Usually, the consultant is a member of one system and the consultee is a part of another. An example of this type of consultation is a relationship between a community mental health center engaged in treating a client or family, and another community institution such as school, social service agency, or courts, who also work with the same client or family. In this situation, sharing of information, mutual planning, cooperative assignment of responsibilities, and joint evaluation of success are desirable outcomes achieved through collaborative consultation.

The emphasis in collaborative consultation is on *cooperative* relationships and pooling of resources and information. The focus is on areas of *joint* responsibility, such as services to the same client, or cooperation in some other kind of joint enterprise. The separateness, equality, and autonomy of each party is kept clearly in view.

The third level of focus for consultation is termed *facilitative*. In this mode the consultant is a professional from outside the client system brought in to form a temporary linkage aimed at improving the functioning of the client. In this model the consultant is clearly interested in broad aspects of the functioning of the client system. Interpersonal relationships, organizational structures, and specific operating procedures are all processes of potential concern. Process consultation is usually at the facilitative level.

In each of these foci of intervention, it is important for the consultant to ensure that appropriate role expectations exist within and around the client system. Out of these expectations the perceived legitimacy of the consulting interventions are established. In this sense the consultant is faced with a need to structure or negotiate his or her role just as this is needed in a counseling relationship. Triadic consultation may be engaged in at the technical, collaborative, or facilitative level. In many situations the most positive or productive outcomes may be associated with the facilitative level. Much greater time and effort may be required to enter and work with a client system at that level, however.

In some situations a consultant may enter a client system at one level and because of new information or opportunities decide to attempt to change the focus. For example, a consultant might be engaged in technical consultation with a local school in providing diagnostic services for a population of children labeled by the school as "emotionally disturbed." In the course of this consultation it might become clear to the consultant and a group of teachers that many of the difficulties of these students are rooted in curricular and class-room management problems in the school. To move from a technical to a facilitative focus for consultation in this instance might well be a very difficult, but rewarding intervention. Obviously, the shift would require a major change in the school's expectations regarding the role of the consultant and perhaps a redefinition of labels and problems confronting the school and students.

A Cognitive Map for Consultation

Because of the complex dynamics involved in consultation, and the fact that consulting relationships often change over time, as in the example above, consultants need to proceed carefully and thoughtfully in their work using as a guide a well-conceived "cognitive map" or guide to action.

To be optimally useful such a cognitive map should allow the user to operate in a systematic and planned sequence of intervention steps and allow for options at each step depending upon the nature of the information available at a given point.

The sequence of activities should be based upon sound psychological principles or sources of gain, and ideally the model should be applicable to a variety of interventions including individual or group counseling as well as consultation, training or organizational development.

The planning model described below is an attempt to provide such a cognitive map. It is useful in virtually any human behavior change situation but is especially important in complex situations such as triadic or process consultation. The term *client system* can refer to an individual group or an organization.

Phase One: Articulation of Goals, Needs, and Objectives. The entry of the consultant into a professional relationship with a client system is a crucial and sometimes difficult step. As we noted earlier, the situations and expectations associated with entry into consulting relationships are often much more varied and less controllable from the standpoint of the counseling psychologist than those associated with the initiation of counseling.

The initial and most important step in the entry phase of the consultation process is for the consultant to be clear and unconflicted in regard to his or her own general professional goals. The consultant must be clear in terms of values associated with systems change processes and in regard to outcome goals. Being aware of and articulating one's own goals in entering a relationship with a client system is necessary to structure that relationship. System members may have varied, unrealistic, and ambiguous expectations for the consultant that must be clarified in the entry phase.

Part of this clarification process involves an articulation of the consultant's purposes and contributions that is clearly related to the needs of the client system. In a real sense the first question to be answered is, "What can I as a consultant offer you the client system in terms of your felt needs?"

Answering this question, then, involves some type of needs-assessment process. This may range in terms of complexity from a relatively simple interview process in a small or simple client system to a formal and lengthy information-seeking process with a large or very complicated organization. In any event, the process of defining goals and assessing needs demands some clarity of thinking. Unfortunately, a certain degree of confusion usually surrounds the process of identifying the needs of human systems.

Basically, a goal is a statement or description of some desired state of affairs. Needs cannot be assessed in the absence of relatively clear goal statements. Strange as it seems, many formal organizations exist for years without articulating in any very comprehensive or direct way their specific goals and purposes. Even when some statement of goals exists within a system, it is unwise to assume that this automatically means that a broad awareness of or commitment to these goals exists within the system.

Needs cannot be assessed in the absence of both goals and some set of assessment procedures that define the existing or immediate situation in relation to the goals or desired state of affairs. A need, then, is a measured discrepancy between a desired condition (a goal) and an existing situation. That is, it represents a gap between "what is" and "what ought to be."

When we have assessed this need discrepancy, we can then set objectives. An objective is a point along a needs discrepancy line that represents a target for movement toward a goal within a given time frame and intervention strategy. Goals thus determine the direction of planned change, while objectives determine distance. Goals are defined primarily by *desirability* while objectives are determined by *feasibility*.

In the entry phase of consultation, the primary task involves structuring the consulting relationship around the resources of the consultant and the needs of the client system. A concrete example of the process of entry may help. A counseling psychologist from a community mental health center was contacted by a local agency devoted to providing family counseling services for families of delinquent and predelinquent youth referred by schools, police, or juvenile courts. In the initial contact the Director of the agency simply stated that he sees his organization having problems in providing appropriate services for many of the highly troubled and disorganized families referred, and he thinks the psychologist might be able to help.

The counseling psychologist scheduled a meeting with the Director and his four counselors to discuss a possible consulting relationship. In the process of this initial session, the consultant, using his group skills, helped the prospective client system clarify its goals with a series of increasingly focused and specific goal statements. The group began with a very global and general statement. "Our job is to improve the quality of family life in this community." This represents, of course, a very high level of generality and abstraction.

The second level of goal statement moved toward somewhat greater concreteness and specificity. "Our goal is to provide counseling services so that troubled families can provide a positive, nurturing environment for their children." Abstraction and molarity were still high, although the goal had now been defined in terms of a set of services to specific kinds of families.

At the next level still greater specificity was introduced. A number of goal statements were generated. One of these suffices for our example. "Our goal is that every referred family leave counseling with a 'family conferencing' plan to provide for increased attention to and communication about the needs of all its members."

We now have a level of goal specificity that can be utilized to begin a needs assessment.

As the latter type of goal statement began to emerge in the

group, the consultant first obtained a crude measure of the existing state of affairs in regard to the goals. The counselors estimated, for example, that roughly one-third of their referrals leave counseling with a family conferencing plan clearly established. They agreed to do a careful study of case files to obtain a more accurate figure. The basis for a needs discrepancy line had now been established and the possibility for establishing objectives in terms of increasing percentages of families engaging in family conferencing was now clear.

The consultant next discussed with the client system her own resources in regard to a situation in which she might offer consulting services to those counselors who would desire to participate around the needs assessed. An entry had been established around an assessed need of the client system, and a consulting relationship was in the process of being structured.

In this entry process the consultant had defined herself to the client system in terms of *credibility* with regard to an assessed need, *concern and respect* for the goals and purposes of the client system, and willingness to *negotiate* her role in relationship to the needs of the client system.

Phase Two: Scanning the Client System. Once entry has been established, the second phase of consultation involves a careful and systematic assessment of the environment represented by the client system. In this process the consultant attempts to become familiar with a variety of characteristics of the client system. In smaller and simpler systems this is accomplished in relatively informal and unobtrusive ways. In more complex systems the consultant might employ questionnaires, structured interviews, an examination of personnel folders, agency policies, case records, or other sources.

The purpose of this phase is for the consultant to learn to understand as thoroughly as possible the social-psychological context or environment in which the client system functions. In a very real sense this process is analogous to the process of coming to understand the personal characteristics, background, and life space of an individual client in one-to-one counseling. In the consulting situation with a complex client system, this phase may take considerable time.

In both situations the process is one of observation and inferences with the latter being couched carefully in tentative and testable terms and checked out against subsequent observations. An axiom of consultation is that *one begins to help a client system by listening to it and helping it to listen to itself.*

Let us return to our concrete example of consulting with the small family service agency. The consultant established with the

Director a schedule of weekly visits. In the first three of these, the consultant arranged for interviews with the Director and each of the counselors. She also sat in on two of their weekly staff meetings and case conferences. She learned about each counselor's academic background, level of experience, and theoretical orientation. The consultant studied the case notes and summaries of several randomly selected families and sat in on two intake interviews. She also learned about the organization of the agency, its funding sources, and its relationship to other community institutions and services.

In the course of these visits, the consultant found that the Director seemed generally supportive and helpful, but was preoccupied with administrative problems and not really in close touch with the day-to-day counseling activities of the agency. Two of the four counselors seemed eager to talk about their cases and very open to suggestions. One seemed relatively disinterested, and the fourth somewhat nervous and even defensive when discussing cases with the consultant. The latter inferences were checked carefully in several different interactions both alone and in group situations.

At this point the consultant began to build an intervention plan that she would propose to the Director.

Phase Three: Choosing an Intervention Strategy.   As we have seen, a variety of possible consulting strategies are possible. Triadic consultation at technical, collaborative, or facilitative levels or process consultation working with the social interaction of a working group or team all represent modes of delivering consultation services. A variety of theoretical content approaches may be drawn from counseling theories.

The choice among these possibilities is not a random or arbitrary matter. As Caplan (1970) pointed out in his pioneering work on consultation, the consultant must attend carefully to what the client system tells him or her. The more the consultant knows about the language patterns, conceptual frameworks, ways of relating, and attitudes toward helping on the part of the client system, the better the consultant will be able to formulate interventions and communicate in a helpful way that will allow the client system to use the input constructively.

An indifference to the perceptions and attitudes of the client system is probably the most frequent cause of failure in the consultation process. As Gordon (1975) pointed out, if the consultant does not understand and respect to some degree the values and concerns of his consultees and is not open to engaging them on their own terms, then all of his knowledge is worse than useless. The consultant's observations, interpretations, techniques, and instruments are simply weapons in the arsenal of an unwanted and even destructive interloper.

Returning again to our example, the consultant now carefully considered the data obtained from her observations and proposed a consultation strategy. This strategy involved triadic consultation with interested counselors around selected families from their case load aimed at helping them to increase the number of client families who engage in regular family conferencing as well as other needs identified in the initial phase of consultation. This proposal was presented first to the Director, then to the counselors for negotiation and reaction. The proposal was accepted and a thorough discussion of expectations indicated that the consultant and the consultees saw the level of focus as facilitative; that is, it would deal with whatever factors seemed relevant to the improvement of their counseling in regard to the specified needs. A schedule of times for consultation was set, and the consultees agreed to tape record sessions and keep careful records of the cases selected for consultation.

Phase Four: Building Communications and Relationships. In the first two consulting sessions with the two counselors who self-selected for the experience, the consultant concentrated upon opening communication and building positive relationships in the consultation group. Using active listening skills, the consultant dealt with the counselors' feelings and frustrations with regard to their cases. She carefully refrained from taking a judgmental position in regard to their therapeutic successes or failures. After the two initial sessions, consultant and counselors were able to talk freely and comfortably about the counseling cases and their own interaction and relationships. The pattern of interaction and self-disclosure in the consultation group led the consultant to infer that considerable trust and cohesion had been developed.

Phase Five: Negotiation of Specific Objectives. In this phase of consultation a careful fine-tuning process of objective setting is initiated around the needs identified earlier. Objectives are set as targets along needs discrepency lines to be reached within given time frames and through specific strategies. The realism of objectives is carefully weighed in terms of feasibility, and the consultant is careful not to set up herself or the consulting group for failure because of unrealistic or impractical objectives. In quite complex consulting situations, a formal feasibility study might be done as part of the objective-setting process.

In our example, the consultant worked with the two consultees to set reasonable objectives in regard to family conferencing and other assessed needs. As the openness of communication developed in the preceding phase allowed some frustrations and doubts to surface, the consultant found that the counselors viewed many of their client families as totally unsuitable for counseling. Some families failed to keep appointments or even dropped out immediately after intake. The counselors believed that many referrals were accepted by the Director more to maintain relationships with referral sources than because a real possibility for helping existed.

As these feelings and perceptions were discussed, it was decided to set an objective for family conferencing at 40 percent of intake families over an eight-week period of time. This represented a modest increase over the 20 to 25 percent base rate that had been identified in a study of case records. We note that this actual figure was slightly lower than the figure first estimated. Similar objectives were set on other assessed needs. At this point the counselors also expressed a desire to accomplish a small-scale study of the characteristics of families who seemed to profit from counseling, and this was incorporated into the consulting plan.

Phase Six: Introducing New Concepts and Behaviors. In many ways, of course, this phase is crucial to the entire consulting model. It is important to note, however, that it is *not* accomplished until a readiness exists in the client system to welcome and accept new ideas and approaches. A major source of failure in consulting interventions is due to the premature introduction of new ideas and consequent demands upon the client system. Only when these ideas and behaviors are clearly accepted by the client system as being in the service of their own needs, goals, and objectives is the motivation for and openness to new learning available.

In our example, the counselor introduced her consultees to new information about contracting with clients and getting specific behavioral commitment to action plans from clients. The consultant furnished the counselors with readings, modeled contracting sessions in role plays, and carefully encouraged their initial attempts in their recorded interviews. Early failures were examined objectively in an open or nonjudgmental way. This process was continued until each counselor had experienced several successful action plan contracts and had seen them successfully followed by families.

Phase Seven: Transferring and Maintaining New Behavior. This phase of the consultation process involves consolidating and providing for the integration of the changes achieved in consultation. It includes efforts to insure transfer and new learning as well as provision for the maintenance of the new learning in the environment provided by the client system. Transfer of training is ensured in several ways. First, the learners are given a cognitive language or set of concepts to use to describe and analyze the new learning. Second, the new learning is tried out in a variety of somewhat different situations that allow the learner to perceive identical elements in the demands and opportunities afforded across the varied situations. Finally, attention is given to the problem of integrating new learning with the learner's previous approach, convictions, and style until the new behavior is experienced as comfortable and natural.

Maintenance of new behavior is made more probable by building in systematic reinforcement and feedback about the new behavior and by scheduling follow-up or "booster" sessions at increasingly long intervals after the end of the acquisition period.

In terms of our example, the consultant encouraged the two counselors to try out contracting procedures with a variety of their client families. They were also encouraged to try contracting with their own children outside of the professional setting. The procedures involved in negotiating, implementing, and evaluating contracts were broken down into a sequence of steps that were clearly defined and labeled. One counselor, particularly, had difficulty using appropriate confrontation techniques when clients did not keep agreements. Considerable time was devoted to helping him become more comfortable in confronting clients and in integrating this with his previous style.

The consultant arranged for the two counselors to establish a schedule for conferring on each other's cases after the termination of regular consultation to give feedback and encouragement. Finally, the consultant scheduled a three-month and six-month follow-up with the counselors to help monitor and assist them in maintaining and evaluating their new approach.

Phase Eight: Evaluating Consultation Process and Outcome. The final phase of the consulting process involves evaluation of both the outcome and the process. When outcomes are stated in terms of needs discrepancies and objectives as implied in the model, evaluation of outcome is usually a rather simple matter. It is also important, however, to examine consultation processes, both to help the consultant improve his own skills and to provide the client system with information about its operation. Successful experiences with consulting processes can help ready the client system to engage in further self-renewing activities.

In our example, the consultant helped the two consultee counselors to assess the frequency with which they were able to get client families to engage in family conferencing on a regular basis prior to termination. Both were able to exceed the 40 percent objective that had been established.

As the consultation process was discussed in the final session, a number of significant points were raised. The counselors kept a careful record of the characteristics of families who had experienced both successful and unsuccessful outcomes from counseling. They felt even more strongly that some of the referrals accepted were clearly inappropriate. Also, they felt that the consultation process had broken down much of the sense of isolation and loneliness that they had previously experienced in the agency.

Both expressed the belief that they had gained a great deal and that they would like to see the positive things that they had experienced be shared by their colleagues. The consultant agreed to attend the next staff meeting and to help her consultees share their experiences with the Director and the remaining counselors.

The planning model for consultation outlined above is more a cognitive map with which to orient consultation activity than a narrow or specific prescription. It allows the consultant to conceptualize his work with a client system and to move forward or backward as data from the client system indicates. The process described is similar in many ways to that used in individual or group counseling. The greater complexity of client systems and the greater variation in client motivation and acceptance of planned change makes a formal process model even more useful in consultation or other organizational work.

Utilized in a systematic way, consultation skills can be an important part of the professional armamentarium of the counseling psychologist. The use of basic counseling skills within a systematic approach and an appreciation of organizational dynamics can make consultation a productive and even indispensable tool in community practice.

Training as a Psychological Intervention

In chapter 1 we traced the evolution of thinking about problems of human psychological functioning from a disease-oriented, essentially medical model to a community-based ecologically and developmentally oriented point of view. It is the latter, of course, that is espoused in this book.

One of the important legacies of the ecological point of view is that many problems and difficulties experienced by individuals can be traced to the basic interactions between that individual and the environment. The notion of person–environment fit as a goal has largely replaced the notion of an intrapsychic restructuring of personality.

Within this view we are careful to avoid the "person-blame" trap of attributing problems that are really based on unjust or inadequate aspects of social organization to personal failures. In reality, however, it is clear that many difficulties experienced by community members are the results of a lack of basic coping skills and strategies needed to handle legitimate and reasonable environmental demands.

In such situations training people may well become, as Carkhuff (1971) put it, a preferred method of treatment. Training interventions have many advantages over traditional intrapsychic approaches. They do not conceptualize the individual as sick or abnormal or inadequate. Rather, they treat the client as a learner who can develop needed skills and who has the potential to cope effectively with and eventually master problematic aspects of the environment.

Lakin Phillips (1978) has explicated a comprehensive view of social skill deficits as essentially a radical revision of notions about abnormal psychology. He believes that a great deal of what we have labeled abnormal, neurotic, or self-defeating behavior can actually be traced to relatively specific skill deficits that are amenable to remediation through training procedures.

Much of what we call, clinically, depression, for example, can be traced to quite understandable reactions to feelings of helplessness and hopelessness arising out of long histories of failure to meet basic social and personal needs because of skill deficits in interpersonal relating. When individuals lack the basic skills to control even minimal aspects of their interactions with the world, they rather obviously can be expected to show strong emotional reactions and perhaps to behave in impulsive and irrational ways.

One of the advantages of a social skills model for understanding and treating dysfunctional behavior is that it causes us to focus directly and immediately upon the individual's interaction with the environment. We can thus develop a set of behavior change objectives.

Most psychotherapeutic interventions with individuals or

groups have elements of social skills training built into them out of necessity. In a sense, a counseling relationship is in itself a kind of laboratory in interpersonal development in which the client learns new skills, styles, and strategies in human relations.

Experience has shown, however, that it is often much more useful and efficient to set up specific programs of social skills training for particular types of clients rather than to deliver them as part of an individually oriented treatment. It is this kind of treatment approach with which we are concerned in this section.

In chapter 4 we discussed laboratory learning as a model of group intervention. As we saw, laboratory learning grew out of a humanistic approach to social psychology and group dynamics. It focused upon experiential learning in social situations characterized by high levels of ambiguity. The purpose of this model was to change attitudes and concepts in order to help the learner change his or her behavior across a wide range of later social and organizational situations.

Social Skills Training

In a sense, social skills training is an approach to interpersonal learning drawn from modern behavioral psychology that represents almost the opposite side of the coin in terms of theoretical rationale and technique (Goldstein, Sprakin, & Gershaw, 1976).

One of the contributions of behavioral psychology to applied situations has been its emphasis on specifying precisely the nature of desired outcomes. One of the first steps in this direction utilizing principles of behavioral analysis was the notion of "behavioral objectives" coined and popularized by Mager (1962) According to Mager, the first step in designing a training or instructional intervention involves specifying objectives. A behavioral objective has three essential components. First, it specifies a set of overt, observable behaviors to be demonstrated by the learner; second, the objective establishes a standard to determine whether the objective was attained, and, finally, the behavioral objective defines the context in which the target behaviors are to be performed by the learner. The focus of this training approach is clearly intended to be upon specificity and objectivity of outcomes.

Identifying Objectives

The first step in designing a social skills training package is the identification of the basic competences or skills that we wish to teach. This may be done by identifying a problematic situation and then arranging to examine the performance of a person acknowledged to be competent in that situation.

Let us suppose that we want to train people to perform well in a job interview situation. We might arrange to observe several people who have been successful in obtaining job offers through interviews in an actual or simulated situation. We might, for example, videotape such a demonstration for careful analysis.

After obtaining the optimal behavior sample, what is called a "component analysis of social skills" (Kelly, 1982) is accomplished. The basic components of the successful performance are analyzed. In the case of the job interview, for example, we might break down the performance into the following components.

1. Appropriate eye contact
2. Appropriate affect
3. Speech fluency and clarity
4. Relevant responding to questions
5. Positive self-statements
6. Relevant questions about the employment situation

Each of the identified components of an optimal performance can then be converted into one or more behavioral objectives. An example of a behavioral objective based upon component 5 above might be:

In a job interview situation the trainee makes at least five positive self-statements about his qualifications that are judged appropriate and relevant by an experienced interviewer.

Enabling and Terminal Objectives

The next step in designing a training intervention is to select a set of enabling objectives through which to attain the terminal or ultimate objectives of the training program. Enabling objectives are the actual learning activities to be performed by the learner in the training situation and out of which the trainer can assess student progress. In terms of our terminal behavioral objective, an enabling objective might be stated in these terms:

In at least two classroom plays of job interview situations, the trainee makes three positive self-statements judged appropriate and relevant by the instructor.

Sequencing Objectives

After the enabling objectives are defined and selected, the next step is to determine an optimal sequence to use. This is in essence the course outline. Objectives may be arranged from simple to complex, from easy to difficult, in a logical or chronological order, or in some sequence observed empirically to be effective. At this point some method should be devised to assess the position of learners in regard to the sequence of enabling objectives. Essentially, this involves some kind of pretest of competence in relation to the enabling objectives. This is sometimes done in an intake interview or in a small group discussion in the initial training session. The important thing is that the trainer has some estimate of the entry level of competence of each learner in regard to the enabling and terminal objectives.

The Training Process

The next and perhaps most important step in the design of training programs involves the actual training process itself. This involves designing a set of instructional activities relevant to each enabling objective in the training package.

Eisler and Fredrecksen (1980) specify four basic elements in the conduct of a training session or unit:

1. *Description and Rationale.* The first step in the training process itself is essentially to describe the enabling objective to the trainees and explain its rationale and relevance in regard to the overall goals of the program and of the learners. This process should include opportunities for the trainees to ask questions, raise fears or doubts, and discuss their feelings of confidence or self-efficacy. Support and encouragement may be given where needed by the trainer or the training group.

In conducting this phase of a training procedure, the trainer should attend to four major points in the explanation or description process:

   a. *Be as specific and clear as possible.* Explain to the trainees in clear and specific terms what is involved and expected in the session. Wherever possible use concrete examples.

   b. *Be positive.* Explain what learners *should* do rather than what they should *not* do. Emphasize that the task is feasible, that continuous help will be available, and that adequate time will be allowed.

   c. *Use small steps.* Break the explanation down into small, discrete steps or parts. Allow time for questions or discussion after each part.

d. *Always explain why.* Always give reasons and rationales. Be sure the learner knows the relevance of each part to the whole.

2. *Demonstration or Modeling.* The second element in the training process involves the demonstration or modeling of the target behavior for the trainees. Where possible, the target behavior should be demonstrated by models who are relatively high in status, at least moderately similar to the learners, and seen to have achieved desirable rewards for their performance. It is desirable where possible to offer both "mastery" models who perform at high levels of proficiency and "coping" models who perform nearer to the level of beginning learners. The presence of only mastery models may discourage entry-level learners.

Again at the conclusion of the modeling session, opportunity should be provided for questions and discussions. Again, learners should be encouraged to discuss their feelings of self-efficacy or confidence in performing the target behaviors. Research (Bandura, 1977) has found that the learners' feelings about ability to perform are crucial in the training situation.

3. *Behavior Rehearsal.* The third phase in the training process involves giving the learners opportunities to try out or practice the target skills and behavior in psychologically safe situations. Usually, this is accomplished in a series of role plays or simulations directly in the training situation under the observation of the trainer. Behavior rehearsal gives the trainee the opportunity to practice, experiment, and try out the target behaviors before attempting them in the higher risk situation of the "real world." In this practice situation, encouragement is available from the trainer and the training group. The role playing or rehearsal phase should be long enough to ensure that each trainee has practiced the target behavior frequently enough to feel reasonably confident and competent.

4. *Feedback.* An important aspect of the training process is *feedback*. Each learner should receive prompt, accurate feedback about performance. In most situations several cycles of rehearsal and feedback may be needed. To be effective, feedback should be given *as soon as possible* after the rehearsal performance. It should be focused only on *relevant behaviors* and should be *specific* and *behavioral*. Finally, feedback should be given in an *emotionally neutral,* matter-of-fact way, within the context of a warm and supportive climate and relationship. The trainer should not allow destructive or innaccurate feedback to be given by anyone in the training situation.

Promoting Transfer and Maintenance

Earlier we made the distinction between terminal objectives and enabling objectives. In a practical social skills training situation, the ultimate success or payoff depends upon whether or not the trainee succeeds with the terminal objectives. That is, the trainee must utilize the newly learned behavior in practical situations in real-world settings. Even though every trainee accomplished all of our enabling objectives in the training situation, we could not be sure that the terminal objectives would ever be mastered. Obviously, if a trainee fails to accomplish even the enabling objectives, we would have little reason to expect success in the terminal objectives.

Sometimes trainers evaluate the success of training programs only in terms of attainment of enabling objectives. This is somewhat akin to the proverbial "shooting fish in a barrel." It leaves the really important questions still unanswered.

Fortunately, there are several steps the trainer can take to help ensure transfer and maintenance of social skill learning and hence the ultimate achievement of terminal objectives. Within the training situation itself, the trainer can first assure that the training behaviors selected are the relevant and effective ones. Sometimes when trainers determine their objectives through an "armchair" process rather than by an actual behavioral analysis process such as that described earlier, transfer and maintenance fail to occur because the newly learned behaviors are not reinforced in the practical situation.

Second, the trainer can facilitate transfer by making the training situation as realistic as possible. Role plays and simulations that are realistic, audiovisual aids that are well done, and models from real-life situations may all contribute to facilitating transfer and maintenance.

Finally, the trainer can be careful to teach not only specific behaviors, but the reasons and rationales behind them and the ways in which the target behaviors fit into the larger context of the trainees' life situation. Even though this kind of attention to careful description and rationale takes longer to accomplish, it is usually well worth the extra time.

A number of additional steps after the conclusion of the initial training sessions can also be accomplished to facilitate transfer and maintenance. These involve later follow-ups and observing the trainee out of the training situation in the natural environment.

One of these is to provide follow-up or booster sessions at gradually increased intervals after the conclusion of the initial sessions.

For example, booster sessions could be scheduled at two weeks, six weeks, and twelve weeks after the conclusion of initial training.

Another useful technique is to involve others who are available normally in the trainee's natural environment to monitor progress and give feedback or encouragement. This might be a spouse, supervisor, or friend. Sometimes this is accomplished by the use of "buddy systems" where trainees are paired and agree to maintain contact after training.

Finally, including self-management skills in training may be effective. The trainee learns to assess his or her own performance, set goals or standards, record progress, and administer self-rewards for performance. This kind of training helps to build into the training process itself elements that facilitate transfer and maintenance.

Practical Applications of Social Skill Training

Social skill training has been used in a wide variety of situations and around a broad range of skills. Perhaps the most widely used and researched area is in what is commonly called "assertiveness training." Essentially, this area involves training individuals to articulate their needs in social relationships, refuse unreasonable demands or requests, and actively negotiate cooperative relationships rather than to submit passively to one-sided or exploitative relationships with others. The voluminous literature on assertiveness training is summarized in a special issue of *The Counseling Psychologist* (Whiteley, 1975) and by Lange and Jakubowski (1976). Unfortunately much of the precision in specifying outcome and evaluating effectiveness promised in the behavioral approach to training has not fully borne fruit in the assertiveness training literature. Definitions of basic concepts and goals sometimes tend to be confused and ambiguous. More clear evidence of the efficacy of these varied approaches in effecting changes in relevant social behavior *in the natural environment* is needed.

Social skill training programs have been developed for a wide range of target behaviors. Job seeking and interviewing skill training has been attempted in a variety of situations. Training programs have been used successfully in teaching dating skills, (Bandes, Steinke, & Allen, 1975; Curran & Gilbert, 1975; Glass, Gottman & Shumrak, 1976; Martinson & Zerface, 1970). Programs have been used to teach career decision-making (Egner & Jackson, 1978) and job seeking and interviewing skills (Hollandsworth, Dressel, &

Stevens, 1977). Training has also been used to effect anxiety reduction (Hollandsworth, Glazeski, & Dressel, 1978; Romano & Cabianca, 1978; Suinn & Richardson, 1971).

Training has also been used in teaching self-control skills (Brown, 1975; Greiner & Karoly, 1976) and control of aggressive behavior (Elder, Edelstein, & Marick, 1979; Frederiksen, Jenkins, Foy, & Eisler, 1976) and in treating marital and family problems (Fensterheim, 1972; Jacobson, 1977; Walder, Cohen, and Breiter, 1971).

Training procedures have been used with a wide range of populations including depressed patients (Libet & Lewisohn, 1973), chronic schizophrenics (Hersen & Bellack, 1976), psychiatric outpatients (Goldsmith & McFall, 1975), disengaged elderly persons (Harris & Bodden, 1978) and alcoholics (Foy, Miller, Eisler, & O'Toole, 1976).

Deliberate Psychological Education

One of the developments in counseling psychology that has considerable relevance to community practice is the movement called "deliberate psychological education" (Sprinthall & Mosher, 1970). Essentially, this model for delivering psychological services conceptualizes the counselor as an educator who actively uses psychological content and technique to facilitate the growth and development of others. The "psychological educator" may work within the framework of existing schools and colleges, offering special courses or collaborating with teachers to enrich regular courses, or he or she may offer special workshops or seminars directly in the community.

A number of writers have conceptualized the educator role as the focus for professional practice (Authier, Gustafson, Guerney, & Kasdorf, 1975; Guerney, Stolack, & Guerney, 1970; Whiteley, 1977). As a process, deliberate psychological education, or "developmental education" as it is also called, tends to be based upon principles derived from cognitive developmental psychology. The work of Kohlberg (1975), Perry (1970), and Loevinger (1976) has been seminal to this approach.

Basically, deliberate psychological education classes tend to be based upon several elements. First, they focus upon some set of general problems, issues, or concerns which are ego-involving and relevant to the life situations of students. These may be ethical or social issues such as racism or sexism, or issues about personal growth and development such as identity development or adolescent problems. The essential elements of the curriculum from a content standpoint are that the material is seen by the students as directly relevant to their lives and that the content can be presented in terms of complex issues and multiple perspectives.

Programs that have been reported in the literature have dealt with the psychological development of women (Erickson, 1975), moral education (Mosher & Sullivan, 1976), high school students' interpersonal relationships (Cognetta, 1977), and identity development in college (Widick, Knefelkamp, & Parker, 1975).

In terms of process, psychological education classes tend to utilize several basic sources of gain. These include:

1. *Facilitating Communcations Skills.* Basic skills in active listening and empathic responding are taught in order for students to be able to understand the perspectives and points of view of people with different cognitive structures.

2. *Higher Stage Modeling.* This involves presenting concepts and approaches at slightly higher levels of complexity, ambiguity, or abstraction than the modal levels of thinking that are habitually used by students. This presents the student with challenges that can be satisfactorily met only by using "higher level" thinking in terms of cognitive stage theory.

3. *Responsible Role Taking.* This technique involves placing students in real-life situations in which they accept responsibility for significant tasks that can be understood and accomplished satisfactorily only by utilizing higher order cognitive structures. Such tasks may involve cross-age teaching situations, cross-cultural helping situations, intervening in situations involving social justice, such as participating in political or governance processes, or interpreting and integrating diverse social perspectives as in a news reporting or personal interviewing tasks.

These three elements are employed in an "action-reflection" cycle that alternates classroom theoretical and skill development activities with practical applications in real-life situations (Mosher, 1974).

Out of this instructional milieu comes cognitive growth as measured typically by changes on cognitive, developmentally oriented instruments such as the Kohlberg (1969) or Loevinger and Wessler (1970) scales. Positive development through the use of psychological education procedures has been reported by a number of researchers (Erickson, 1977; Rustad & Rogers, 1975; Widick et al., 1975). This general line of research is reviewed in Mosher (1979).

Training Community Helpers

A use of training procedures that is of equal importance to its role as a mode of treatment is in its impact in facilitating the effectiveness of community helpers. Successful training procedures have been used to improve the effectiveness of a wide variety of community people including probation offices (Novaco, 1980), day-care workers (Ennis & Mitchell, 1970), police (Bard & Berkowitz, 1967), telephone "hot line" workers (Gray, Mida, & Coonfield, 1976), high school peer group facilitators (Cooper & Cherchia, 1976), and crisis intervention para-professionals (Getz, Fiigita, & Allen, 1975).

The use of training programs for enhancing the resources available within a community is undoubtedly one of the most rapidly expanding activities of community-based professionals. It seems probable that the design, implementation, and evaluation of a wide variety of training programs with both consumers and providers of community services will constitute a major responsibility of counseling psychologists in community settings.

Carkhuff's Human Relations
Training Model

Carkhuff (1969) expanded upon the client-centered or Rogerian model of psychotherapy to develop a general approach to training helpers. Implicit in this approach is the notion that individuals have the greatest opportunities for personal growth at certain crisis points in their lives. Helping relationships are characterized by the presence of certain "core conditions." At some of these crisis points it may be difficult or even impossible for some community members to enter relationships with psychotherapists or other highly specialized professionals.

Carkhuff reasoned, then, that one of the most powerful ways to improve the quality of community environments would be to identify and train wide variety of "natural helpers" who would be available to provide "core conditions" to others when and where they are most needed in the natural environment. Carkhuff then developed a simple, direct model for helping that could be taught and implemented with minimal expense and involvement of professionals.

The Helping Model has two principal phases: First is the "downward" or "inward" phase in which a basic relationship is established and the helpee explores his or her own area of greatest concern.

Second is the phase of "emergent directionality" in which attempts are made to search out and implement specific courses of action.

In the first phase it is important that the helper provide the facilitative conditions of (1) empathy, (2) respect, and (3) concreteness. In the second phase, helpers concentrate on a set of "action oriented" dimensions. These include: (1) genuineness and self-disclosure, (2) confrontation, and (3) immediacy.

Carkhuff has described a training model for teaching these specific helping skills in practical and immediately applicable ways. The training model utilizes a text and trainer's guide that outlines a set of training exercises for each basic set of skills. The model is not unlike the general social skills training model outlined earlier in this chapter. It essentially involves giving an overview, working through specific exercises, and reviewing the skills learned. The training model also includes some outside assignments such as writing a review of the specific behavioral steps involved in a given task.

The skills training program also includes procedures and instruments for evaluating outcomes. This aspect of the Carkhuff model is especially laudable. It provides for evaluating knowledge about needed skills, mastery of the skills themselves, and the ability to apply the skills.

The Egan Model of Skilled Helping

Another somewhat similar model for training helping skills is that developed by Gerard Egan (1975). In some ways it is more psychologically sophisticated and better elaborated than the model described above. Egan has developed a basic text and an exercise book that provide very clear guidelines for training. A major advantage of the Egan model is that it is psychologically sophisticated enough to be useful at even a beginning graduate level, yet simple enough to be used with some kinds of paraprofessionals or well-educated lay helpers.

The Egan model is centered around a basic concept of psychological growth and development that examines the interactions among perceptions, cognitions, and overt behaviors or actions. According to Egan, development involves challenges which demand new patterns of behavior. Development proceeds out of a balance or equilibrium between these environmental challenges and the availability of resources with which the individual can meet these challenges. Environmental resources include the presence of empathic and supportive human relationships, needed knowledge, and a repertoire of specific behavioral skills.

Egan's program is intended to train helpers to move through a well-defined set of steps in facilitating the development of others. The model is set up in terms of a four-step process.

The first step is a diagnostic and focusing stage in which the client carefully reviews his or her situation and attempts to sort out positive and negative elements. The helper facilitates this process through the use of active listening and relationship-building skills.

The second step in the model involves goal-setting. In this process the client may restructure and redefine problems and concerns to make them amenable to his or her own control and to allow the establishment of specific behavioral goals. The skilled helper assists in this process of cognitive restructuring and goal-setting.

The third stage of the model involves the development of an action plan or program through which the client can reach goals. This is a practical, action-oriented phase in which the helper focuses on encouraging clear, firm, and decisive goal-relevant action on the part of the client.

The final step in the model involves implementation and evaluation of the plan. In this phase the helper helps the client be responsible and accountable for following through on plans and commitments made earlier. Evaluation is based upon the completion or attainment of behavioral goals and objectives.

Egan's people-in-systems model (Egan & Cowan, 1979) is a comprehensive and relatively sophisticated program that can be utilized either for preservice or in-service training of a variety of human services workers or lay helpers in the community.

Other Training Models

Ivey (1980) has developed a sophisticated model for training helping skills based upon what is often called "micro-counseling." Essentially, micro-counseling involves a careful analysis of counseling processes to identify crucial counseling skill components at the simplest possible level. These skills are identified and trained with a set of techniques involving explanation, videotape modeling, role-playing, and feedback. Comprehensive packages of training tapes and print materials are available to implement this package.

A similar approach, developed by Kagan (1980), is called Interpersonal Process Recall. This procedure again uses video recordings of counseling as well as supervisory and feedback sessions to define and demonstrate a basic set of skills and understandings. Complete packages of training materials are again available commercially.

All of the approaches described above offer valuable resources to the counseling psychologist interested in enhancing the number and quality of helping resources available within the community. When such programs are successfully implemented, they may literally multiply the human services resources of a community. They thus are very high in potential payoff. The ultimate effects of these programs are relatively difficult to research and evaluate in systematic ways. There are some dangers in using training procedures in mechanical or superficial ways. Careful selection of trainers is an important consideration, and sufficient time and other resources should be available to ensure that training programs are thorough and of high quality.

References

Authier, J., Gustafson, K., Guerney, B. G., Jr., & Kasdorf, J. A. The psychological practitioner as a teacher: A theoretical-historical and practical review. *The Counseling Psychologist*, 1975, *5*, 31–50.

Bandes, K. W., Steinke, G., & Allen, G. J. Evaluation of three dating-specific treatment approaches for heterosexual dating anxiety. *Journal of Consulting and Clinical Psychology*, 1975, *43*, 259–265.

Bandura, A. Self-efficacy: Toward a unifying theory of behavior change. *Psychological Review*, 1977, *84*, 191–215.

Bard, M., & Berkowitz, B. Training police as specialists in family crisis intervention: A community psychology action program. *Community Mental Health Journal*, 1967, *3*, 315–317.

Brown, S. D. Self-control skills training. *Professional Psychology*, 1975, *6*, 319–330.

Caplan, G. *The theory and practice of mental health consultation*. New York: Basic Books, 1970.

Carkhuff, R. R. *Helping and human relations* (2 vols.). New York: Holt, Rinehart & Winston, 1969.

Carkhuff, R. Training as a preferred mode of treatment. *Journal of Counseling Psychology*, 1971, *13*(2), 123–131.

Cognetta, P. V. Deliberate psychological education: A high school cross-age teaching model. *The Counseling Psychologist*, 1977, *6*(4).

Cooper, P. G., & Cherchia, P. J. Effects of communication skills training on high school students' ability to function as peer group facilitators. *Journal of Counseling Psychology*, 1976, *23*(5), 464–468.

Curran, J. D., & Gilbert, F. S. A test of the relative effectiveness of a systematic desensitization program and an interpersonal skills training program with date anxious subjects. *Behavior Therapy,* 1975, *6,* 510–521.

Danskin, D., Kennedy, C. E., & Friesen, W. S. Guidance—The ecology of students. *Personnel and Guidance Journal,* 1965, *45,* 130–135.

Egan, G. *The skilled helper.* Monterey, Calif.: Brooks-Cole, 1975.

Egan, G., & Cowan, M. A. *People in systems: A model for development in the human-service professions and education.* Monterey, Calif.: Brooks-Cole, 1979.

Egner, J. R., & Jackson, D. J. Effectiveness of a counseling intervention program for teaching career decision-making skills. *Journal of Counseling Psychology,* 1978, *25*(1), 45–52.

Eisler, R. M. & Fredereksen, L. W. *Perfecting social skills.* New York: Plenum, 1980.

Elder, J. P., Edelstein, B. A., & Marick, M. M. Adolescent psychiatric patients: Modifying aggressive behavior with social skills training. *Behavior Modification,* 1979, *3,* 161–178.

Ennis, K., & Mitchell, S. Staff training for a day-care center. In J. Fagan & I. Shepherd (Eds.), *Gestalt therapy now.* New York: Harper & Row, 1970.

Erickson, V. L. Deliberate psychological education for women: A follow-up study. *The Counseling Psychologist,* 1977, *6*(4).

Erickson, V. L. Deliberate psychological education for women: from Iphigenia to Antigone. *Counselor Education and Supervision,* 1975, *14*(4), 297–310.

Fensterheim, H. Assertive methods and marital problems. In R. D. Rubin, H. Fensterheim, J. D., Henderson, & R. P. Walman (Eds.), *Advances in behavior therapy.* New York: Academic Press, 1972.

Foy, D. W., Miller, P. M., Eisler, R. M. & O'Toole, D. H. Social-skills training to teach alcoholics to refuse drinks effectively. *Journal of Studies on Alcohol,* 1976, *37,* 1340–1345.

Frederiksen, L. W., Jenkins, J. O., Foy, D. W., & Eisler, R. M. Social skills training in the modification of abusive verbal outbursts in adults. *Journal of Applied Behavior Analysis,* 1976, *9,* 119–125.

Getz, W. L., Fiigita, B. N., & Allen, D. The use of paraprofessionals in crisis intervention: Evaluation of an innovative program. *American Journal of Community Psychology,* 1975, *3,* 135–144.

Glass, C. R., Gottman, J. M., & Shumrak, S. H. Response-acquisition and cognitive self statement modification approaches to dating skills training. *Journal of Counseling Psychology,* 1976, *23,* 520–526.

Goldsmith, J. B., & McFall, R. M. Development and evaluation of an interpersonal skill-training program for psychiatric outpatients. *Journal of Abnormal Psychology,* 1975, *84,* 51–58.

Goldstein, A. P., Sprakin, R. P., & Gershaw, N. J. *Skill training for community living: Applying structured therapy.* New York: Pergamon Press, 1976.

Gordon, J. S. Coming together: Consulting with young people. *Social Policy,* 1975, *5*(2), 40–52.

Gray, B., Mida, R. A., & Coonfield, T. J. Empathic listening test: An instrument for the selection and training of telephone crisis workers. *Journal of Community Psychology,* 1976, *4,* 199–205.

Greiner, J. M., & Karoly, P. Effects of self-control training on study activity and academic performance: An analysis of self-reward and systematic planning components. *Journal of Counseling Psychology,* 1976, *23*(6), 495–502.

Guerney, B. G. J., Stolack, G., & Guerney, L. A format for a new mode of psychological practice. *The Counseling Psychologist,* 1970, *2,* 97–109.

Harris, J. W., & Bodden, J. An activity group experience for disengaged elderly persons. *Journal of Counseling Psychology,* 1978, *25*(4), 325–330.

Hersen, M., & Bellack, A. S. A multiple-baseline analysis of social skills training in chronic schizophrenics. *Journal of Applied Behavior Analysis,* 1976, *9,* 239–245.

Hollandsworth, J. G., Dressel, M. E., & Stevens, J. The use of behavioral versus traditional procedures for increasing job interview skills. *Journal of Counseling Psychology,* 1977, *24,* 503–510.

Hollandsworth, J. G., Glazeski, R. C., & Dressel, M. E. Use of social-skills training in the treatment of extreme anxiety and deficient verbal skills in the job-interview setting. *Journal of Applied Behavior Analysis,* 1978, *11,* 259–269.

Ivey, A. Counseling and psychotherapy: Skills, theories, and practice. Englewood Cliffs, NJ: Prentice-Hall, 1980.

Jacobson, N. S. Problem solving and contingency contracting in the treatment of marital discord. *Journal of Consulting and Clinical Psychology,* 1977, *45,* 92–100.

Kagan, N. Influencing human interactions: Eighteen years with IPR. In A. K. Hess (Ed.), *Psychotherapy supervision: Theory, research and practice.* New York: Wiley, 1980.

Kelly, J. A., Laughlin, C., Claiborne, M., & Patterson, J. A. A group procedure for teaching job interview skills to formerly hospitalized psychiatric patients. *Behavior Therapy,* 1979, *10,* 299–310.

Kelly, J. A. *Social-skills training.* New York, Springer, 1982.

Kohlberg, L. Counseling and counselor education: A developmental approach. *Counselor Education and Supervision,* 1975, *14*(4), 250–257.

Kohlberg, L. Stage and sequence: The cognitive developmental approach to socialization. In D. Goslin (Ed.), *Handbook of socialization theory and research.* Chicago: Rand-McNally, 1969.

Lange, A., & Jakubowski, P. *Responsible assertive behavior: Cognitive behavior: Cognitive behavioral procedures for trainers.* Champagne-Urbana, Ill: Research Press, 1976.

Libet, J. M., & Lewinsohn, P. M. Concept of social skill with specific reference to the behavior of depressed persons. *Journal of Consulting and Clinical Psychology,* 1973, *40,* 304–312.

Loevinger, J. *Ego development.* San Francisco: Jossey-Bass, 1976.

Loevinger, J., & Wessler, R. *Measuring ego development* (Vol. I.) San Francisco: Jossey-Bass, 1970.

Mager, R. F. *Preparing instructional objectives.* Palo Alto, Calif.: Fearon Publishers, 1962.

Martinson, W. D., & Zerface, J. P. Comparison of individual counseling and social programs with non-daters. *Journal of Counseling Psychology,* 1970, *17*, 36–40.

Mosher, R. L. Knowledge from practice: Clinical research and development in education. *The Counseling Psychologist,* 1974, *21*, 73–81.

Mosher, R. L. (Ed.). *Adolescent's development and education.* Berkeley, Calif.: McCutchan Publishing Co., 1979.

Mosher, R. L., & Sullivan, P. A curriculum in moral education. In D. Purpel & Ryan (Eds.), Moral Education: It comes with the territory. Berkeley, CA: McCutchan Publishing Corp., 1976.

Novaco, R. W. Training of probation counselors for anger problems. *Journal of Counseling Psychology,* 1980, *27*(4), 385–390.

Patterson, G. R. Behavioral intervention procedures in the classroom and in the home. In A. E. Bergin & S. L. Garfield (Eds.), *Handbook of psychotherapy and behavior changes.* New York: Wiley, 1971, pp. 751–775.

Perry, W. *Intellectual and ethical development in the college years.* New York: Holt, Rinehart & Winston, 1970.

Phillips, L. *The social skills basis of psychopathology.* New York: Grune and Stratton, 1978.

Romano, J. L., & Cabianca, W. A. EMG Feedback training versus systematic desensitization for test anxiety reduction. *Journal of Counseling Psychology,* 1978, *25*(1), 8–13.

Rustad, K., & Rogers, C. Promoting psychological growth in a high school class. *Counselor Education and Supervision,* 1975, *14*(4), 277–286.

Sprinthall, N. & Mosher, R. Psychological education in secondary schools: A program to promote individual and human development. *American Psychologist,* 1970, *10*, 911–924.

Suinn, R. M., & Richardson, F. Anxiety management training: A non-specific behavior therapy program for anxiety control. *Behavior Therapy,* 1971, *2*, 498–510.

Tharp, R. G., & Wetzel, R. J. *Behavior modification in the natural environment.* New York and London: Academic Press, 1969.

Walder, L., Cohen, S., & Breiter, D. Teaching behavioral principles to parents of disturbed children. In A. M. Graziano (Ed.), *Behavior therapy with children.* Chicago: Aldine-Atherton, 1971.

Whiteley, J. (Ed.), Assertion training, special issue. *The Counseling Psychologist,* 1975, *5*(4). Whole issue.

Whiteley, J. M. (Ed.), Developmental counseling psychology. *The Counseling Psychologist,* 1977, *6*(4). Whole issue.

Widick, C., Knefelkamp, L. L., & Parker, C. A. The counselor as a developmental instructor. *Counselor Education and Supervision,* 1975, *14*(4), 286–297.

Wrenn, C. G. *The counselor in a changing world.* Washington, D.C.: American Personnel and Guidance Association, 1962.

6
Working with Community Organizations

In chapter 1 we pointed out the fact that American psychology has never really dealt with the challenge presented nearly fifty years ago by Lawrence Frank to view society as the patient. In a recent article, Sarason (1981) traced the history of American psychology and noted the relative dominance of theoretical formulations designed to explain individual behavior. He drew attention to the lack of awareness given to problems involving social interaction and the behavior of people in groups and organizations.

Perhaps this imbalance of attention is, indeed, simply an accident of the development of psychology as a science, or perhaps it is indicative of the deep ambivalence with which our society approaches the vicissitudes of organizational life generally.

We all exist, rather obviously, in a world that is dominated, if not defined, by organizations. We are born, work, live, love, and die within the webs woven by myriad organizations that touch and shape our lives. Our communities are essentially clusters of organizations welded together by an ever-growing bond of economic, social, and political interdependence. The story of our social and technological progress is one of proliferation of formal organizations.

For most of us the geography of our life space is best delineated by tracing our patterns of memberships in organizations. The rivers, mountains, and valleys of our lives are drawn in terms of the roles and relationships that define our participation in groups and organizations. Unfortunately, the life-long love affair that we maintain with these organizations seldom runs smoothly. We join, we participate, we even structure our lives around organizations, but seldom do we find in organizational life a well-paved path to personal security and fulfillment.

In chapter 5, on consultation and training, we described process consultation as a psychological intervention aimed at improving the

149

functioning of work groups through facilitating their social interactions around the tasks or goals that they were intended to achieve. We limited the definition of process consultation to those work groups characterized by routine, face-to-face, personal interaction. We know, however, that the complexity of our communities and the size of many of our vital institutions and agencies means that many times we are faced with the fact that malfunctioning in large organizations leads to devastating consequences to community members. In such organizations, productive interventions must transcend simple, face-to-face relationships in small groups and deal, instead, with the complex dynamics of a many-layered organizational bureaucracy. Indeed, as we have seen in chapter 2, our principal conceptual tool for understanding community life, general systems theory, causes us to look at the relationships among the various levels of a large organization as important determinants of their effectiveness.

As we engage in the study of organizational behavior, we cannot help but be struck by the deep ambivalence in outlook and attitudes alluded to earlier. This ambivalence manifests itself in many ways. Most of us, for example, harbor anemic aspirations for the organizations to which we belong. Membership on a new committee is greeted with undisguised disgust. We jokingly define a committee as a group that keeps minutes and wastes hours. Yet attempts at reorganization that seem rational and moderate to outsiders are often greeted with deep suspicion and distrust from within. Our organizational structures, no matter how we curse at them ourselves, somehow take on the form of anchors to our personal identities that must be defended and protected like a worn-out suit of clothes about to be thrown on the trash heap by an overzealous housekeeper.

Years of attempting to understand and constructively intervene in a variety of organizational problems leads to the conclusion that in organizational behavior we witness the collision of powerful and competing themes in human motivation and, indeed, human existence.

For some years psychology has accepted a view of human motivation that focuses upon the proactive, stimulus-seeking nature of the organism. This view sees individuals as possessing basic tendencies or drives to explore, manipulate, and control significant aspects of their environments. White's (1959) concept of "competence" or "effectance motivation" was a pioneering statement of this view. Basically, White and a host of researchers who followed him have studied and elaborated upon the notion that human beings have strong and perhaps innate needs to reach out to understand, predict, and, ultimately, to control novel, complex, ambiguous, or problematical elements in their environments. This basic quest for control is seen as a central and uniquely important human characteristic, and one that constitutes a basic source of motivation and energy for individual and social development. Over the past quarter century attribution theorists (Heider, 1958), social learning theorists (Bandura, 1974), cognitive theorists (Kelly, 1963), and applied psychologists (Mahoney, 1974) have elaborated and extended this basic view.

It seems evident, then, that human beings are organisms that need to perceive and experience themselves as having control over significant aspects of their interaction with the environment. They need to recognize the impact of their efforts in terms of effects upon their world. Without some of this feeling of effectance, people tend to become vulnerable to the helplessness-hopelessness syndrome that is the breeding ground of depression and dispair (Maier & Seligmann, 1976).

In the contemporary world it is also obvious that for one to experience these feelings of power, control, and effectiveness, he or she must be able to engage effectively in a variety of social roles generated out of formal organizations. In our complex and interdependent world to be truly alone and isolated is to be largely powerless, vulnerable, and ineffective.

We are thus inexorably drawn toward organizations because of the opportunities they offer us to extend our influence and control over the environment. A few years ago one of the authors counseled with a young woman who was very much a "campus activist." She expressed this view eloquently when she said, "organizations are for me like the cheerleader's megaphone—they amplify my voice. I don't really like them, but without them, I would feel helpless and alone."

It is the need to feel some sense of expectance and control as well as purely practical considerations that propels us toward organizations. Yet, as we sense the pull of the group, another equally powerful set of motives comes into play. We sense the threat of the group to our own individuality and autonomy. If we surrender too much of ourselves for the sense of power, purpose, and potency afforded by the organization, we risk losing ourselves—our independence, freedom, and autonomy.

Richard de Charms (1968) and his associates have compiled an impressive array of evidence that points to the very powerful motivational impact of the human need to experience autonomy. In a variety of experimental situations, this research shows that people often respond negatively to situations that are perceived and experienced as manipulative. In such situations they resist or withdraw cooperation even in the presence of very desirable rewards or presumed incentives. Indeed, this line of research indicates that one of the most powerful ways to reduce a human being's intrinsic motivation for a task or activity may be to reward performance in the activity in a systematic way. Levine and Fasnact (1974) reviewed evidence for this phenomenon as it operates in behavior modification situations, and Notz (1975) reported similar findings in a review of the job performance and supervision literature. It seems rather clear, then, that the push–pull, approach–withdrawal elements in organizational behavior have a rather firm basis in both the reality of direct experience and the findings of systematic research. We also know from research with both animals and human beings that when they are put in alternatively punishing and rewarding situations, it is possible to condition neurotic, stupid, or self-defeating behavior.

When we look at the level of effectiveness or, more aptly, ineffectiveness of many human organizations, it seems all too obvious that something like this occurs in many people and in many organizations. Two examples of this phenomenon may serve to clarify it.

A few years ago one of the authors was hired by a large urban school system to supervise a major evaluation project. This city had its full share of urban ills and problems. Racial tensions, delinquency problems, drug abuse, and all of their related social malfunctions had made their presence felt in the schools and in the community.

The school system itself had made a valiant and determined response to these problems. A large number and wide variety of special, innovative programs had been launched if not floated. Indeed, the central administration building was a veritable kettle of alphabet soup. Programs ABC, XYZ, and SOS, together with almost every other combination of consonants and vowels, occupied lonely little offices along the back corridors of a factory-like administration building. As one senior school official put it, "there is hardly a major educational innovation that hasn't been tried here over the past ten years."

Part of the research project involved visiting more than twenty schools and interviewing a sample of several hundred teachers. The feeling generated out of these interviews was disillusioning and unforgettable. A very large percentage of these intelligent, well-educated, and at one time dedicated men and women had been reduced to apathy, resignation, and hopelessness. They felt trapped in a situation where nothing seemed to work. Their sense of personal and organizational effectiveness and worth had been steadily eroded by a history of unrelieved failure and disappointment. Hopes had been raised and dashed countless times by countless promises of help with overwhelming problems. Their faith in the organization as a source of mutual strength and power to deal with problems and meet needs was nearly gone.

Another, somewhat similar example involved the clinical staff of a large, chronic, neuropsychiatric hospital with whom one of the authors had a continuing consulting relationship over a period of several years. In the course of perhaps a dozen one-day consulting visits, the consultant began to realize that the scenario was always the same. Sessions began with a discussion of recent research findings and new approaches to treatment. Within a couple of hours a subtle change would begin to occur in the group. Feelings of frustration, defeat, and helplessness would begin to be vented. The revolving door phenomenon with patients would always come up in the discussion. Successes seemed inevitably to turn into failures. The lack of caring and concern for patients in the hospital and in the outside society would be described. Hopes for new treatment approaches seemed always to fade with time and experience.

Gradually, the consultant came to realize that his role was not to bring in new ideas, or even to work with the staff's problems in regard to professional practice. Rather, the role was clearly to serve as a group therapist for a staff of highly educated, superbly intelligent depressives. Somehow the helplessness-hopelessness syndrome had insidiously been transmitted from patients to healers.

When we examine the destructive and wasteful impact that so many of our organizations have upon both their members and the public these organizations are intended to serve, nagging and disturbing questions are raised. Why have we failed so frequently and so miserably in our organizational endeavors? We acknowledge the fact that we as human beings are social animals. Our philosophies and our religions point up a need for each other. Yet in so many settings, from family to factory, we fail, and do psychological violence to ourselves in the act of failing.

The need for systematic institutional self-renewal in the organizations that combine to form our communities seems overwhelmingly obvious. So many of the people whom we try to serve clearly trace their own upset and unhappiness to malfunctioning organizations. Such inadequate and destructive systems in families, classrooms, neighborhoods, or job settings seem to chew people up and spit the bloody remnants back at us in the helping professions. We band-aid and then feed them back into the dehumanizing hopper of organizational reality.

Unfortunately, our own organizations in the human services seem to fare little better in terms of their capacity to generate humane and nurturant environments than do those found in other parts of the community. One of the most disillusioning experiences in the life of a young professional in the human services occurs when he or she is brought face to face with that unhappy reality. Psychologists, for example, seem to fight and bicker among themselves just like other people. We, who ought to be immune and enlightened, are as susceptible to the ills of organizational entropy as any of our fellows.

We have studied organizational life through the medium of the social and behavior sciences for about a century. The history of that process of investigation pretty well reflects the clash of human needs and tendencies described above.

Classical Organization Theory

The first great thrust in the study of organizational behavior has often been termed the "economic rational movement." Its founding father was Max Weber, and its illuminating ideal was that of the rational, orderly, and logical bureaucracy.

In this model of human organization, administrators exist to administer in direct, clear, efficient ways. A policy should exist for every rule, a rule for every action, and a designated official should be present to ensure compliance with the rules. Duties should be specified, authority and responsibility delegated, relationships formalized, and merit rewarded.

The emphasis in this movement, which merged into the classical school of organization theory, was clearly centered around the human motivation to achieve control of the environment through orderly, cooperative, rational behavior. While today it may be fashionable to deprecate this approach, we should face the fact that it worked and often worked well. This approach to human organization largely built the great industrial machine whose fruits (some not altogether sweet) we enjoy today. This approach to human organization did give men and women the power to control their environments in previously undreamed of ways.

Basically, the classical approach was built around several central notions or concepts, as described below.

Hierarchical Structure.   Almost all complex systems—physical, biological, or social—are organized in terms of some hierarchical kind of structure. Johnson, Kast, and Rosenzweig (1967) point out that there is apparently something fundamental in this structural principle that goes beyond the peculiarities of human organizations. Almost any type of system having sufficient complexity can apparently be analyzed in terms of the box within a box analogy. As we saw in chapter 2, general systems theory helps us to focus upon and understand the relationships among various levels within a hierarchical system.

In human systems or social organizations, relationships between levels are often defined primarily in terms of the concepts of *authority* and *leadership*. Authority is defined as the capacity to invoke compliance in subordinates by virtue of position. The captain of the ship sets the course and gives the orders precisely because he is the captain, not necessarily because of superior wisdom, knowledge, or experience. Authority, then, tends to be impersonal and to be legitimized in terms of a position within a hierarchy rather than in terms of individual personality traits or qualities. Leadership, on the other hand, is the charismatic quality that induces compliance in others regardless of legally vested position. A leader exists primarily in the eyes of the beholder.

As we work with community organizations, we need to be able to understand and analyze both the authority and the leadership hierarchies within the system. They are not always identical by any means. Organizations typically function optimally when those in authority also exercise a reasonable degree of leadership. Paralyzing conflicts may arise when authority and leadership are sharply divided. On the other hand, when those in authority constrict or impede all opportunities for leadership in the organization, they may severely limit the total human resources of the system and reduce its ability to cope with change or handle emergency or crisis situations.

Since leadership arises primarily out of the perceptions of the leader held by other members, it may be withdrawn or transferred by members as situations and perceptions change. Leadership resources thus add tremendously to the flexibility and adaptability of an organization.

Functional Specialization.   Functional specialization is a concept that is extremely important in organization theory. The nature of specialization, or the ways in which the division of labor or tasks is accomplished, heavily influences the structure of the organization.

The theory of functional specialization that an organization holds is reflected in the division of the organization into departments or other units. It also largely determines the hierarchical elements of the the system and consequently the lines of authority and responsibility.

In many human services organizations, for example, the theory of functional specialization may be rudimentary or be based on outmoded perceptions of professional specialties and preparation. Many community mental health systems are organized around a theory of specialization traditional to the practice of medicine. Such a model presents the psychiatrist as the natural authority figure and views other professionals such as psychologists, social workers, and public health nurses as clearly subordinate figures who can function effectively only under close supervision. When such a theory of specialization is clearly outmoded and out of contact with the realities of the professional development of a field, the seeds of conflict and discord are certain to be present.

In the human services generally, the level of communication and understanding among disciplines and professions is typically so low that much energy is devoted to attempting to develop structures that tap the unique resources of each member without doing violence to legitimate needs for recognition and autonomy. One of the major organizational tasks of the counseling psychologist in community practice is to communicate a clear sense of his or her professional identity to other professionals and in turn be sensitive to their professional role conceptions. Out of a productive and open dialogue, more harmonious and effective models of functional specification can grow.

Span of Control.   Span of control is a concept from classical organization theory that is useful in understanding the role of supervision and consultation within organizations. Classical organization theory held that the span of control, that is, the number of subordinates that any one administrator can supervise, should be small, typically from five to seven people. More modern approaches to organizational analysis have pointed out that in a large organization this may create a highly elongated vertical structure with many levels, thus creating communication problems. The flow of information from bottom to top in such a system is notoriously difficult, and communications failures may result in bad decisions being made far from the actual site of operations.

Tight spans of control also may limit the autonomy of workers and hence their sense of commitment and satisfaction with the organization.

Organizations with predominantly professional workers, such as schools and other human services agencies, may have very broad spans of control. The principal of a school may, for example, supervise as many as a hundred teachers in addition to being the primary link between the system and the rest of the community.

Span of control problems in such organizations are alleviated by the distinction made between *line* and *staff* functions. The line function represents the primary flow of legitimately or legally vested authority. The original concept of staff was a military one, essentially that of providing the commander with an extra complement of aides or assistants. These staff people were seen originally as extensions of the administrator's personality, giving him, in a sense, extra sets of arms and legs or eyes and ears, so that he could figuratively manage to be everywhere at once.

Gradually, the concept of staff functions has broadened to include a wide variety of direct inputs into the system. In many organizations staff functions of a specialized nature are performed by a variety of professionals. In schools, for example, guidance counselors, nurses, social workers, and psychologists among others work directly with teachers and students as well as in advising administrators.

The concept of mental health consultation discussed in an earlier chapter was in a sense a device to bring into a human services agency extra staff or supporting resources in the form of outside consultation. The consultant essentially plays a temporary quasi-staff role in the client system.

The distinction between line and staff roles is a powerful one in modern organizations, but it is not without problems. Sometimes the lines between supporting staff work and direct supervision are easily blurred, the resulting confusion causing conflict and dissension. An important task for counseling psychologists involved in performing staff functions in a community organization is to keep lines of communication open and constantly to clarify their own roles and responsibilities.

The classical approach to organizational behavior made substantial contributions to the understanding of problems of formal organizational structure. This approach called attention to problems of nepotism, incompetence, indecisiveness, and favoritism that often afflict badly managed organizations. It provided an impetus for reforms in personnel selection and promotion on the basis of merit that we take for granted today. In a sense, it created the model of the professional manager or administrator (Blau & Scott, 1962).

In this country men like Frederick Taylor took the classical approach to organizational analysis further, into the area of time and motion studies. Taylor helped to inaugurate the era of the "efficiency expert." He envisioned organizations functioning at peak efficiency through total adherence to carefully prescribed working methods, conditions, and equipment (Taylor, 1957). He and those who followed him developed the principles of "scientific management."

The classical approach to organization theory fully clothed in the garments of "scientific management" soon ran afoul of the second great theme of organizational behavior to which we alluded earlier. Its tendency to treat workers as interchangeable units to be manipulated by omniscient authorities, the "scientific managers," soon brought a deluge of criticism from many sources. Gross (1964) called the ultimate extension of classical organization theory the "gospel of efficiency." Critics of the view contended that human beings are not interchangeable parts, but should be seen as persons with feelings, attitudes, ideas, and aspirations that cannot and should not be brought under the presumed control of a set of "puppet masters" in the guise of scientific management.

The Human Relations Approach

A study of Max Weber's writings shows that even he sensed the dangers and disillusionments inherent in his approach. Weber too recognized and longed for something more than "bureaucratic man."

The urge to recognize that "something more" pushed its way into the study of organizational life about fifty years ago. Studies of worker morale, productivity, and satisfaction brought into focus an alternative view of organizational life that is often termed the *human relations* approach. Beginning with the oft-quoted Hawthorne, California, or Western Electric studies (Roethlisberger & Dickson, 1939) of the 1930s, a powerful new body of organizational theory and research was advanced. This new approach soon found itself squarely astride the second great theme of human motivation that we discussed earlier. These researchers focused upon human needs for autonomy, independence, and individual recognition. Scores of studies reported results to indicate that the productivity of workers was more a function of their morale and social interaction than of wages, hours, working conditions, or closeness of supervision.

Etzioni (1964) pointed out that the human relations approach was centered around the burgeoning array of evidence that pointed to four basic phenomena in human interaction. These are:

1. The amount of work accomplished by a worker is a product not of his physical capacity but of his "social capacity."
2. Noneconomic or psychological rewards play a central role in the satisfaction and motivation of workers.
3. High degrees of specialization and resulting isolation are not always the most efficient methods for division of labor.
4. Members of an organization do not react to it and its norms and rewards solely as individuals, but rather as members of groups.

Basically, the human relations approach highlighted the fact that the behavior of people in an organization is primarily a product of their social interactions with each other, and with the outside environment. What follows from this fact is that the most important component of that interaction is determined by the interpersonal resources of members, and that these resources can never be fully tapped through the use of fear, coercion, or for that matter totally external and impersonal rewards and reinforcements.

Perhaps the most eloquent and influential expression of the human relations approach to organizations was articulated by McGregor (1960) in his famous distinction between the X and Y views of human tendencies and the managerial styles that flowed from them. He vividly contrasted two sets of managerial attitudes, one of which pictured workers as essentially lazy, unmotivated, untrustworthy, and incompetent. The other and obviously preferable view envisioned the same workers as motivated, responsible, creative, and committed. These two sets of managerial philosophies or attitudes were seen as setting into motion forces within an organization that caused their premises and predictions to become self-fulfilling.

The vastly changed perspective to the study of organizational behavior provided by the human relations school brought forth a veritable avalanche of new findings. Generally, this line of research showed that the attitudes, communications processes, and group dynamics involving workers tended to be more potent determinants of their productivity than are the formal structural properties of the organization. The new approach promoted a relatively sweeping reevaluation of organizational practices. Much greater emphasis was put upon wide participation in decision making, the importance of face-to-face relationships in communication, and mutual confidence rather than vested authority as the major integrative force in the organization. The role of the supervisor was seen more as a facilitator of communication and problem solving than as an agent of authority and unilateral decision maker (Johnson et al., 1967).

The human relations approach thus broadened the scope of organizational theory from a framework with which to examine the formal structure of an organization as it appears on organizational charts to a much more encompassing tool with which to study a wide range of social behavior as it occurs within organizational contexts.

Bernard (1938), in examining social organizational structure from the human relations point of view, suggested that there are really two intimately related and intertwined structures in any large, formal organization. One is the formal, consciously established and maintained structure that is often represented on wall charts. The other is informal, fluid, and indefinite, but tremendously important and significant in the life of the organization. The latter *informal* structure may have few apparent, permanent and distinct subdivisions. Bernard insisted, however, that no large organization could long exist without the development of this informal system or alternative structure.

The informal elements of the organization grow out of the inevitable interpersonal relationships and attitudes that each organization member builds up in regard to every other member. These attitudes may exist at relatively low levels of personal awareness. The nature of the informal structure is, however, a potent determinant of how information flows through the organization, how opinions will be formed and maintained, and how and to what extent compliance will be given to suggestions and directives. It also determines how readily accurate information will feed into decision-making processes. Finally, it will also shape perceptions of those who will be seen as sources of help and advice and those who will be viewed as threatening or meddlesome.

Formal and Informal Behavior

Dubin (1958) analyzed organizational behavior into a series of dimensions that are conceived out of the division of formal and informal structure noted above. He described the formal behavior system as those behaviors that are emitted in conscious response to explicit rules and directives. Part of this formal behavior can be called "technical" since it arises from the specific job function of an organization member. For example, counseling clients, doing psychological assessments, attending case conferences, keeping case notes and records may all be part of the technical behavior of psychologists in a typical agency setting.

Operating at the same time, however, are other sets of behaviors that may actually deviate from formal expectations, but which are very important to the actual operation of the system. Dubin called these behaviors "nonformal" and pointed out that while they may deviate from formal expectations, they often serve to bypass red tape and may ensure efficient operation.

Examples of such behavior in a community agency may include informal consultation between therapists, covering the appointments of an absent staff member, communicating informally with a referral source, seeing a client in a crisis situation without a prior appointment, and the like. This type of behavior actually ensures smooth operation because it is more flexible and adaptive than responses generated out of a formal and cumbersome bureaucratic procedure. In another sense it represents an assertion of autonomy against what may be perceived as the tedious constraints of the formal system.

A second kind of unofficially sanctioned behavior that goes beyond mere technical behavior is what Dubin termed "informal." This consists largely of socializing activities that have significant, if indirect effects on organizational operations. Such informal behaviors include conversations at coffee breaks, around the water cooler, in the lunchroom, or before and after meetings. These conversations provide the basis for a communication system usually called the "grapevine." As research has shown (Davis, 1953), the grapevine is a ubiquitous organizational phenomenon that supplements and sometimes supplants other more official channels of communication. Sometimes, in fact, the formal channels of directives, memos, and announcements seem only to exist to provide official validation for what is already common knowledge.

The nonformal and informal kinds of behaviors are extrememly important to the operation of an organization (Cornell, 1954) and must be studied and understood by those who plan to intervene to improve it. These behaviors are often crucial in determining the ways in which members respond to innovative ideas or practices, or how the system reacts to crisis and challenge. Without a healthy and responsible informal structure, an organization is apt to become rigid and sterile with minimal communication, little stimulation, and an almost paralyzing degree of conformity to formal edicts and procedures. In such organizations, morale is often very low and members may function in automatic, ritualistic, totally unenthusiastic ways.

Another important aspect of the informal structure is that it is often the structure that influences the opinions and attitudes of members most significantly. Precisely because the informal structure grows out of the personal and social needs of members, it has great influence over their behavior. Within the small groups of the informal structure are the "articulators," to use Iannacone's (1962) term. These articulators or opinion clarifiers are extremely influential individuals in the informal structure who serve as spokespersons for and representatives of their informal groups. They often hold no position of authority in the formal hierarchy, but are extremely influential because of their leadership roles in the informal system. Because of their high status in the informal structure, they may be relatively immune to the influence or authority of the formal hierarchy. Sometimes this allows them to communicate very clearly and honestly with administrators. Sometimes, however, they can represent formidable centers of resistance and opposition to the formal structure. When such resistance is intense, it can virtually paralyze the operation of the entire organization. Since these people are communication clarifiers and opinion makers, their behavior must be understood and reckoned with by anyone who hopes to improve the organization.

Compliance Systems

One of the contributions of the human relations school of organizational theory is its attention to problems of compliance within social systems. The classical approach tended to take for granted that compliance arose directly and simply out of the legitimate and vested authority of administrators. In fact, compliance involves a set of complex and far-reaching phenomena within every social organization.

Etzioni (1961) categorized social organizations into three groups in terms of the kind of compliance they seek to elicit from members. He called those organizations that seek to influence the attitudes and feelings of members as *normative* organizations. Obvious examples of normative organizations are churches or political parties. *Utilitarian* organizations are defined as those that seek to change or influence the cognitions and skills of members. Trade schools, businesses, or factories are examples of utilitarian organizations. *Coercive* organizations are those that exercise very strong overt controls to provide custodial care aimed primarily at preventing nonconforming behavior from going beyond tolerable limits. Prisons, some kinds of mental hospitals, and peacetime military establishments all, at times at least, fall into this category.

Many community agencies such as schools, welfare agencies, mental health centers, youth centers, and juvenile justice systems have unique problems because they represent at given times all three of these categories. Schools, for example, are coercive organizations in one sense. They contain captive populations of children and youth who are compelled by law and parental pressure to stay. They undeniably perform a custodial function that at times seems to degenerate into little more than glorified babysitting.

At the same time schools try to be normative organizations discharging obligations to socialize young people to the values and ethical and moral standards of the community. Clearly, they are also utilitarian in the sense of transmitting essential knowledge and skills to equip young people to cope with the demands of adult occupational roles.

Other community agencies share the problems of the schools. Welfare and correctional agencies attempt to reform and rehabilitate yet are also charged with enforcing laws and procedures. Even mental health agencies become involved in questions of custody, competence, sanity, and so forth that bring them into the category of coercive systems.

Etzioni (1961) pointed out that ample evidence attests to the fact that the more an organization relies upon coercion, the less it is able to influence changes in attitudes and feelings. He pointed out that we can identify two primary forms of communication within organizations. *Instrumental* communication tends to be cognitively oriented and is aimed at changing overt behavior. It is of the "close the window, open the door" variety. *Expressive* communication, on the other hand, involves a sharing of emotions and attitudes. The use of coercion in an organization tends to suppress expressive communication. In extremely coercive institutions such as maximum security prisons, for example, inmates often develop their own codes or languages and learn to speak almost without lip movements to suppress the level of direct expressive communication between themselves and the authority structure. Such institutions are, of course, notoriously ineffective in changing the attitudes and values of their inmates, as witnessed by high rates of recidivism.

Unfortunately, something of the same phenomenon tends to occur in many other community agencies and institutions. As this occurs we see a breakdown in communication and a resulting alienation between the community institution and the public it was intended to serve. At times, one of the most important functions of the counseling psychologist may be in the form of constructive organizational interventions in schools, welfare agencies, police departments, or mental health agencies to help reverse the forces that promote alienation and conflict.

Communication Systems

The human relations movement made its greatest contribution to the understanding of organizational behavior in terms of the focus it placed upon communications processes. Although most sensitive people in society are more or less acutely aware of the importance of good communication in dyadic relationships, many are remarkably ignorant of the vital role that communication plays in the life of an organization.

One of the most effective ways to understand the dynamics of any human system is to study the flow of communication within and around that system. The capacity of a human system to engage in planned, purposeful change processes is often a function of its capacity to communicate with its members and with the outside environment.

Communication is one of the major processes that holds groups together. Formal social organizations usually structure patterns of communication into clear-cut channels, but they depend upon communication for cohesiveness just as much as small informal groups do. One indication of the significance of communications processes within organizations is in the speed with which rituals and traditions are built up and informal channels of communication established to supplement the formal network.

A major function of communications processes is to help establish consistency of expectations. Human systems expend great amounts of time and energy in communications processes precisely because these processes perform an important psychological purpose. People are often unable to function comfortably and effectively in relationships with each other unless they have the security of knowing that every new situation does not have to be treated as though it were an encounter with a being from another planet.

Often, members of large, complex organizations find this security in small groups or cliques where members know each other well and consequently feel very safe. In these subsystems, members come to develop a common view or "story" of what is happening. The security generated by this common way of perceiving and construing events is jealously guarded. Outsiders or outside perceptions that threaten to invalidate this view may be rejected out of hand. Much of the resistance to planned change that we discussed in chapter 2 stems from efforts to protect the security and cohesiveness of these subsystems. Similarly, the power and strength of the informal structure of an organization is rooted in the motivation to maintain the security provided by these cohesive and closely knit support groups.

In organizations, communication must move across distances that are measured in social-psychological as well as physical distances. Small support groups are very close in terms of social-psychological distance so that communication is rapid and fairly simple. As social-psychological distance increases, problems of communication tend to become more and more difficult.

Optimal system functioning generally requires effective communication across a number of organizational dimensions. A useful way to conceptualize problems of organizational communication is to think about the amount, direction, and nature of communication that can be carried through any communication network at a given time. A channel of communication can thus be viewed as a sort of pipeline that is capable of carrying certain kinds of signals in given directions with a specific degree of clarity and volume at any particular time.

It is easier to understand this concept of a communications network when we think of indirect patterns of communication. The administrator who communicates to his staff through mimeographed memos or who recites a list of announcements over a public address system is obviously operating through a communications network that facilitates only one-way communication and which limits even that kind of communication severely.

Limitations of time and space impede communication and allow nonverbal behavior that may communicate much meaning to be lost or misinterpreted. Even when communication is direct and face to face, however, there are other severe limitations on the kinds of information that are likely to be carried in a communications channel between any two people. As we saw earlier, one useful way of classifying messages is in terms of the "expressive–instrumental" distinction. Instrumental messages are intended to produce some specific response in the receiver, while expressive messages merely convey the feelings or inner state of the sender. Similarly, both categories of messages may be either positive or negative either in terms of do's and don'ts, or of feelings that are pleasant or unpleasant.

Effects of Social Distance

The nature of communications processes are, as we have noted, powerfully affected by the social context in which they occur. When social distances between people or stations in a communications network are wide, many kinds of communications, particularly of the negative, expressive type are directly inhibited. The new member of the typing pool may be no more likely to tell the company vice president that she is confused about his policy on performance ratings and reviews than he is likely to communicate his ambivalent feelings about the plunging neckline of her new dress.

Some of the effects of vertical social psychological distance on communications patterns are evident when we examine the differences between individual and group effectiveness in problem-solving situations (Blau & Scott, 1962). Basically, group problem-solving processes tend to be superior to individual performances in certain task situations when three types of interaction processes operate. These processes occur when: (1) A sifting and evaluation of ideas and suggestions through social interaction serves as an error-correction mechanicsm. (2) Social support furnished in social interaction facilitates creative and critical thinking. (3) Competition among members for respect and recognition mobilizes their energies for contributing to the task.

Differences in status, backgrounds, or affiliations—that is, those differences that combine to produce what we called social-psychological distance—appear to curtail these three group processes that are necessary to harness fully the human resources available in an organization.

First, when social-psychological distance is great, social interaction and social support are reduced. Research has shown, for example, that social interaction typically follows status lines and is inhibited across status boundaries. Lower-status members tend to direct their friendship choices heavily toward upper-status members. Since these upper-status members tend not to reciprocate, but rather to direct their choices to others also high in status, lower-status members receive only low levels of the social support needed for stimulating thought and making suggestions.

Second, formal status differences tend to undermine the process of competition for respect and recognition. Lower-status members may give up any effort to win increased recognition from the group. Other social-psychological differences may similarly result in members feeling valued or devalued in terms of characteristics that override consideration for their actual contribution to the organization.

In community organizations the potential contributions of low-status members may be almost completely lost when they feel that respect and appreciation for their efforts are restricted by various forms of prejudice and bias.

Similarly, social-psychological differences may distort the error-correcting function of communication within an organization. It is not easy for members to oppose the judgments of high-status figures in the group. Even when members have needed information that might correct errors in decision making, they may be unable or unwilling to share that information. The result is that ideas and decisions may go untested or unchallenged even when the necessary information is available in the organization. The actual effects of changes in welfare programs, for example, are often mistaken by decision makers simply because no messages from recipients are ever received.

Open communications processes as they are enhanced by the organizational and social structure of a human system influence many of the dynamics that determine an organization's effectiveness, including its capacity for decision making, problem solving, and planning.

Band Width in Communication Networks

The ability of a communications channel to carry a variety of kinds of messages can be called "band width." When channels can carry positive, negative, instrumental, and expressive messages, we consider them to be wide-band channels. The ability of a communications channel to carry the full range of messages is heavily a function of the quality of interpersonal relationships within the system. When interpersonal relationships are characterized by openness, trust, and respect, the communications network can also carry negative expressive messages that may provide stimulation and warning for badly needed changes in the system. Many times communities do not have the wide-band communications channels that are required to carry negative expressive messages across the social-psychological gaps that separate the rank and file of community members from the policy and decision makers in the social and political hierarchy. In such situations the first warning of system breakdowns may take the form of social explosions such as riots, strikes, or disruptive demonstrations.

Conversely, when band widths are wide, the communications

channels can carry positive, expressive messages about what is right in the system. These messages can serve as reinforcements for innovations and reforms accomplished in the system. Sometimes the seeming cynicism and indifference of people in a power hierarchy is the result of the failure of the communications network to carry positive expressive messages about needs met and jobs well done.

Myths about Communication

Some system difficulties in regard to communication result from myths held by people in the power hierarchy. One of the most obvious and most crucial symbols of power in any organization is the ability to control formal channels of communication. In any organization administrators tend to control and monitor formal communication channels. They normally schedule and determine agenda for staff meetings and control the flow of announcements, memos, newsletters, or other formal media of communication. In this process administrators often inhibit the flow of communication within formal channels because of mistaken beliefs about the consequences of letting certain kinds of messages "surface" within formal channels. Thus, they deliberately narrow the band width of formal communications channels and sometimes even undermine the credibility of these channels.

Because they control the formal channels of communication and because they are separated by considerable social distance from lower positions in the vertical hierarchy, administrators are often insulated from important feedback about the consequences of decisions or policies. They may even view this insulation from negative expressive feedback as a sign of system health rather than as a symptom of the breakdown of communications within the system. The flow of negative expressive communication upward through a power hierarchy is the most difficult kind of communications problem in a human system. It is, however, a necessary ingredient in really effective planning, problem solving, or decision making—that is, the control function within a social system.

The Grapevine

When administrators narrow band widths in communications networks, the result is to force many kinds of messages into the informal channels or "grapevine." The grapevine is a communications channel within the informal structure of an organization that is notoriously innaccurate in transmitting messages. It is a network that consists of long chains of word-of-mouth relays that follow varying and indirect pathways through the system. At each relay point gross distortions and exaggerations are apt to occur. Since all relay points tend to be face to face, however, social-psychological band width can carry all sorts of expressive messages very readily and rapidly. No provision for error correction is available within the grapevine since its chain of relays tends to consist of two-person situations. Thus, while it performs an inevitable function in the informal system, it can be a dangerous source of deviation amplification in the overall system. In times of community crisis, the rumor mill or grapevine may distort messages and escalate conflict.

Flow of Communication

One of the most significant characteristics of communication networks stems from the fact that messages do not flow with equal speed and accuracy in all directions. As we noted earlier, negative expressive messages do not tend to flow upward through a power hierarchy. Status, prestige, and popularity are generally the most important factors that influence information flow, although sheer geographic or physical location or accessibility may also be important factors. Members of a system who are middle level in terms of status or prestige or popularity may often perform important communications functions as relayers of messages through power hierarchies or across lateral groupings.

One of the most significant communications problems in a complex organization is in arranging for two-way communication. Many people actually believe that it is safer to communicate complex, difficult, or tension-arousing messages in one-way, indirect channels rather than in two-way face-to-face situations. Considerable research evidence exists to refute this assumption.

Bavelas (1948) studied the effects of one-way versus two-way communication in a cooperative problem-solving task. Partners with partial diagrams were asked to arrange a set of dominoes in a prescribed way. The dyad partners were physically separated and all communication was by telephone.

Not surprisingly, results of the experiment showed that when only one-way communication was allowed, no dyad succeeded in accomplishing the task. When the second partner was merely allowed to respond with a simple push-button signal for "yes" or "no," the task was accomplished.

More interesting, however, were the effects of restriction of communication on the feelings and attitudes of dyad partners toward each other. When communication was one-way, each member tended to view the other as stupid. When the experimenter allowed full two-way communication by telephone, partners not only accomplished the task, but spontaneously expressed liking and respect for each other.

The importance of effective, broad-band, two-way channels of communication within an organization is considerable. No human system can long operate in consistent and purposeful ways unless it can exchange information within its internal and external environments.

Communication patterns within an organization are not random. Members' positions within the physical and social structure of the organization determine with whom they communicate and the kinds of messages sent and received. As system size increases and physical distance becomes greater, the probability that all group members will have face-to-face contact obviously decreases.

Communications Networks

Organizational psychologists chart and study patterns of communication within an organization in terms of what are called communications networks. A communication network has a shape and size determined by the number of members and the flow of messages through it. In some networks all information must flow through a central position and thence out to other positions in a pattern reminiscent of the hub and spokes of a wheel. In others the flow of communication may follow a circular pattern with messages flowing across and between members in a relatively evenly distributed way. A small leaderless discussion group or a counseling group would be examples of a circular network. The "grapevine" network that we discussed above is essentially a chain-like pattern.

Social psychologists have identified several important properties of communications networks that are determined by the shape of the network and that have important consequences for the performance and satisfaction of members. The first property of a communications network is *centrality*. The concept of centrality relates to the position of members in a network and the distance between them.

In this case distance is measured not in physical terms but in terms of the number of communications links or stations that must be utilized to transmit a message from one member to another. One's centrality in a system is measured by his or her closeness to all other group members in terms of communications. It is, therefore, also a measure of the relative availability of information to a given member. Since information is usually necessary for group problem solving, a high degree of centrality often means high influence, status, and satisfaction as a group member.

Sometimes, however, high-status members in an authority hierarchy may actually have low centrality in that they are cut off from much information by the presence of a group of subordinates who screen information and buffer the administrator from contacts with others. In such situations the person in the organization with the greatest authority and heaviest responsibility may literally be the last to know the bad news. Political leaders such as mayors of large cities are often in this situation.

Another related concept that helps us to understand communications networks is *independence*. This concept refers to the ease or difficulty with which any individual can obtain information from any other. Generally, members higher in a status or authority hierarchy can demand and obtain information from those lower in the hierarchy, while the converse is not always true. The person with high independence clearly is able to act more freely and is less constrained than is the member who must wait for information to filter through to his station in the network. Research (Shaw, 1964) indicates that high independence, like centrality, is associated with greater commitment to tasks and satisfaction with group role.

Still another relevant concept about communications networks is *saturation* (Gilchrist, Shaw & Walker, 1954). This concept is based upon the fact that any individual or station in a communication network can process or handle only a limited number of messages within any given time span. Observers of organizational behavior noted that when the number of messages addressed to any particular position in a network exceeded an optimal number, the level of performance and satisfaction of that member tended to decrease even though centrality and independence remained high.

The level of saturation in a particular station is determined by the total requirements placed upon that position. It varies with the communication and information-processing demands. The former is measured by the number of messages feeding into the station and the latter by the task complexity that is represented in the messages.

When task complexity is high—for example, when many messages require major policy decisions or complicated data analyses—saturation in a central position may be reached quickly.

Administrators who are reluctant to delegate and who demand very high levels of centrality and independence for themselves in all of the communications networks to which they belong are of course very vulnerable to saturation.

In any organization high saturation in the key authority and leadership positions not only induces stress in the occupants of those positions but also undermines the confidence and respect of other members for their leaders or authority figures. Particularly when organizations experience crisis conditions, saturation occurs in central positions of the key communications networks with a resulting breakdown of both communications and confidence.

Sometimes administrators suffering from saturation problems tend to distance themselves to reduce the volume of messages. Because they enjoy high independence, they may be able to do this even though the overall system performance suffers.

Often a more effective strategy for reducing saturation is to decentralize communications networks by giving greater centrality and independence to other positions. A wider distribution of both line and staff responsibilities may solve this kind of problem.

Often the shape and impact of a given communications network can be observed and studied by charting the source and flow of information from one office to another. Another simple device is simply to ascertain through interviews how a message of high interest or importance passed through a network, recording how each member heard the message and from whom it was received.

Perhaps the greatest contribution of the human relations approach to organizational theory is the knowledge and awareness that it generated about the importance of human communications processes to organizational behavior.

Organizational Development

Just as the classical school of organizational theory spawned the "efficiency expert" busily engaged with stopwatch and clipboard in doing time and motion studies, so too has the human relations approach given birth to a method of organizational intervention. Organizational development, or OD as it is often familiarly called, largely grew out of a merger between the human relations approach to organizational behavior and the study of group dynamics generally. In the 1950s the National Training Laboratories developed a set of approaches in training people to understand better the impact of human relationships and social interactions upon their own behavior and that of significant others in a variety of settings. These approaches were known by various terms such as "sensitivity training," T-groups, or the most generic term—"laboratory education." This approach has been discussed in the chapter on group work, above.

Laboratory education principles provided the intervention mode or vehicle for the systematic effort to improve the kind of organizational functioning that we call organizational development. The OD movement came from a strong humanistic base that reflected the positive view of human beings and their potentials for cooperation and productivity that, as we have seen, was fundamental in the human relations approach. Organizational development also reflects the preferences inherent in the human relations school for decentralized planning and control, open lines of communication across organizational levels, and the need for warm, personal, and informal relationships between workers and managers.

The OD approach to intervention, then, focuses upon the informal structure of the organization and attempts to open communication and build trust across levels and departments. A typical OD intervention pattern begins with laboratory education groups involving managers. In these sessions participants are trained in basic concepts and skills in interpersonal communication, relationship building, and group dynamics. In accordance with laboratory-training precepts, this education focuses heavily on direct experiential learning that involves "here and now" experiences in group situations in handling ambiguity, conflict, competition, or anxiety. In many OD laboratories, where "in house" groups of managers or workers from the same organization are brought together, members are encouraged gradually to deal with more and more significant and sensitive reality-based problems. The trainer facilitates the group processes among members and uses the material generated in the group to teach basic concepts of human relations and group dynamics.

In an intensive OD program, relatively large numbers of key personnel are trained in the laboratory education model. As organization members become more comfortable in the model and more confident of their skills, more and more heterogeneous groups are formed and more and more difficult or emotionally charged problems are examined in the laboratory sessions.

Eventually, as the human resources of the organization are

enriched by this process, new ways of communicating, relating, solving problems, and making decisions are learned and institutionalized within the organization. These innovations may or may not involve reorganization of the formal structure, but they are clearly intended to revitalize the informal structure and the patterns of communication in the organization.

Organizational development and the human relations approach have certainly made major contributions to organization life. Unfortunately, the research evidence about the effectiveness of OD approaches is less compelling than we might hope. Campbell and Dunnette (1968) found some evidence for positive organizational effects from human relations training directly on participants and concluded that powerful and positive results do occur. Friedlander (1967) was cautiously optimistic in assessing the evidence for lasting and significant changes from sensitivity training, while Perrow (1972) has raised questions about both the effectiveness of OD interventions in producing positive, lasting changes and the adequacy of its theoretical and methodological base.

Clearly, OD approaches do not constitute miracle cures or panaceas for problems of organizational ineffectiveness, or the destructive effects of organizational stress upon individual members. Organizational development, is, however, a useful and potentially powerful tool in the professional repertoire of the counseling psychologist in community practice.

The most important problem for the counseling psychologist is first to be able to *understand* the dynamics of community organizations, including his own, and their impact on the lives of community members. Both the classical and human relations approaches to organizational behavior have made major contributions to this understanding. The legacies left by both of these approaches need not be discarded.

The emphasis upon logical and clearly defined structural and functional relationships within an organization is important. Job descriptions, written policies, and logical divisions of labor and responsibility are important attributes of effective and humane organizations.

People *are* legitimately motivated by both economic rewards and the sense of accomplishment, purpose, and worth that comes from the successful completion of group tasks. People are capable of making rational decisions and engaging in cooperation on the basis of long-term self-interest.

Similarly, the human relations approach has given us an increased understanding of the role of social interaction and communication in behavior. The need for individual participation and recognition in decision making and planning is real. Open and honest communication can increase cooperative behavior and enhance satisfaction and productivity. Perhaps most important, the OD movement has shown that successful interventions into community life can be based upon educational and developmental goals and can operate on collaborative rather than coercive models.

A social systems point of view elaborated out of the knowledge generated in both the classical and human relations approaches can enable us to help people shape to human purposes and needs the organizational environments in which they live.

As we have seen, many sources of tension within community organizations are inevitable and not totally undesirable. Tension is not necessarily pathological in the organization, nor does it arise solely from the presence of pathological people. Tension can energize both organizations and individuals toward positive growth and change. When we understand organization, we as counseling psychologists can begin to tap the tremendous well-springs of power and motivation inherent in organizational life for the service of developing human beings.

References

Bandura, A. Behavior theory and models of man. *American Psychologist,* 1974, *29,* 859–869.

Bavelas, A. Some problems of organizational change. *Journal of Social Issues,* 1948, *4,* 48–52.

Bernard, C. C. *The functions of the executive.* Cambridge: Harvard University Press, 1938.

Blau, P. M. & Scott, W. R. *Formal organizations.* San Francisco: Chandler Publishing Company, 1962.

Campbell, J., & Dunnette, M. Effectiveness of T Group experiences in managerial training and development. *Psychological Bulletin,* 1968, *79,* 72–104.

Cornell, F. G. Administrative organization as social structure. *Progressive Education,* 1954, *30,* 29–35.

Davis, V. Management communication and the grapevine. *Harvard Business Review,* 1953, *31,* 43–49.

de Charms, R. *Personal causation: The internal effective determinants of behavior.* New York: Academic Press, 1968.

Dubin, R. *The world of work.* Englewood Cliffs, N.J.: Prentice-Hall, 1958.

Etzioni, A. *Complex organizations.* New York: Free Press, 1961.

Etzioni, A. *Modern organizations*. Englewood Cliffs, N.J.: Prentice-Hall, 1964.

Friedlander, F. The impact of organizational training upon the effectiveness and interaction of ongoing work groups. *Personnel Psychology*, 1967, *20*, 289–307.

Gilchrest, J. D., Shaw, M. E., & Walker, L. C. Some effects of unequal distribution of information in a wheel group structure. *Journal of Abnormal and Social Psychology*, 1954, *49*, 554–556.

Gross, B. M. The scientific approach to administration. In D. E. Griffith (Ed.), *63rd National Society for the Study of Education yearbook*. Chicago: University of Chicago Press, 1964.

Heider, J. *The psychology of interpersonal relations*. New York: Wiley, 1958.

Iannacone, L. An approach to the informal organization of the school. In D. E. Griffith (Ed.), *63rd National Society for the Study of Education yearbook*. Chicago: University of Chicago Press, 1962.

Johnson, R. A., Kast, F. E., & Rosenzweig, J. E. *The theory and management of systems*. New York: McGraw-Hill, 1967.

Kelly, G. A. *A theory of personality: The psychology of interpersonal constructs*. New York: Norton, 1963.

Levine, F. M., & Fasnact, G. Token rewards may lead to token learning. *American Psychologist*, 1974, *29*, 816–820.

Mahoney, M. *Cognition and behavior modification*. Cambridge, Mass.: Ballinger, 1974.

Maier, S. F., & Seligmann, M. E. P. Learned helplessness: Theory and evidence. *Journal of Experimental Psychology: General,* 1976, *105*, 3–46.

McGregor, D. M. *The human side of management*. New York: McGraw-Hill, 1960.

Notz, W. W. Work motivation and the negative effects of extrinsic rewards: A review with implications for theory and practice. *American Psychologist*, 1975, *30*, 884–891.

Perrow, C. *Complex organizations*. Glenview, Ill.: Scott, 1972

Roethlisberger, F. J., & Dickson, W. J. *Management and the worker*. Cambridge: Harvard University Press, 1939.

Sarason, S. An asocial psychology and a misdirected clinical psychology. *American Psychologist*, 1981, *36*, 827–835.

Shaw, M. E. Communications networks. In L. Berkowitz (Ed.), *Advances in experimental social psychology* (Vol I). New York: Academic Press, 1964.

Taylor, F. W. *Scientific management*. New York: Harper & Row, 1957.

White, R. Motivation reconsidered: The concept of competence. *Psychological Review*, 1959, *66*, 297–333.

PART III
DIAGNOSIS AND ASSESSMENT OF INDIVIDUALS AND ENVIRONMENTS

Psychological Diagnosis

A long-standing problem of psychological intervention programs oriented toward a mental health or a medical model is the problem of reliability of diagnosis. As we noted in chapter 1, it seems clear that simple, easily recognized, and concretely defined disease entities in the area of psychological functioning tend to be the exception rather than the rule. If this is the case, it is not surprising that we encounter serious problems in establishing adequate levels of reliability for mental health diagnoses.

Spitzer, Endicott, and Robins (1975) identified five sources of low reliability in mental health diagnosis:

1. Subject variance. Patients exhibit different conditions at different times.
2. Occasion variance. Patients are at different stages of the same condition at different times.
3. Information variance. Clinicians have different sources of information about their patients.
4. Observation variance. Clinicians presented with the same stimuli differ in what they notice.
5. Criterion variance. Clinicians differ in the inclusion and exclusion criteria used to summarize patient data into a diagnosis.

Spitzer et al. argue that the largest source of diagnostic unreliability is criterion variance and that improvements in psychiatric diagnosis will result from reducing criterion variance.

Some kind of diagnostic system is important because it is an integral part of classification systems in scientific disciplines. The study of classification systems is usually divided into three areas: (1) taxonomy, or the theoretical study of classification; (2) classification, or the process of forming groups from a large set of units; and (3) identification, or the process of assigning an entity to a category in an existing classification (Blashfield & Draguns, 1976). In psycho-pathology, the term *diagnosis* is used as a synonym for *identification*.

A classification system is the product of the process of classifying entities. Such a system has the following components. First, there are entities (people) being classified. Second, there are categories or classes of people. Third, the categories are organized into a hierar-chical system. An *extensional* definition of a category enumerates all the individuals who comprise it, and an *intensional* definition of a category lists the characteristics which individuals must possess to be members of the category.

Four criteria can be used to evaluate a diagnostic classification system: (1) reliability, (2) coverage, (3) descriptive validity, and (4) predictive validity (Blashfield & Draguns, 1976). Reliability refers to the variability in accuracy from user to user and has generally been equated with agreements among diagnosticians. Coverage refers to the applicability of a classification system to the entire domain of people for which it was intended. Descriptive validity refers to the degree of homogeneity of the categories of behaviors, symptoms, personality characteristics, social history data, and other kinds of information which are used to make a diagnosis. Predictive validity identifies the variables in the diagnostic categories which are related to differential response to treatment. The two primary purposes of diagnostic classification systems are to facilitate communication and to improve prediction. However, these goals can be in conflict. In order to facilitate communication, a system should have a simple structure, making it easy for clinicians to use, while to improve prediction a classification system may need to be highly complex. The criteria for evaluating a diagnostic system in counseling psychology will probably differ somewhat from those preferred in clinical psychology and psychiatry because of the differences in professional orientations and missions. (Schacht and Nathan, 1977). Also, the criteria for evaluating a diagnostic system are not the same as the criteria to be used in evaluating the diagnostic *process* itself. Some years ago, one of the authors (Blocher, 1965) suggested that all counselors diagnose, but that their diagnostic activities contribute most when they are continuous, tentative, and testable. Diagnosis is a continuous process integrated within counseling, which is tentative or subject to revision, and testable in that diagnostic inferences are operationally defined so that they may be confirmed or rejected through prediction. These criteria have to do with the *process* of diagnosis rather than the structure or content of the system. In evaluating a diagnostic system, consideration should also be given to the impact of the system on the quality of the clinician's thinking. A good diagnostic system should improve the quality of the counselor's and the client's thinking and problem solving.

The Importance of Diagnosis

Before we can deal with issues regarding the importance of diagnosis in counseling, we need to recognize that counseling psychologists differ considerably in their definitions of diagnosis and its role in treatment.

Rogers (1946), in discussing the significant aspects of client-centered therapy, argued that diagnostic knowledge and skill were *not* necessary for good therapy. He tells a parable about a prominent allergist who decided to have all medical histories taken by a non-medical person trained in nondirective techniques in order to get a true picture of the client's health, "uncluttered by the bias and diagnostic evaluation" which is almost inevitable when a medical person takes a history and unintentionally distorts the material by his premature judgments. For Rogers, the act of diagnosis appeared to be inherently error-ridden and biased. He believed that the kind of thinking traditionally involved in diagnosis was to be avoided because it involves evaluation and judgment!

Later, Patterson (1948) explained more fully the reasons that nondirective psychotherapy was not dependent on diagnosis. Nondirective therapists assume that all maladjustment is similar in origin and thus knowledge of the content of conflicts is unessential and is not a prerequisite for effective therapy. For Patterson, techniques of therapy do not depend on the nature or content of a conflict but upon the presence of conflict and resulting tensions.

In a large measure, client-centered theorists have argued that the same treatment is indicated for all human concerns. Certain attitudes of the therapist constitute the necessary and sufficient conditions of therapeutic effectiveness. If the same principles of psychotherapy are applied to all clients, then differential diagnosis is not necessary. Trait and factor theorists, particularly Williamson (1939), differed with the client-centered view about diagnosis. Diagnosis was a step in the counseling process and involved the logical thinking of the counselor. The goal of diagnosis was to "tease out" from a mass of data about a client a consistent pattern of meaning and an understanding of the client's assets and liabilities, together with a prognosis or future judgment. The process of diagnosis involved making inferences from data and then synthesizing the results of these inferences to make a prognosis. The client was to participate in the task of understanding himself in so far as he was intellectually able and emotionally willing to do so.

The trait and factor model of diagnosis (Williamson, 1939) involves identifying the problem, discovering the causes, and indicating counseling treatments. The counselor collects facts about a client, reviews them, and tries to identify a recurring theme, consistent meaning, or valid diagnosis. Williamson warned that cautiousness and tentativeness were needed in making a diagnosis. For him, the outcome of a good diagnosis was a structured summary of significant case data, and not a verbal label which is treated as if it had an existence separate from the client. Evaluative labeling was not to be confused with diagnosis.

Williamson never developed a diagnostic category system, for his interest was more in the process of diagnosis. However, a number of counseling psychologists attempted to develop such systems of diagnostic categories.

Bordin (1946) described a system which included the following categories: (1) dependence, (2) lack of information, (3) self-conflict, (4) choice anxiety, and (5) no problem. He also suggested three criteria to determine whether a set of diagnostic categories was valid. First, the constructs should allow the clinician to make comprehensive predictions about an individual by assigning him to a class. Second, the constructs should vary independently. Third, the constructs should form the basis for treatment. Definitions of categories should include a statement as to how the condition can be modified. Pepinsky (1948) evaluated the Bordin system and proposed a more elaborate model. The no problem category was changed to lack of assurance and a new category, lack of skill, was proposed. Byrne (1958), Callis and Clyde (1960), and Robinson (1963) made further revisions in the list of diagnostic constructs. Since the late 1960s there has been very little interest among counseling psychologists in developing systems of diagnostic categories.

The eclectic approach as described by Thorne (1955) was based on the use of a medical model of diagnosis. Treatment without diagnosis was characterized as nothing but guesswork. Diagnosis was to involve the assessment of all clinically and socially significant behaviors and was to employ all suitable operational approaches that would offer valid contributions relating to all levels of behavior organization. Levels of organization specified included the morphological, the biochemical, the physiological, the psychological, and the psychosocial.

The objectives of diagnosis were: (1) to establish the existence of a pathological process, (2) to establish the nature and relationship of etiologic factors, (3) to locate the disorder in the various organizational levels of personality and behavior, (4) to evaluate the severity of the disorder, (5) to determine the prognosis, (6) to provide a rational basis for psychotherapy, (7) to provide a scientific basis for classification and analysis of data, and (8) to diagnose the resources of the environment.

Behavioral Assessment and Diagnosis

As behavioral theories of intervention came into prominence, they produced behaviorally oriented assessment procedures. Behavioral assessment develops a model of client social learning. The aim is to discover functional relationships between behavior and environment by observing relevant behaviors and environmental conditions.

Behavioral assessment leads to a functional analysis in terms of the S-O-/R-K-C model (Kanfer & Saslow, 1965). In the model, *Stimulus* events include physical, social, and internal stimuli. *Organismic* variables include the biological condition of the individual. *Responses* include the following systems: motor, cognitive, and physiological. These may be overt or covert responses. *Contingency* (K) relationships describe the arrangement of behavior and consequences. This relationship has been called the "schedule of reinforcement." *Consequences* are positive or negative events that follow the responses.

Two major principles in behavioral assessment are the principle of direct sampling and the principle of operational definitions. Problematic behaviors are not viewed as signs of an underlying disturbance but rather as the problem itself. The second imperative is to operationalize terms. Vague or general terms are translated into operational definitions.

Behavioral assessment is an integral part of therapy. The process involves: (1) problem definition, (2) measurement and functional analyses, (3) matching treatment to client, (4) assessment of ongoing therapy, and (5) evaluation of therapy (Keefe, Kopel, & Gordon, 1978). Problem identification involves: (1) pinpointing presenting problems, (2) determining response characteristics, (3) obtaining a history of the problem, (4) identifying probable controlling variables, and (5) selecting tentative targets for modification.

The first task is to operationalize presenting problems in behavioral terms. "Feeling depressed" can be defined in several ways. Depression may be described in terms of motor, cognitive, or physiological responses. Responses can be categorized along the dimensions of frequency, intensity, duration, and appropriateness. A history of the problem will include developmental history, current environment, and factors related to drugs, intellectual capacities, and physical limitations. In order to identify controlling variables, it is necessary to gather information about conditions which occur immediately before and after the problematic behaviors. The phase of the initial assessment is to select tentative targets for assessment.

The second stage of behavioral assessment is to collect more refined measures of problem behaviors and situational determinants. A static analysis measures the characteristics of the behavior itself, while a functional analysis includes measures of antecedents, behaviors, and consequences. Data collection includes questionnaires, self-observation, naturalistic observation, and laboratory observation (i.e., role-playing).

In the functional analysis, antecedents are events or situational conditions present immediately prior to the problem behaviors. The antecedents may include chains of behaviors. Consequences are events or situational factors that follow the problem behaviors. For example, what does the individual obtain or avoid when he engages in the problem behaviors?

Cognitive mediational responses can be antecedents or consequences. Causal attributions, labels, and self-perceptions can contribute to the maintenance of problem behaviors. These could include covert self-instructions. The outcomes of the functional analyses are a baseline measure of target behaviors, a conceptualization of the functional relationship, and an indication of targets to modify.

The third state of assessment involves selection of treatment procedures. First, it is necessary to assess client motivation and decide how much therapist control should be included in a treatment. The second step is to assess the client's resources. The third step is to choose the treatment procedure that will be simplest and least disruptive. Also, it is important to choose a procedure that best fits the client's style of perceiving and solving problems. For instance, what kinds of positive reinforcers would be most effective for this particular client?

The next phase of the assessment process involves an information-sharing conference with the client. At this time, the counselor reviews and discusses the description of the problem, as well as its history and functional analysis. During treatment there should also be a systematic assessment of the use of techniques, a monitoring of the effectiveness of treatment, and, if necessary, modifications of treatment.

The final step in behavioral assessment is to evaluate the outcomes. The sequence might involve: (1) collecting baseline data, (2) monitoring treatment procedures, (3) returning the target behaviors to baseline behavior levels, and (4) reinstatement of treatment.

The functional analysis begins with the gathering of data on antecedent and consequent conditions and identifies the relationships of behaviors to environmental events. The behavioral approach to diagnosis in counseling psychology emphasizes the role of the environment in determining human behavior as well as the significance or meaning of behavior to the client (Osipow, Walsh, & Tosi, 1980). A functional analysis describes both the stimulus and reinforcing conditions for problem behaviors. Counseling strategies may involve adding, weakening, or strengthening responses. The functional analysis defines the antecedents, behaviors, and consequences of behavior control. Mediational constructs are used for defining unobservable events.

Diagnosis involves the assessment of target behaviors which are in need of modification. In the selection process, the psychologist chooses from: (1) the relevant antecedent, situational events that may have elicited the maladaptive behavior, (2) the mediational responses and cues which because of the individual's previous learning experiences have become associated with these situational events, (3) the observable maladaptive behavior itself, and (4) the consequent changes in the environmental situation including the reactions of others to the maladaptive behaviors. The decision as to which aspect of this environmental–mediational–behavioral complex is most relevant in any case should be determined by which, if effectively manipulated, is most likely to alter the client's maladaptive behavior (Goldfreid & Pomeranz, 1968).

A second aspect of diagnosis involves selection of appropriate therapeutic techniques. The behaviorally oriented psychologist chooses an approach for a particular client from such techniques as systematic desensitization, assertiveness training, aversive conditioning, role-playing techniques, modeling procedures, and in vivo desensitization. The selection of an approach may be a function of the target behavior or the situational determinant in need of modification. For example, modeling may be particularly effective in cases where, due to inadequate social learning, certain desired behavior patterns are low in the individual's repertoire.

For the behavioral therapist, the most fundamental problem in diagnosis is to identify the specific factors that are functionally related to the problematic behaviors. In the functional analysis, the psychologist gathers data on antecedent and consequent conditions, the relationship of behavior to environmental variables, and the significance or meaning of behavior (Osipow et al., 1980). The purpose of functional analysis is to conceptualize the current controlling or maintaining variables.

Diagnosis: To Do or Not To Do Is *Not* the Question

The issue of whether counseling psychologists should or should not make a diagnosis is an elusive one (Blocher, 1965). There are really two issues. First, what kind of cognitive activities of the clinician are most effective in understanding a client? Second, what diagnostic system or theoretical model is most useful in developing an accurate model of the client? The word *diagnosis* has carried odious connotations regarding authoritarianism, stereotyping, and labeling which are not necessarily part of the process. The meaning of diagnosis is "to know" the client in terms of both internal and external perspectives.

For us, diagnosis is an essential and inevitable part of effective counseling. Some time ago, one of the authors (Blocher, 1965) described diagnosis as a hypotheses-testing operation which is an inevitable part of the counselor's cognitive process. Diagnosis involves the quality of the clinician's cognitive processes. Obviously, there are individual differences in diagnostic skills, and our efforts should be focused on developing an understanding of how these processes take place and how they can be improved.

Clinical and Actuarial Data in Diagnosis

A major issue regarding diagnosis in counseling psychology has to do with the contributions of clinical and actuarial data. Meehl (1954) reviewed a number of studies involving a comparison of clinical and actuarial forms of prediction. In all but one study, predictions based on actuarial methods were either approximately equal or superior to those made by a clinician. Although further research is needed to ascertain those situations in which each method is most efficient, Meehl did conclude, "it is clear that the dogmatic complacent asser-

tion sometimes heard from clinicians that 'naturally' clinical prediction being based on real understanding is superior, is simply not
justified by the facts collected to date." In about half of the studies,
the two methods were equal; in the other half, the clinician was
definitely inferior. No study established clearly that the clinician
was better.

In order to interpret this research, it is necessary to define the
two methods. The actuarial method of prediction involves ordering
the individual to a class or set of classes on the basis of objective facts
concerning his life history, his scores on psychometric tests, ratings,
and checklists, or judgments gained from interviews. Then, after
combining this data, the subject is classified and a statistical table
gives the statistical frequencies of behaviors of various sorts for
persons belonging to that class. The actuarial method of prediction
involves a mechanical combining of information for classification
purposes and a probability figure which is an empirically determined
relative frequency.

The clinical or case study method of prediction relies on interview impressions, case history data, and some psychometric information. Using this data, a psychological hypothesis is formulated regarding the structure and dynamics of an individual. The model and
certain expectations about other events are used to formulate a
prediction.

In 1957 and 1965 Meehl again reviewed the studies comparing
clinical and actuarial methods of prediction. The results had not
changed. However, the interpretation of the findings is not clear-cut
because the comparison of the two types of predictions may not make
clear their unique contributions to the diagnostic process. For instance, do clinical and actuarial predictions have the same purposes?

Sarbin (1944) argued that the clinician was always predicting
actuarially and from classes. For him, the clinician was doing a
second-rate job of actuarial prediction. This position assumes no
logical differences between the clinical and actuarial methods of
prediction. The only difference is that the actuarial method is more
explicit and precise.

In contrast, Meehl (1954) differentiated between clinical and
actuarial prediction. In order to explain his viewpoint, he distinguished between the context of justification and the context of discovery (Meehl, 1954). The former refers simply to the usual scientific
procedures for establishing the empirical validity of predictions. This
validity is established by the same empirical standards that apply to
statistical procedures. The context of discovery is concerned with the
psychological processes that are used to engender predictions about

the nature of the client system. The context of discovery involves the clinical activities of formulating inferences and developing hypotheses about the client system. The context of justification involves the analyses of the verifiability of the knowledge which has been discovered. Meehl (1954) described how these two diagnostic spheres are related to each other:

> Having once conceived of a particular hypothesis concerning a patient, we must, if we are scientific (I should be inclined to say even rational), subject this hypothesis to the usual canons of inference. That is, we must see whether the hypotheses will entail more of the known facts than others, a greater range or diversity of known facts, will enable us to make predictions that will square with general principles arrived at by previous inductions, can be fitted into the nomothetic scheme at the next lower level in the explanatory hierarchy and so on [p. 66].

Clinical prediction involves the invention of structural, dynamic hypotheses. The clinician uses a theory of human behavior to describe structural relationships between various internal and external stimuli and responses. In statistical prediction, the clinician uses data regarding the probabilistic relationships that exist between certain stimuli and responses. The deductions follow from the classification of input data. In clinical prediction, the hypotheses are not a straightforward consequence of the data.

The two types of prediction are both important in clinical judgment. The clinician first develops an approximate model of the client based on a series of clinical predictions. These hypotheses have to do with the status of the client in reference to a theory of human behavior. Inclusion and exclusion rules are used to describe whether specific client behaviors are instances of classes or categories of behaviors in the theory of behavior. The task is to recognize when a unique event is an instance of a general class of behaviors which have lawful relations with criterion behaviors. The clinician invents a hypothesis regarding the state of the hypothetical variables in a client. Some kind of personality theory then is used to generate specific predictions.

The logic of discovery has to do with hypotheses formation. This is a psychological event, not a matter of inference from either propositions or experience (Vance, 1968). The process of clinical prediction is not necessarily a logical activity; it may be intuitive. The psychologist is organizing clinical information for action. The clinician needs imperatives which cannot be inferred from propositions. He or she needs to know "what to do" with the client (Vance, 1968).

Although Meehl's distinction between the context of discovery and the context of justification makes considerable sense, the research still raises questions about clinical judgment. Sawyer (1966) recategorized all published studies comparing clinical and actuarial prediction based on mode of collecting data—that is, judgmental or mechanical—and mode of combining data—that is, clinical or statistical (see Table 7.1). He reported that for each method of measurement, the statistical combination is superior. The best method of prediction involves the statistical combination of both judgmental and mechanical data. Even though clinicians are a valuable source of data, they should not be the sole source of data.

TABLE 7.1
Wiggins' Classification of Prediction Methods

Mode of Data Collection	Mode of Data Combination	
	Clinical	Statistical
Judgmental	Pure clinical	Trait ratings
Mechanical	Profile interpretation	Pure statistical
Both	Clinical composite	Mechanical composite
Either or both	Clinical synthesis	Mechanical synthesis

Wiggins, *Personality and Prediction: Principles of Personality Assessment*, © 1973. Addison-Wesley, Reading, Mass. Page 197. Reprinted with Permission. Also in Sawyer, Measurement and prediction, clinical and statistical. *Psychological Bulletin*, 1966, *66*(3), 178–200.

The Process of Diagnosis

In order to clarify the difference between clinical and actuarial prediction, it is necessary to have a model of the clinical process. Research suggests that a good judge of others uses appropriate norms, has both general and social intelligence, and is motivated and free to make accurate judgments (Wiggins, 1973).

In our model of the diagnostic process, there is a series of hypothesis-testing activities which lead to a model of the client and a series of hypothesis-testing activities regarding future behaviors of the client. The psychologist uses decision rules for developing the model and actuarial data for making the predictions.

The major variables in the diagnostic process are observations, inferences, and hypotheses (Pepinsky & Pepinsky, 1954). An observation denotes the characteristics of an object or event by which it can be recognized. The process of making observations resembles a hypothesis-testing procedure. Three functions of observations are: (1) to serve as a basis for inferences about client behavior, (2) to facilitate the restatement of inferences as meaningful hypotheses, and (3) to afford a means of verifying hypotheses or predictions by checking them against independent observations.

Clinical observations can be either general or specific (Pepinsky & Pepinsky, 1954). General observations regard the social conditions and the culture in which the client lives. The clinician may also make general observations regarding the specific subcultures to which the client belongs. Another source of general observations is the clinician's professional knowledge and experiences.

Specific observations can be made by direct or indirect methods. A direct observation can be made of counselor behaviors, client behaviors, and counselor–client interactions. Indirect methods of observation include social histories, test scores, and anecdotal records.

Inferences are tentative conclusions based upon the data acquired through specific and general observations. Inferences are translated into hypotheses. These need to specify the procedures whereby they are to be tested and the conditions under which they are considered to be verified. Inferences should be based on communicable observations made under described conditions.

In the diagnostic process, hypothetical constructs such as "anxiety" or "risk-taking ability," for example, are used to refer to an event, process, or entity which is not in itself observed. These constructs can be used effectively in making inferences when antecedent conditions and consequences are identified.

Inferences can be used to relate observations and to formulate hypotheses. One type of inferential statement relates antecedent conditions to each other and to present client behavior. Another type of inferential statement relates successive or independent observations to each other. Inferential statements can also be translated into answerable questions about either the client system or the future behavior of the client. The questions must be stated in language that denotes observable events and permits specification of procedures by which needed data can be obtained. Support for hypotheses is always tentative.

To summarize, clinical and actuarial hypotheses have different functions in the diagnostic process. Clinical hypotheses are concerned with describing the state or condition of the client to which observable events are supposed to conform. Actuarial hypotheses are concerned with the frequency of occurrence of certain behaviors.

Actuarial prediction is concerned with determining the likelihood of certain alternative client behaviors at some future time.

In many community settings that tend to be oriented toward the medical model, diagnostic activities center around procedures that may be relatively foreign to the value orientation of counseling psychologists. Because one of the purposes that we have noted for diagnostic systems is to improve communication among helping professionals, the counseling psychologist has little choice but to learn to understand and communicate using the dominant model. This does not mean, however, that the counseling psychologist must accept without question all of the values, assumptions, or logical relationships implied in a psychiatric model.

DSM III

The American Psychiatric Association has published three editions of the *Diagnostic and Statistical Manual of Mental Disorders*. The third edition, which took five years to complete, is designed to be a more reliable system for diagnosing mental disorders (Spitzer, Williams, & Skodol, 1980).

The *Third Diagnostic Manual* (DSM III) includes more specific and operationally defined criteria than were found in the first two manuals. It should be understood that for most of the categories, the criteria are based on clinical judgment and have not yet been fully validated. The authors of the system caution that with further experience and study, the criteria will, in many cases, need to be revised.

The DSM III is more comprehensive than the two earlier manuals. The system covers a wide range of human concerns, including developmental, educational, and vocational. The manual defines a mental disorder as a clinically significant behavioral or psychological syndrome or pattern that occurs in an individual and that is typically associated with a painful symptom (distress) or impairment in one or more important areas of functioning (disability).

The DSM III is a multiaxial system providing information on five dimensions, the last two intended to be helpful in planning treatments and predicting treatment outcomes. The first three axes constitute the official diagnostic assessment. The first axis includes clinical syndromes and conditions not attributable to mental disorders which are the focus of treatment. Disorders listed on Axis Two are personality disorders and specific developmental disorders. In some cases, individuals will have a disorder listed on both axes.

Multiple diagnoses can be made on both axes and they can be made within the same class or category of a disorder. If no personality disorder is noted, Axis Two can be used to indicate specific personality traits.

When an individual receives more than one diagnosis, the principal diagnosis is the condition chiefly responsible for the evaluation or the condition responsible for the client seeking treatment. The system also allows for deferring a diagnosis or making a provisional diagnosis.

The diagnostician indicates any physical disorder or physical condition which is relevant to understanding the case on Axis Three. These conditions may or may not have etiological significance.

Axes Four and Five provide information to supplement the official DSM III diagnosis. On Axis Four, the overall severity of stressors which have been a significant contributor to the development or exacerbation of the disorder is coded. The rating is based on the severity of the stressors in reference to the stress an "average person" in similar circumstances and with similar sociocultural values would experience from the particular stressors. The evaluation involves the following factors: the amount of change in a person's life caused by the stressor, the degree to which the event is desired and under the person's control, and the number of stressors. A stressor may either be a specific event which occurred in the past year or involve the anticipation of a future event. The seven-point scale is a rating of the summed effect of all stressors.

Axis Five is a means of describing the individual's highest level of adaptive functioning for at least a few months during the past year. Adaptive functioning is a composite rating of three areas: social relations, occupational functioning, and use of leisure time. The evaluation of leisure time affects the overall rating only when there is no significant impairment in social relations and occupational functioning, or when occupational opportunities are limited or absent (retired or handicapped persons). Adaptive functioning is rated on a seven-point scale ranging from superior to grossly impaired.

Another important feature of the DSM III is the inclusion of diagnostic criteria which appear at the end of the text describing each specific diagnosis. These operational definitions should promote better diagnostic agreement among clinicians. For instance, the criteria for diagnosis of a simple phobia include all of the following:

1. Avoidance of the irrationally feared object or situation. If there is any element of danger in these objects or situations, it is reacted to in a fashion out of proportion to reality.

2. The avoidance has a significant effect on the patient's life adjustment.
3. The patient has complete insight into the irrational nature of his fear.
4. The phobic symptoms do not coincide with an episode of depressive disorder, obsessive compulsive disorder, or schizophrenia, nor are they limited to a period of two months prior to or two months after such an episode.

The DSM III diagnostic criteria are to be employed even when the clinician does not have sufficient information to satisfy all the criteria for a diagnosis. In these cases the diagnosis is to be made on the basis of criteria perceived as clinically probable.

In a reliability study (Spitzer, Forman, & Nee, 1979), the Kappa statistic was used to index chance-corrected inter-rater agreement. These kinds of reliability studies involved joint and separate use of DSM III by two clinicians. Based on joint interviews, the Kappa statistic for all major classes on Axis One was .78, and the Kappa statistic for all major classes on Axis Two was .61. When the diagnoses were made separately, the Kappa statistic was .66 for Axis One and .54 for Axis Two. The Kappa coefficient for Axis Four was .62 for joint interviews and .58 for separate interviews (Spitzer & Forman, 1979). The Kappa coefficients for Axis Five were .80 for joint interviews and .69 for separate interviews. Although the reliability coefficients for DSM III are an improvement over those for DSM I and DSM II, there is still a high percentage of disagreement between diagnosticians, suggesting important issues regarding the validity of DSM III diagnoses for individuals.

Major Classes of Disorders

The DSM III includes seventeen major classes of disorders. Each class will be described briefly.

1. *Disorders usually present in infancy, childhood, or adolescence.* Adults will occasionally be given a diagnosis from this class. The diagnoses are divided into five major groups based on the dominant area of disturbance. The groups are: intellectual, behavioral, emotional, physical, and developmental. One category in the intellectual group is mental retardation. The behavioral group has two categories: attention deficit disorders and conduct disorders. The emotional disorders include a large number of diagnoses related to anxiety and identity problems. The physical disorders include eating

disorders, stereotyped movement disorders, stuttering, enuresis, and sleep disturbances. The fifth group of disorders includes pervasive developmental disorders such as the childhood type of schizophrenia and specific developmental disorders in reading, language, arithmetic, and articulation. The specific developmental disorders are coded on Axis Two.

2. *Organic mental disorders.* Eight organic syndromes are delerium, dementia, amnestic syndrome, organic delusional syndrome, hallucinosis, organic personality syndrome, intoxication, and withdrawal. Dementias which are due to certain neurological diseases and which characteristically appear in the senium as well as substance-induced organic brain syndromes are grouped together, and diagnoses are made on Axis One. Organic mental disorders in which the etiology or pathophysiological process is infection, tumor, metabolic disturbances, or those in which the process is unknown are diagnosed on Axis One and Axis Three. The specific organic brain syndrome is noted on Axis One and the specific physical disorders are noted on Axis Three.

3. *Substance-use disorders.* These disorders involve behavioral changes associated with the use of substances that affect the central nervous system. These disorders include abuse and dependence. Abuse is defined by a pattern of pathological use for at least one month that causes impairment in social or occupational functioning. Dependence is defined by the presence of tolerance or withdrawal. For alcohol and cannabis dependence, impairment in social or occupational functioning is also required to constitute abuse. Course of the illness is noted as continuous, episodic, in remission, or unspecified.

4. *Schizophrenic disorders.* A diagnosis of schizophrenia requires: (1) a period of active psychotic symptoms such as delusions, hallucinations, or certain characteristic thought disturbances and (2) a six-month duration of the disturbance or impairment including prodromal, active, and residual phases. Subtypes are as follows: disorganized, catatonic, paranoid, undifferentiated, and residual. The course of the illness can be chronic, subchronic with acute exacerbation, chronic with acute exacerbation, or in remission.

5. *Paranoid disorders.* The predominant symptoms are persistent, persecutory delusions or delusional jealousy not accounted for by another psychotic disorder. By definition, a paranoid disorder requires duration of at least six months. Three kinds of paranoid disorders are paranoia, shared paranoid disorder, and acute paranoid disorder.

6. *Psychotic disorders not elsewhere classified.* These disorders

include schizophreniform disorders and atypical psychosis. The essential clinical features of a schizophreniform disorder are the same as those of schizophrenia except the duration is less than six months, but more than two weeks. The schizoaffective disorder is the only specific diagnosis that does not have diagnostic criteria. With the atypical psychosis, there are psychotic symptoms—such as delusions, hallucinations, incoherence, loosening of associations, marked poverty of thought content, markedly illogical thinking, or behavior that is grossly disorganized or catatonic—that do not meet the criteria for any specific mental disorder.

7. *Affective disorders*. Three subclasses are major affective disorders, other specific affective disorders, and atypical affective disorders. The major affective disorders include manic episode, major depressive episode, bipolar disorders, and major depression. Other specific affective disorders are a cyclothymic disorder and a dysthymic disorder. A cyclothymic disorder involves periods during the last two years when symptoms characteristic of both the depressive and manic syndromes were present but were not of sufficient severity or duration to meet the criteria for a major depressive or manic episode. With a dysthymic disorder or depressive neurosis, symptoms characteristic of the depressive syndrome are present but are not of sufficient severity or duration to meet the criteria for a major depressive episode.

Bipolar disorders involve a manic episode (a period of predominantly elevated, expansive, or irritable mood) which lasts at least one week and a depressive episode (a period of loss of interest or pleasure in all or almost all usual activities and pastimes). The category of major depression is used only when there has never been a manic episode.

8. *Anxiety disorders*. This category includes all disorders in which anxiety is experienced directly. The phobic disorders are agoraphobia (a fear of being alone in public places from which escape might be difficult or help not available in the case of sudden incapacitation), social phobia (a fear of situations in which the individual is exposed to possible scrutiny by others and fears acting in a way that may be embarrassing or humiliating), and simple phobia (phobic objects are often animals or situations such as heights or closed spaces).

Anxiety states include panic disorders (a discrete period of apprehension or fear without symptoms such as choking, dizziness, or sweating), generalized anxiety disorders (symptoms include motor tension, autonomic hyperactivity, apprehensive expectations, and hyperattentiveness), and obsessive-compulsive disorders (obsessions include recurrent, senseless ideas, thoughts, or impulses which are not experienced as voluntarily produced). Compulsions are repetitive and seemingly purposeful behaviors that are performed according to certain rules or performed in a stereotyped fashion. The behavior is designed to produce or prevent a future event.

Post-traumatic stress disorders involve the presence of a recognizable stressor that would evoke significant symptoms of distress in almost anyone.

A residual category is labeled atypical anxiety disorder.

9. *Somatoform disorders.* These disorders include a history of physical symptoms of several years' duration beginning before the age of thirty for which no demonstrable organic findings or known physiological mechanisms account for the disturbance. Somatization disorders involve recurrent and multiple somatic complaints of several years' duration beginning before the age of thirty. There is preoccupation with symptoms.

Conversion disorders involve a loss of or alteration in physical functioning suggesting a physical disorder. There may be a temporal relationship between an environmental stimulus that is related to a conflict or need and the exacerbation of the symptoms. The symptom may allow an individual to avoid an activity or it may allow the person to get attention and support.

Psychogenic pain disorders involve pain that is inconsistent with anatomic distribution of the nervous system and excessive complaints about pain when there is some related organic pathology.

Hypochondriasis involves an unrealistic interpretation of physical signs or sensations as abnormal leading to preoccupation with the fear or belief of having a serious illness.

A residual category is labeled "atypical somatoform disorder." An example would be a client who is preoccupied with imagined defects in physical appearance that is out of proportion to an actual physical abnormality.

10. *Dissociative disorders.* These disorders feature a sudden, temporary alteration and loss in functioning or consciousness, identity, or motor behavior. Psychogenic amnesia is a sudden inability to recall important personal information that is too extensive to be described as forgetfulness. Psychogenic fugue involves sudden unexpected travel away from home or place of work with an inability to recall the past. Multiple personalities involve two or more distinct personalities, each of which is complex and integrated with its own unique behavior patterns and social relationships. Depersonalization disorder involves a loss of a sense of reality. The residual category is labeled atypical dissociative disorders and includes trancelike states and disassociated states that may occur in people who have been subjected to periods of prolonged, intense, coercive persuasion (brain washing, thought reform, and indoctrination).

11. *Psychosexual disorders.* Gender identity disorders include transsexualism, childhood gender identity disorder, and atypical gender identity disorder. These disorders usually involve a sense of discomfort and inappropriateness about one's anatomic sex.

Paraphilias include fetishism, transvestism, zoophilia, pedophilia, exhibitionism, voyeurism, sexual masochism, sexual sadism, and atypical paraphilia. In paraphilias, the deviation is in that to which the individual is attracted. These include nonhuman objects, humans who are suffering or who are humiliated, or nonconsenting or inappropriate adults.

Psychosexual dysfunctions are inhibited sexual desire, inhibited sexual excitement, inhibited female orgasm, inhibited male orgasm, premature ejaculation, functional dysparluma (pain), functional vaginismus (involuntary spasm), and atypical psychosexual dysfunction. The essential feature of the psychosexual dysfunctions is inhibition in the appetitive, psychophysiological changes that characterize the complex sexual response cycle.

12. *Factitious disorders.* These disorders involve individuals who can simulate physical or psychological symptoms in order to assume the patient role. The actions of these individuals are compulsive and voluntary. Their goal is usually not understandable in light of the environmental circumstances. Factitious disorders can involve either physical or psychological symptoms.

13. *Disorders of impulse control not elsewhere classified.* These disorders involve: (1) a failure to resist an impulse to perform an act which is harmful to the individual or others and (2) an increasing tension before committing the act and an experience of pleasure or release at the time of committing the act. Examples are pathological gambling, kleptomania, pyromania, intermittent explosive disorder, isolated explosive disorder, and atypical impulse control disorder.

14. *Adjustment disorders.* These disorders are characterized by a maladaptive reaction to an identifiable psychosocial stressor that occurs within three months of the onset of the stressor. The maladaptive nature of the reaction is indicated by either of the following: (1) impairment in social or occupational functioning or (2) symptoms that are in excess of a normal and expectable reaction to the stressor. The adjustment disorders can involve a depressed mood, an anxious mood, mixed emotional features (i.e., a combination of depression and anxiety), a disturbance of conduct, mixed disturbance of emotions and conduct, work or academic inhibition, or withdrawal.

15. *Psychological factors affecting physical conditions.* Environmental stimuli are temporally related to the initiation or exacerbation of a physical condition. The physical condition has organic pathology or a known pathophysiological process. The physical condition is recorded on Axis Three.

16. *Personality disorders coded on Axis Two.* These involve an enduring pattern of relating to, perceiving, and thinking about the environment and oneself that has become inflexible and maladaptive, causing significant impairment in social or occupational functioning or subjective distress. Types of these disorders are:

1. Paranoid. There may be pervasive, unwarranted suspiciousness, hypersensitivity, and restricted affectivity.
2. Schizoid. There may be emotional coldness, indifference to praise or criticism, few close friendships, and no eccentricities of speech, behavior, or thought.
3. Schizotypal. There may be magical thinking, ideas of reference, social isolation, recurrent illusions, odd speech, inadequate rapport, undue social anxiety, and suspiciousness.
4. Histrionic. There may be overly dramatic behavior which could include irrational, angry outbursts, incessant drawing of attention to oneself, and a craving for activity.
5. Narcissistic. There may be a grandiose sense of self-importance, exhibitionism, and a preoccupation with fantasies of unlimited success, power, or brilliance.
6. Antisocial personality disorder. The current age is at least eighteen years and the onset was before fifteen. Before the age of fifteen there could be history of delinquency, persistent lying, vandalism, or thefts. Since age eighteen years, there might be some of the following behaviors; inability to sustain consistent work behavior, lack of ability to function as a responsible parent, failure to accept social norms regarding lawful behavior, and failure to honor financial obligations.
7. Borderline. The symptoms may include impulsivity, unstable interpersonal relations, inappropriate anger, intolerance of being alone, and identity disturbance.
8. Avoidance. The symptoms may include hypersensitivity to rejection, desire for affection, low self-esteem, and social withdrawal.
9. Dependent. Symptoms may include allowing others to assume responsibility for major areas of one's life, lack of self-confidence, and tolerance of abuse.

10. Compulsive. Symptoms may include an inability to express warm and tender emotions, perfectionism, excessive devotion to work, and indecisiveness.
11. Passive aggressive. Symptoms may include resistance to demands for adequate performance. There may be procrastination, dawdling, and stubbornness.
12. Atypical, mixed, or other. "Atypical" should be used when the clinician judges that a personality disorder is present but there is insufficient information for a specific diagnosis. "Mixed" is used when an individual has symptoms from several disorders. "Other" is used when the disorder is not included within the DSM III.

17. In some cases, clients may not have a mental disorder or the scope of the diagnostic evaluation has not been adequate to determine the presence or absence of a disorder. Yet the reason for contact must be noted. In other cases, the client may have a mental disorder but the focus of treatment is on a condition not due to the mental disorder. In all these instances, V codes are used and noted on Axis One. The conditions include Malingering, Borderline Intellectual Functioning, Adult Antisocial Behavior, Childhood or Adolescent Antisocial Behavior, Academic Problems, Occupational Problems, Uncomplicated Bereavement, Noncompliance with Medical Treatment, Phase of Life Problem, Marital Problem, Parent–Child Problem, Other Specified Family Circumstances, and Other Interpersonal Problems.

Additional codes include Unspecified Mental Disorders which are not psychotic, an indication of no diagnosis on Axis One or Axis Two, and a deferred diagnosis on Axis One or Axis Two.

Conclusion

The diagnostic process involves both the context of discovery and the context of justification, and, for us, it is not clear how the DSM III is related to these two different prediction problems. Since the authors claim that the DSM III will reduce criterion variance, you might surmise that the DSM III is primarily concerned with clinical prediction and the context of discovery. However, this issue needs to be clarified.

We also assume that effective diagnosticians differentiate between observations and inferences. However, with the DSM III, the authors seem to use observations and inferences interchangeably and do not seemingly treat them as different. The DSM III calls for observations and at other times for inferences, specifying the basis for them. Finally, the structure of the DSM III does not lend itself to a dynamic, hypothesis-testing model of diagnosis. The descriptive data and diagnostic criteria could be differentiated depending on their relative importance in testing and evaluating diagnostic hypotheses.

Psychologists in community mental health settings will need to understand the DSM III system in order to communicate effectively with their colleagues in health-related fields. Still, the continued development of the DSM III raises several issues regarding the implicit assumptions about diagnosis in this particular medically based system.

First, the DSM III is predicated on the assumption that effective diagnosis is a necessary first step in effective treatment. Diagnosis is viewed as a description of the characteristics of the client which should be the basis for a choice of treatment. This definition of diagnosis only indirectly refers to the social context and does not deal with the generation of causal attributions through diagnosis. When diagnosis is viewed as a descriptive process, clinicians tend to overinterpret descriptive statements as causal attributions. Traits are categories for the systematic *description* of human behavior. However, they are often inappropriately used to make causal inferences. Personality, interest, and aptitude traits are best used to *describe* individual differences.

A second assumption underlying the DSM III regards the importance attached to clinical observations and medical tests as the sources of data for making a diagnosis. DSM III makes no mention of standardized psychological tests or statistical procedures for combining clinical and actuarial data.

Third, the DSM III system deals only with the content of a diagnostic system without consideration of how the system is used in the diagnostic process. A diagnostic system such as the DSM III needs to be related to a model of the diagnostic process and to the characteristics of the diagnostician. For instance, counseling psychologists at different levels of cognitive complexity, with different models of the diagnostic process, probably make different diagnostic decisions regarding similar clients. If the diagnostic process resembles hypothesis testing, then a diagnostic system needs to consider how clinical observations, inferences, and different types of hypotheses are systematically related. It is also not clear whether the DSM III is primarily to be used in the process of discovering the client's characteristics and developing a model of the client, or if it is to be used for the process of validating hypotheses based on a hypothetical model of the client.

At this point the counseling psychologist may well view DSM III as a descriptive system useful primarily in communicating with other clinicians in a medically oriented treatment setting. Using the system as a primary guide for making causal inferences and treatment decisions about clients should be undertaken with great caution and awareness of both the scientific and the philosophical issues involved.

References

Blashfield, R. K., & Draguns, J. G. Evaluative criteria for psychiatric classification. *Journal of Abnormal Psychology,* 1976, *85,* 140–150.

Blocher, D. Issues in counseling: Elusive and illusional. *The Personnel and Guidance Journal,* 1965, *63,* 796–800.

Bordin, E. S. Diagnosis in counseling and psychotherapy. *Educational and Psychological Measurement,* 1946, *6* (1), 71–172.

Byrne, R. H. Proposed revision of the Bordin-Pepinsky diagnostic constructs. *Journal of Counseling Psychology,* 1958, *5,* 184–187.

Callis, R., & Clyde, R. J. A two-dimensional diagnostic classification plan. Paper presented at the Tenth Annual Conference of College and University Counseling Administrators. Air Force Academy, October 31, 1960.

Diagnostic and statistical manual of mental disorders (3rd ed.). American Psychiatric Association, 1980.

Goldfried, M. R., & Pomeranz, D. M. Role of assessment in behavior modification. *Psychological Reports,* 1968, *23,* 75–87.

Kanfer, F. H., & Saslow, G. Behavioral analysis. *Archives of General Psychiatry,* 1965, *12,* 529–538.

Keefe, F. J., Kopel, S. A., & Gordon, S. B. *A practical guide to behavioral assessment.* New York: Springer Publishing Co., 1978.

Meehl, P. E. *Clinical versus statistical prediction: A theoretical analysis of the evidence.* Minneapolis: University of Minnesota Press, 1954.

Meehl, P. E. When shall we use our heads instead of the formula? *Journal of Counseling Psychology,* 1957, *4,* 268–273.

Meehl, P. E. Seer over sign: The first good example. *Journal of Experimental Research in Personality,* 1965, *1,* 27–32.

Osipow, S., Walsh, W., & Tosi, D. *A survey of counseling methods.* Homewood, Ill.: The Dorsey Press, 1980.

Patterson, C. H. Is psychotherapy dependent upon diagnosis? *The American Psychologist,* 1948, *3,* 155–159.

Pepinsky, H. B., The selection and use of diagnostic categories. *Applied Psychology Monograph,* 1948, No. 15.

Pepinsky, H. B. & Pepinsky, P. N. *Counseling theory and practice.* New York: The Ronald Press, 1954.

Robinson, F. P. Modern approaches to counseling diagnosis. *Journal of Counseling Psychology,* 1963, *10,* 325–333.

Rogers, C. R. Significant aspects of client-centered therapy. *The American Psychologist,* 1946, *1,* 415–422.

Sarbin, T. R. The logic of prediction in psychology. *Psychological Review,* 1944, *51,* 210–228.

Sawyer, J. Measurement and prediction, clinical and statistical. *Psychological Bulletin,* 1966, *66* (3), 178–200.

Schacht, T., & Nathan, P. E. But is it good for the psychologist? Appraisal and status of DSM-III. *The American Psychologist,* 1977, *32,* 1017–1025.

Spitzer, R. L., & Forman, J. B. DSM III field trials: II. Initial experience with the multiaxial system. *American Journal of Psychiatry,* 1979, *136,* 818–820.

Spitzer, R. L., Forman, J., & Nee, J. DSM III field trials: I. Initial interrater diagnostic reliability. *American Journal of Psychiatry,* 1979, *136,* 815–817.

Spitzer, R., Endicott, J., & Robins, E. Clinical criteria for psychiatric diagnosis and DSM III. *American Journal of Psychiatry,* 1975, *132,* 1187–1199.

Spitzer, R. W., Williams, J. B., & Skodol, A. E. DSM III: The major achievements and an overview. *The American Journal of Psychiatry,* 1980, *137,* 151–163.

Thorne, F. D. Principles of psychological examining: A systematic textbook of applied integrative psychology. *Journal of Clinical Psychology,* 1955, 494.

Vance, F. L. The psychological interview as a discovery machine. In C. L. Parker (Ed.), *Counseling theories and counseling education.* Boston: Houghton Mifflin, 1968.

Wiggins, J. S. *Personality and prediction: Principles of personality assessment.* Reading, Mass.: Addison-Wesley, 1973.

Williamson, E. G. *How to counsel students: A manual of techniques for clinical counselors.* New York: McGraw-Hill, 1939.

8

Assessment and the Use of Tests

James Cattell is given credit for inventing the term *mental test*. The original "tests" were psychophysical measures which he used (unsuccessfully) to predict the academic success of Columbia University freshmen. Since that time (1890) tests have been at the center of numerous professional and public controversies in the United States (Cronbach, 1975). At different times in the last eighty years, tests have been alternately praised and damned for either contributing to or alleviating social ills or progress. For the most part, these discussions of the values of testing have shed more heat than light.

To begin with, there is considerable confusion in the public mind about the nature of tests. To be sure, tests *are not* "windows into the mind," but that fact does not preclude the possibility of their being useful in the assessment of human situations and development of plans for helping.

Tests are devices for systematically observing behaviors. The observations can then be used to make various kinds of inferences. Observations based on tests are only one source of clinical inferences. An important term that must be contrasted with testing is *psychological measurement,* which is the process of determining individual variations along the dimensions of a trait or attribute. Measurement involves the rules used to assign numbers to objects in order to represent quantities of given traits or attributes. In a sense, concepts of measurement represent a refinement and systematization of the fundamental process of observation. Pepinsky and Pepinsky (1954) defined scores on tests and inventories as *indirect* observations and warned that the counselor's task may be to sort through the "inferential camouflage" or diagnostic labels and descriptions associated with some tests.

Tests may be used to sample certain important criterion behaviors. In this case, the behaviors on the tests are considered to be representative of the class of criterion or ultimately crucial behaviors. Tests also can be used as signs. Test behaviors should be significantly related to criterion behaviors. However, the test behavior and the criterion behaviors may not necessarily resemble each other in obvious ways. In the latter case, test behaviors may have empirical relationships to criterion behaviors, rather than face relationships. Items on the test are not always assumed to be directly representative of the behaviors of ultimate interest.

Interpreting Tests

The four traditional purposes for giving tests are: (1) prediction, (2) selection, (3) classification, and (4) evaluation (Cronbach, 1970). The assumption seems to be that the clinical use of test information is subsumed under one or more of these purposes. We will argue that when counselors use test information with clients, their primary purpose is to facilitate the quality of mutual counselor–client thinking and problem solving. Test interpretations thus need to be an integral part of the counseling process. We assume that counseling, like most complex human behaviors, is rule governed, and that counselors therefore need to have conscious rules or principles for using test information effectively. Specifically, they need rules for dealing with the following issues in test interpretation: (1) providing the client with an effective orientation to the use of tests; (2) inducing a high level of conscious client control and involvement regarding the use of test information; and (3) teaching clients to use test information to improve the ways in which they think about their problems and situations (Biggs & Keller, 1982).

The first issue in test interpretation concerns the client's cognitive framework for the use of tests. An orientation process is needed to provide the client with a conceptual framework in personal terms for the use of tests. For instance, a client has indicated a need for help in making a vocational decision. After some preliminary discussion, the counselor might make the following statement. "You have told me that you would like some help in making a career decision and you have indicated that you are not quite sure how your quantitative skills compare to individuals in various technical training programs. You have also indicated that you are not quite sure if you have interests which are similar to those of people in the technical field or to individuals in scientific fields. I would suggest a test might be used to help you make some comparisons of your skills to those of several groups of people in different kinds of technical training course programs. A test may also be used to compare your likes and dislikes to the distinctive likes and dislikes of people in several families of occupations. You will be able to use this information along with other information we have discussed in your decision making." This framework should be plausible to the client and its acceptance should naturally lead to the taking and interpretation of tests. It is most important that the framework is credible in light of the client's presenting problem.

The second issue in test interpretation concerns the need to promote high levels of client involvement in the process. An important reason to promote client involvement is to ensure client willingness to deal with the test results. The likelihood of test information being discredited by a client is probably inversely proportional to the level of client involvement in the counseling process. So in order to reduce the possibility of client rejection, the counselor must reinforce client involvement and ownership for the decision to use and interpret tests.

Counselors' rules regarding promoting client involvement in the test interpretation process should be compatible with recent research on client self-control in the counseling process. For example, the decision to use tests should be viewed as promoting those cognitive processes in clients that are needed to develop controlling actions that alter the factors influencing their behavior. The counselor might say, "Our purpose in using this test is to give you additional information about yourself that you may find helpful in solving your problem. What does this new information mean to you and what might it suggest as to where you need to go from here?" Clients should perceive test information as a means of promoting, not abdicating, self-control. Tests are described as samples of behaviors about which clients can make specific observations to use in developing inferences and hypotheses which they will be responsible for evaluating.

The third issue in test interpretation concerns the use of test information to improve the quality of client thinking. This is the most important criterion for evaluating the effectiveness of test interpretations. Other criteria used in studies of the effectiveness of different modes of test interpretation have included: (1) increased congruence between self-estimates of characteristics and test scores, (2) accurate memory of test results over different periods of time, and (3) realism of vocational choice. Still, all these criteria have obvious limitations including inadequate methods of measuring criterion behavior and the lack of meaningful theories which can relate various methods of test interpretation to different counseling outcomes. We encourage counselors to acquaint themselves with different models for communicating test information. The problem with all of these models, however, is that they, to one degree or another, put too much emphasis on describing the counselor's activities in communicating test information. There are no models for describing how clients interpret and use tests to improve their thinking. Although the counselor plays a significant role in this communication process, it is always the client who interprets the test information and the real problem is to help clients use test information to improve *their* thinking. Test interpretation provides an excellent opportunity to teach clients to think rationally about their own problems. However, counselors need some specific rules for using tests to improve client thinking.

Such rules should consider how tests, as observations of behavior, can be used as a basis for developing and evaluating inferences and hypotheses. For instance, clients can learn how to apply the scientific method to evaluate their present models of human functioning and for making inferences and hypotheses about themselves and their future courses of action.

Many naive models of normality or healthy personality which clients hold do not allow them to integrate aspects of themselves that are not mature or healthy signs of psychological adjustment. Clients may have inadequate cognitive decision rules for classifying and making inferences about whether their behaviors are normal or abnormal, healthy or unhealthy. Issues dealt with during the discussion of test results can include the use of dysfunctional attitudes, irrational beliefs, and maladaptive thoughts in self-evaluation. Test information presents an opportunity to observe client self-evaluation processes and to correct such problems as irrational self-censure or inappropriate generalizations. Interests, personality, and aptitude can all be operationally defined in terms of client behaviors. Hypothetical constructs can be questioned in terms of their applicability to the client and the client's present life situation.

Normative Interpretations

The interpretation of test information often involves the use of social comparison data to help clients examine and hopefully to improve their methods of making self-evaluations. Test information is used to generate inferences about a client's characteristics in relationship to relevant groups and to make predictions about future client perform-ances. First, test information can be used to generate normative or status inferences about a client. In this instance, test behaviors of a client are compared to test behaviors of various norm groups. Com-monly, percentiles are used to make such comparisons. However, one problem with these scores is that they tend to exaggerate score differences in the middle of distributions and to minimize differences at the extremes of distributions. Descriptive information may also be used to generate causal inferences regarding client situations. For example, a client might use test information to infer that a low interest score indicates low motivation and that this fact may be influencing the client's level of achievement in a given course or activity.

Test information can also be used to generate inferences about client satisfaction. In this case a comparison is made between a client's test behavior and the "distinctive" test behaviors of indi-viduals in different educational and/or occupational groups. Test scores of a client are thus used to examine and differentiate among educational and occupational alternatives. These interpretations may help a client identify alternatives with which he or she may be most satisfied and in which he or she will most satisfactorily meet role expectations.

Test information can also be used in combination with other data to generate inferences about future client behavior. These actuarial test interpretations use statistical means such as regression equa-tions or expectancy tables to predict future client status in defined social situations.

Reliability

Two criteria used in evaluating test information are reliability and validity. Reliability concerns the consistency or precision of any measure. To the degree to which errors of measurement are associ-ated with the test scores, unreliability is present. A major problem in assessing consistency is that test scores may be reliable for one population and not reliable for another population. Reliability is specific to a particular group or population.

Theories of reliability define observed scores as having a "true" component and an error component. Although there are different definitions of "true score," all assume that a "true score" exists for a specific set of conditions. Moreover, a true score for an attribute on one test is assumed to be equal to the true score for that attribute on a parallel test (Wiggins, 1973). The traditional definition of reliability rests on the concept of the correlations among parallel tests. Generally, there has been little restriction on the types of measurement procedures that have been called parallel. For example, when different parts of data obtained on a single occasion are considered parallel, a coefficient of internal consistency may be computed. When parallel forms of a test are used, the correlation between forms is known as a coefficient of equivalence. When the same form is administered on two occasions, the correlation between obtained scores is known as a coefficient of stability. Obviously, these different methods of computing reliability account for different sources of error and this fact should be taken into account when interpreting tests.

Since the counseling psychologist often uses test information with individual clients, he or she needs to assess the accuracy of individual observed scores. The standard error of measurement provides an estimate of the size of the error factor in the observed scores of an individual. The standard deviation of observed scores is called the standard error of measurement. An error of measurement is a difference between a person's "universe score" and his score on any one observation.

Another view of reliability is based on the concept of generalizability, that is, generalizing from the test observations to some other class of observations. Wiggins (1973) cautioned that since a given measure can be generalized to many different "universes," the investigator must be able to specify the particular universe in which he is interested before he can study "reliability." To determine the generalizability of a personality inventory, we should obtain a random sample of persons who would presumably be representative of the populations to whom we would like to generalize—for instance, society at large. To determine the reliability of a psychiatric screening device, on the other hand, we would obtain a random sample of, for example, psychiatric patients. Assessing reliability of such a device on college sophomores would violate the principle (Wiggins, 1973). In estimating reliability under a specific set of conditions (test items, test forms, stimuli, observed occasions, or situations of observation), we are interested in the extent to which we can generalize from one set of conditions to the universe of which the conditions are a sample. The extent to which one can generalize from one sample of raters to the other also falls within the theory of generalizability.

For a given sample of persons and given set of conditions, we obtain only an observed score for a given person in a given condition. For each person, a universe score can be conceptualized as the mean of observed scores over all possible conditions. A generalizability study would assess a measuring technique in terms of the relationship between the observed scores and the universe scores to which they are to be generalized. A subsequent decision study would provide the basic data from which decisions about individuals or groups could be made.

Validity

The concept of validity is somewhat controversial (Ebel, 1961) and confusing because concepts about validity are used loosely. Validity is concerned with the usefulness of test information for specific purposes. The counseling psychologist uses test data to make different kinds of inferences about clients. Thus, the validity data for an instrument is important because it deals with the issue of what can be appropriately inferred from a test score. Validity itself is inferred and the psychologist must always make a judgment about its adequacy.

Validity has to do with inferences about what is being measured by a test and about the usefulness of the measure as a predictor of other variables. The inferences made from test scores require various kinds of evidence and not merely different aspects of validity (Messick, 1980). We wish to second Messick's (1980) point about the importance of validity: "Validity is the overall degree of justification for test interpretation and use" (p. 1014). He goes on, "Although it may prove helpful conceptually to discuss the interdependent features of the generic concept (validity) in terms of different aspects or facets, it is simplistic to think of different types or kinds of validity" (p. 1014). We will be describing a number of terms used in connection with validity. However, they should be considered different aspects of the general concept of validity and not different *types* of validity. Three aspects of validity are: (1) content validity, (2) criterion-related validity, and (3) construct validity (Betz & Weiss, 1975).

Content validity refers to how adequately a particular sample of test behaviors used to measure a trait or characteristic reflects performance or standing on the whole domain of behaviors that constitute the trait. In establishing content validity, items should be chosen from a well-defined behavioral domain. Content validity is often indirectly evaluated by assessing the degree to which the test shows high internal consistency, reliability, or homogeneity.

Criterion-related validity usually refers to the extent to which a measure of a trait demonstrates an association with some external measure of the same trait. The external measure is usually called the *criterion* and represents the class of behaviors of interest. We use test scores to predict or compare status or performance on the criterion. *Predictive* validity concerns measurment of the criterion some time after scores are obtained on the predictor measures. *Concurrent* validity is the term used when the predictor and criterion scores are obtained at the same time. Criterion-related validity concerns the direction and extent of the observed relationship between a measure of a trait and other measures or variables which may or may not reflect the same trait. Data on mean differences between groups and correlation data are used to establish criterion-related validity. These resulting data must be interpreted in terms of a hypothesis derived from the "nomological net" or expected relationships among measures of the trait being studied. In other words, the measures must be related to our assumptions about how the trait relates to actual performance on the criterion.

The basic source of information regarding the *construct* validity of a psychological test derives from empirical evidence concurring its relationships with *other* variables. Construct validation is a process of studying the empirical network of relationships of the test scores with other variables, and of verifying, modifying, or proposing a theoretical system of constructs and hypotheses that allow for logical interpretations of empirical results. If empirical data support the theoretical predictions regarding the trait, there is evidence for both the theory of the construct and the hypothesis that the test measures the construct.

Two key concepts in establishing construct validity are convergent and discriminant validity. Convergent validity indicates evidence that scores on a particular instrument correlate appropriately with independent measures of the same trait. Discriminant validity, on the other hand, provides evidence for a lack of relationships with irrelevant or contaminating factors or variables.

Messick (1980) has presented a convincing argument that construct validity is the overall unifying concept of validity, integrating criterion and content considerations into a framework for testing theoretical hypotheses. Meaningfulness or interpretability of test scores is seen as the goal of the construct validation process. The basic evidence for test interpretation and test use is derived from construct validation studies.

In the rest of this chapter, we will discuss various kinds of psychological tests. In some instances, we will provide fairly detailed information about specific tests. Our reason for providing this information is that a counseling psychologist in a community agency works with a wide variety of professionals in different settings who may use tests. In a community mental health agency, the psychologist is often called upon to interpret psychological reports which contain test information. We will now provide brief descriptions of some of the major psychological tests used in psychological reports.

Measures of Intellectual Functioning

In 1905, Alfred Binet developed a scale of thirty items arranged in order of increasing difficulty. He argued that the scale differentiated between those children who could or could not function adequately in a classroom. In 1908, his "Measuring Scales of Intelligence" included fifty-nine tasks grouped by age levels from three years to thirteen years. Each item had to be appropriate for a modal age level, and he then gave mental age credits for items passed. The credits were summed and the total score was called a mental age. In 1912, William Stern developed the concept of a mental quotient, which was computed as the proportion of the mental age over the chronological age. This model for making inferences about intelligence assumed that rate of intellectual development is highly related to intelligence. Later, Goddard translated the scale into English, and Terman revised the scale. The resulting scale was really the first standardized individual intelligence test. Arthur Otis subsequently built a paper-and-pencil or group-administered version of the scale (Linden & Linden, 1968).

Since that time, intelligence tests as well as theories of intelligence have been the basis for a vast and controversial literature in psychology. In an essay dealing with various concepts of intelligence, Tyler (1976) observed that "until a decade or so ago, the measurement of intelligence was generally considered to be one of psychology's major success stories." Today, the old debates about theories and measures of intelligence are again resurfacing in the professional and popular literature (Garcia, 1981).

Carroll and Horn (1981) cite problems with IQ tests that need to be kept in mind by practitioners. To begin with, no IQ test is known that measures the "true or best" construct of intelligence. Different IQ tests in effect measure different "intelligences." An IQ for one individual can be based on a combination of high and low scores for component abilities that is quite different from the configuration yielding the same IQ for another individual. There is very little evidence that these different configurations have the same implications across situations or tasks. Moreover, the assumption that because different abilities increase with age, they continue to represent the same factor of intelligence is dubious. Finally, basing test construction on relatively homogeneous samples makes the definition of intelligence used relevant only to those particular populations.

Garcia (1981) recommends that mental testing should be based on specified sets of operations and efforts made to eliminate cultural bias and inappropriate generalizations. Use of single scores and dimensions should be deemed scientifically invalid and prohibited from use in legal and bureaucratic regulations. Finally, performance should be described with profiles bearing some resemblance to specific brain functions and/or to actual social role performances in various community situations. We would like to echo the latter suggestion.

Individual Intellectual Tests

The Stanford Binet is the oldest intelligence measure available. The 1960 version (Form L-M) yields a deviation IQ with a mean of 100 and a standard deviation of 16. Form L-M can be administered to any appropriate person from age two to adult. There are half-year tests between the ages of two and five, and there are year tests from ages five to fourteen. There is also an "average adult" test and three "superior adult" tests in the total scale (Terman, 1916).

The tasks on the Stanford Binet are mostly of a verbal nature. However, there are some memory, reasoning, and spatial ability tasks. For younger clients, the Stanford Binet administration time is about thirty to forty minutes and about one to one and a half hours for older age groups. The age at which all items are passed is called the *basal* age, while the age at which all items are failed is the *ceiling* age. The resultant score is the *mental age*. With adults the chronological age of eighteen is used in entering the norm tables. In 1971–72, the norms for the Stanford Binet were updated.

The validity and reliability for the Stanford Binet is mostly based on internal consistency data and correlational studies between the 1960 and 1937 versions. Because of the size of the standard error of measurement of a Stanford Binet IQ, it is customary to use approximately a ten-point band on either side of the obtained IQ to take into account chance variation due to unreliability (Shertzer & Linden, 1979).

A final point concerns the construct validity of the Stanford Binet. Results of factor analyses indicate that performance on the Stanford Binet is largely explained in terms of a single common factor. Additionally, the common factor found at adjacent age levels was essentially the same. This common factor becomes increasingly verbal as the higher ages are approached (Cronbach, 1970).

The Wechsler-Bellevue Adult Intelligence Scale was published in 1939 (Wechsler, 1958). Its author, David Wechsler, thought that the other intelligence scales were less relevant for adults in that they relied too much on verbal tasks and overemphasized speed of performance. In 1955, the test was published as the Wechsler Adult Intelligence Scale (WAIS) for ages sixteen years and older. The WAIS is composed of six verbal and five performance subtests that are combined to obtain the full-scale deviation IQ. The raw scores on the subtests are transformed to weighted standard scores (mean = 10; standard deviation = 3) which are summed to obtain a verbal, performance, and full-scale IQ (Shertzer & Linden, 1979).

Wechsler tests are sometimes used in assessing mental retardation and organic brain dysfunction. Some psychologists interpret discrepancies on the subtest profile to assess personality characteristics.

The latest edition of the instrument is the Wechsler Adult Intelligence Scale—Revised (WAIS-R) published in 1981. The norm samples include an equal number of men and women distributed over nine age levels from sixteen to seventeen years to seventy to seventy-four years.

In the interpretation of WAIS-R IQs, it should be remembered that above-average individuals tend to score higher on the Stanford Binet than on the Wechsler scales. In contrast, below-average individuals score higher on the Wechsler than the Stanford Binet. The Wechsler does not discriminate as well as the Stanford Binet at the extremes of the IQ range.

The Wechsler Intelligence Scale for Children (WISC-R) contains ten subtests plus two alternatives. The verbal and performance items are given in alternating fashion.

The WISC-R is used with children ages six through sixteen years. A child's performance on each of the subtests is summed and transformed into normalized standard scores (using the child's own age group) with a mean of 10 and a standard deviation of 3. Scaled subscores are summed and translated into verbal, performance, and full-scale deviation IQs with a mean of 100 and a standard deviation of 15. A difference of 15 score points or more between the verbal and performance IQs is often viewed to have diagnostic significance.

The Wechsler Preschool and Primary Scale of Intelligence (WPPSI) is designed for children ages four to six and a half years. The WPPSI has eleven subtests grouped into a verbal and a performance scale. As with the WISC, the Stanford Binet correlates higher with the Verbal IQ than with the Performance IQ.

Group Intelligence Tests

Among paper-and-pencil intelligence tests, the Otis-Lennon is one of the most frequently used. The latest edition of the Otis-Lennon was published in 1979–1980 and is available at all levels from grade one through grade twelve (1976). The items are grouped into three parts: (1) classification, (2) analogies, and (3) omnibus. The third category involves following directions, quantitative reasoning, and verbal comprehension. The test has two equivalent forms. At each level, scores are expressed as a School Ability Index, which is in effect a standard score with a mean of 100 and an S.D. of 16. Concurrent and predictive validity against achievement test scores and end-of-year grades in different subjects range from .40 to .60.

Examples of tests which are particularly useful in community mental health settings are the Wide Range Intelligence and Personality test, which assesses ability as well as behavior, The Wonderlic Personnel Test, which is useful in business and industrial settings, and the Full Range Picture Vocabulary Test, which is useful with clients having reading problems.

The Wide Range Intelligence and Personality Test is a battery of ten subtests including vocabulary, number series, coding, picture reasoning, space series, verbal reasoning, social concept, arithmetic, space completion, and spelling (Jastak, 1971). The entire series takes about fifty minutes to complete. Raw scores are converted to standard scores. Norms are based on a wide range of individual's ages: nine and one half to fifty-four years.

The Wonderlic Personnel Test includes fifty items covering areas such as analogies, analysis of geometric figures, arithmetic problems, disarranged sentences, sentence parallelism with proverbs, similarities, logic, definitions, judgment, direction following using clerical items, spatial relations among others (Wonderlic, 1970). There are fourteen forms of the Wonderlic. Raw scores can be converted to percentile ranks. The age range of the norm samples is from sixteen years to sixty-five years. There are high school and college norms, norms for seventy-five occupational groups, and norms for both Caucasian and Black applicants.

The Full Range Picture Vocabulary Test assesses individual intelligence using sixteen plates, each with four pictures on it (Ammons, 1949–1950). The examiner states a word and the subject responds by indicating the picture on the plate which corresponds to the word. This test is helpful when a client has limited comprehension or communication resources.

The concept of aptitude is often used erroneously to infer a static trait not within the control of an individual. More accurately, aptitude is the ability to *acquire* certain behaviors given appropriate training. An aptitude is a construct which postulates a relationship between an observed pattern of present test behaviors and a pattern of future criterion performance. There are complex issues regarding the influence of training in determining aptitudes. Mathis (1969) criticized the ambiguous concept of aptitude and pointed out that aptitudes are affected by specific test experience as well as general training and experience. He has demonstrated that all nine of the General Aptitude Test Battery aptitudes are correlated with an index of previous environmental experience.

The General Aptitude Test Battery (GATB) measures nine aptitudes: (1) intelligence, (2) verbal aptitude, (3) numerical aptitude, (4) spatial aptitude, (5) form perception, (7) motor coordination, (8) finger dexterity, and (9) manual dexterity. Eight of the twelve tests are paper-and-pencil tests and four are performance tests (U.S. Department of Labor, 1967). The GATB utilizes multiple cutoff points. Aptitude test scores are to be considered in relation to specific occupations and the cutoff points are chosen on the basis of criterion correlations as well as means and standard deviations of workers in that occupation and observations of job analysts. The object is to identify two to four aptitudes, with appropriate cutting scores for each occupation. The aptitudes with their specific cutoff scores are called a Special Aptitude Test Battery (SATB). Occupations having similar aptitude requirements are grouped into a small number of job families. Cutoff scores are identified for the three most significant aptitudes for each family. These are called Occupational Ability Patterns (OAPs)

The nine-factor scores are converted into standard scores with a mean of 100 and an S.D. of 20.

The Non-Reading Aptitude Test Battery (NATB) was designed

to yield the same nine aptitude scores as the GATB (Droege, Shorober, Bemis, & Hawk, 1970). The NATB requires no reading or writing and is supposed to be especially useful with educationally and culturally disadvantaged adults. The battery has not proven to be very effective and it does not correlate highly with the GATB.

The Differential Aptitude Tests are used for educational and vocational counseling of students in grades eight to twelve (Bennett, Seashore, & Wesman, 1973). The DAT yields the following eight scores: verbal reasoning, numerical ability, abstract reasoning, clerical speed and accuracy, mechanical reasoning, space relations, spelling, and language usage.

Percentile rank and stanine score norms are available. Normalized standard scores can be transformed into a stanine scale with a mean of five and a standard deviation of approximately two. The name stanine (a contraction of standard nine) is based on the fact that the scores run from one to nine (Anastasi, 1982). The profiles show a percentile band for each score, such that the chances are 90 out of 100 that an individual's true score lies within the band. Test scores whose percentile bands do not overlap can be regarded as significantly different. The total of verbal reasoning and numerical ability subtests provides an indication of the subject's general scholastic aptitude. This index correlates in the .70s and .80s with composite criteria of academic achievement. While many of the validity coefficients for the subtests are high, some are low, a reminder of the fact that validity is specific to identified norm groups. The counseling psychologist should also be cautious about using this battery for differential prediction.

A DAT Career Planning Program is available. The report includes a client's DAT scores, with appropriate explanations and interpretive statements that relate the DAT scores to a client's expressed interests and plans.

Achievement Tests

An achievement test measures the outcomes of learning which are a result of experiences in a relatively controlled learning or training situation. Three assumptions are made: (1) The skill and content domains can be defined behaviorally. (2) The test measures important behaviors which are an outcome of learning. (3) The individual taking the test has had adequate exposure to the material being tested.

Three types of achievement tests are: (1) survey, (2) diagnostic, and (3) readiness. Survey tests estimate overall performance in a content area. Content may be defined primarily as factual material, as skills, or as a combination of both. The important point is that survey tests should be an adequate and a representative sample of the content area. Diagnostic tests assess relative strengths and weaknesses in a content area. These tests should be divided into subtests which have logical implications for remediation. Readiness tests indicate whether an individual has the content and skills to learn material at a higher level.

When selecting an achievement test, the counseling psychologist needs to consider whether the level of difficulty of the test is appropriate for the client. Is the test "too difficult" or "too easy" for a particular client? Does the test have appropriate norms for this client? The groups used in the reliability and validity studies should be relevant to the client.

It should be kept in mind that standardized achievement tests, too, constitute systematic procedures for observing certain behaviors. When selecting an achievement test the psychologist needs to identify carefully the behaviors which are being observed. Caution should be exercised because tests with similar titles may not necessarily be measuring the same skills and behaviors. Thus, it is important to ascertain whether the client has had adequate exposure to the critical skills and behaviors being measured on the test chosen. Also, the psychologist needs to ascertain the importance of the kinds of skills tapped with a given test. For instance, tests differ in their emphasis on recall of specific information, interpretation and drawing inferences, and problem solving.

A final consideration in selecting an achievement test concerns the purposes for testing the client. If the goal is placement, the test must allow one to identify the educational status of the client in order to place him or her in an appropriate training program or class. If the goal is diagnosis, the specific kind of educational diagnosis should be identified: That is (1) general diagnosis, (2) analytic diagnosis, or (3) case study diagnosis. General diagnosis usually involves standardized group tests of ability and achievement. Analytic diagnosis systematically explores specific strengths and weaknesses in background knowledge and skills. Case study diagnoses often include diagnostic tests, individual intelligence tests, evaluation of health and physical condition, and environmental assessment.

In a community mental health setting, the psychologist may use achievement tests in vocational and educational counseling of adults.

A very useful battery of achievement tests is the Tests of General Educational Development (Dressel & Schmid, 1951). These tests are used to appraise the educational development of adults who have dropped out of school and seek to obtain high school equivalency certificates. This battery has five tests covering English Composition, Social Studies, Natural Sciences, Literature, and Mathematics.

Reading deficiencies are a source of difficulty for many adults. Causes of reading difficulties are varied and reading disabilities are not simple to diagnose. Physical, social, and psychological factors can be involved. Diagnosis can involve four reading levels:

1. Independent reading level. At this level an individual can read with no more than one error in word recognition in each 100 words and has a comprehension score of at least 40 percent.

2. Instructional reading level. At this level, the individual can read with no more than one word recognition error in each twenty words and has a comprehension score of at least 75 percent.

3. Frustration reading level. At this level, the individual reads orally without rhythm and in unnatural voice and comprehension is no more than 50 percent.

4. Probable capacity reading level. At this level, the individual can comprehend 75 percent of the material when it is read aloud by the examiner (Betts, 1957).

In diagnosing learning problems, the psychologist should use reading tests to assess accurately strengths and weaknesses. Many misjudgments of client capability could be avoided if counseling psychologists would pay more attention to diagnosing reading difficulties.

For instance, the Wide Range Achievement Test is a series of three subtests which can be used with adults (Jastak & Jastak, 1965). Two are oral and one is paper-and-pencil as well as oral. The three subtests are: reading with recognition and naming of letters and the pronunciation of words; spelling, which includes copying marks resembling letters, writing the name, and writing words from dictation; and arithmetic, which includes reading number symbols, solving oral number problems, and performing written computations. The Wide Range Achievement Test can be used with other assessment devices for assessing achievement problems of adult learners and for job placement.

Measures of
Habitual Performance or
"Interests"

The first attempt to measure interests was probably made by E. L. Thorndike in 1912. However, the work of C.S. Yoakum at Carnegie Institute of Technology had a major impact on interest measurement as we know it today (Campbell, 1971).

The construct of interest is frequently used by both lay people and professionals, but it is poorly understood. This construct can be defined in affective terms involving both perception and evaluation. Interests are stimuli in the form of objects, social and physical activities, and people, which are responded to with positive or negative feelings. They are inferred from an analysis of a client's history of choice or preference behavior. These behaviors include accepting and rejecting; liking and disliking; and approaching and avoiding certain things, people, and activities. Positive interests are directed toward objects and processes and these can be preferentially ordered to assess relative strength of interests.

Three criteria for defining interests are as follows:

1. *Attention*. Interests can be inferred from the things or activities to which people attend. However, interests are not the only inference that can be made from observing attending behavior.
2. *Choice*. Interests can be inferred from observations of situations in which individuals choose among equally available alternatives. Although people tend to choose the alternative which most interests them, other factors also influence choices.
3. *Persistence*. Interests can be inferred from observing activities at which people tend to persist or not persist. Again, interest is not the sole factor which influences persistence.

The psychological concept of "interest" is a hypothetical construct used in making causal inferences about behavior. It is often wrongly used to make indiscriminate causal inferences which imply that interests are personal characteristics of a static nature and not within the control of the client. This is clearly not the case! If interests are used for causal attributions, they should be viewed as modifiable and within the control of the person. It is clear, for example, from the research of Heider (1958) that individuals who attribute their level of performance to their own efforts (an internal/controllable attribution) tend to be more motivated to continue to perform tasks.

Individuals who attribute causes of their behavior to a static characteristic such as interests over which they assume they have no control are less likely to continue to perform tasks. If interests are to be used as causal attributions they should be used to promote change, self-control, and achievement motivation. Interests are then merely inferences about certain kinds of client behaviors. Obviously, in many cases, there may be other more appropriate inferences that can be made about the same behaviors. Interests are most useful in systematically describing client behavior. They are very inadequate as the basis for theories of causality.

Two major methods of measuring interests involve viewing them as expressed and inventoried interests. Expressed interest is the direct verbal statement of interest in an occupation or activity. The inventory method employs a variety of items, differential weighting of items, and a scoring method that relates to occupational or educational norm groups. Dolliver (1969), in a comparison of the Strong Vocational Interest Blank and expressed vocational interests, reported: (1) moderate degree of overlap between the results of the Strong Vocational Interest Blank and the results of an expressed interest method; (2) reliability of the Strong Vocational Interest Blank exceeding that of expressed interests; (3) the predictive validity of expressed interests at least as great as the predictive validity of the Strong Vocational Interest Blank; and (4) expressed interests that develop early in an individual's life as highly predictive of future behavior.

Interest inventories have been constructed on the basis of logical or theoretical considerations, on the basis of the empirical relationship between measured interests and various external criteria, and on the basis of empirical evidence that the interest scales are homogeneous. When using interest measures, it is important to remember that the scales describe or measure directionality rather than strength or intensity of interests.

Holland (1980) examined the research regarding the influence of interest inventories on respondents. First, a group of experiments indicated that people who took interest inventories listed more vocational choices, increased their satisfaction with a current choice, and reported increased self-understanding. Another group of experiments suggested that different vocational assessment devices have similar or identical effects. A third group of experiments indicated that increasing the number of vocational assessment devices is no more effective than using each of the individual devices singly. Finally, a group of experiments reported no significant mean differences between males and females when the directions for an interest inventory were radically revised and an attempt was made to render all the items gender neutral.

Holland (1980) also reported the results of a poll of high school students. Both females and males indicated that what they wanted most from an interest inventory was "reassurance" about an aspiration they already had. "Wanting more alternatives" ranked well below this desire. Overall, there is no experimental evidence that documents any negative effects of taking interest inventories. Interest inventories have small but apparently beneficial effects for a wide range of populations.

The Strong-Campbell Interest Inventory (Campbell, 1974) integrates Holland's theory of career development with the traditional empirical scales of the older Strong Vocational Interest Blank. A total of 179 scales averaging approximately forty-five items each are used. The occupational scales are classified according to Holland's letter codes, which are arranged in descending order of importance. The twenty-three basic occupational scales range in length from five to twenty-four items. Sex differences are indicated by mean scores and significant percentile point benchmarks that are presented for each sex on the profile sheet.

The occupational theme scales attempt to measure Holland's types of personality and occupational environments. These are (1) realistic, (2) investigative, (3) artistic, (4) social, (5) enterprising, and (6) conventional (see chapter 10). Each scale has twenty items and has been standardized with a mean of 50 and a standard deviation of 10 on a combined sample of men and women. However, there are also printed statements based upon separate male and female norms. Each of the Holland Theme Scales is highly correlated with at least one basic area scale.

The Kuder Preference Records represent another important set of interest inventories (Kuder, 1970, 1979). Kuder's Form C has scales with homogeneous item content, which are significantly intercorrelated and reflect specific areas of interest. All the Kuder forms have employed a forced-choice, triad-item response format. The client selects the item in the triad liked most and the one which is least preferred. Form E is the General Interest Survey suitable for ages seven through sixteen and adults and includes the same scale as Form C. They are: outdoor, mechanical, computational, scientific, persuasive, artistic, literary, musical, social service, and clerical. The items in Form D and Form DD include the ten occupational areas from Form C and Form E as well as items from the Kuder Personal Form (Form A) and some new items. Form D has fifty-two empirically derived scales each based upon representative responses of men in a given occupation. In Form DD, there are also scales for thirty-three college majors. For men there are seventy-nine occupation scores and twenty-five college major scores and for women there are fifty-six occupation scores and twenty college major scores (Kuder, 1979). The percentile norms for the occupational groups and the college major groups include only those individuals who reported satisfaction with their choice of occupation or college major.

Other relevant interest inventories are the Career Assessment Inventory (Johansson, 1976), which can be used with clients interested in immediate career choices or careers requiring technical, business school, or some college training. This inventory has theme scales, basic interest area scales, and occupational scales.

The Self-Directed Search allows the client actively to engage in his or her educational and occupational planning (Holland, 1973). The questionnaire has a series of questions related to occupational daydreams, preferences for activities and occupations, competencies, and self-estimates of abilities in different occupations. There is also a comparison booklet, *The Job Finder.*

Career and Vocational Developmental Assessment

Career development and vocational maturity are two important concepts in vocational assessment. The concept of stages of vocational development is based on the work of Piaget and assumes that there are stages of development with appropriate tasks for each stage. It is essential to resolve the tasks at each stage if an individual is going to proceed to the next, higher stage. Super (1955) compared the vocational coping behavior of an individual to his or her age peers, while Crites (1973) compared individuals with the oldest individuals in the same vocational life stage (see chapter 10).

Super (1955) defined the concept of vocational maturity as including five dimensions: (1) orientation to vocational choice, (2) information planning, (3) consistency of vocational choice, (4) crystallization of trade, and (5) wisdom for vocational preferences. For him, the process of career development progressed through orientation, exploration, decision making, and reality testing. To determine objectively the stages of career development, Crites constructed the Career Maturity Inventory (Crites, 1973). This inventory has two sections: Career Choice Attitudes and Career Choice Competencies. The former assesses clients' attitudes toward career choices: (1) involvement, (2) independence, (3) orientation, (4) decisiveness, and (5) compromise. Career Choice Competencies measure: (1) self-appraisal, (2) occupational information, (3) goal selection, (4) planning, and (5) problem solving. All items are related to either chronological age or school grade, and it is assumed that they measure the developmental variable—career maturity.

The Career Development Inventory was designed by Super and Forrest (1972) for assessing vocational maturity of adolescent boys and girls. There are three scale scores: planning and orientation, resources for exploration, and information and decision making. High school and college forms of this test are available.

Personality Inventories

Robert Woodworth is often credited with developing the first structured personality inventory (Linden & Linden, 1968). During World War I, he collected hundreds of symptoms of neurotic tendencies and constructed a questionnaire which was tried on 1000 recruits. This self-report device was the forerunner of a number of adjustment inventories. The assumption underlying these inventories is that the responses to the questions are an accurate representation of the client's condition. The two major approaches to personality measurements are self-report techniques and projective techniques. The former assumes that the individual is in the best position to describe his behavior. The latter assumes that individuals will interpret or impose structure on ambiguous stimuli and these meanings will provide significant insights regarding personality structure and dynamics.

Self-Report Scales

Three methods of constructing self-report personality scales are: logical, empirical, and factorial. Using the logical method, the inventory constructor chooses items which have either *face* validity or theoretical validity as measures of a hypothesized trait. Most early personality inventories were of this sort. However, in 1934, Landis and Katz reported that "normals" answered the neuroticism items on the Bernreuter Personality Inventory in the deviant direction more frequently that did "neurotics." Since that time, psychologists have been increasingly aware of the effects of test-taking attitudes on the validity of inventory items and scales.

A second method of constructing personality scales is to develop empirical keys. Items are selected on the basis of their empirical relationship to criterion behaviors. Responses to items are significant verbal behaviors which can be used to distinguish between various criterion groups. These inventories tend to be atheoretical and to allow the psychologist to compare the client responses with those of various criterion groups. The Minnesota Multiphasic Personality Inventory and the Strong-Campbell Interest Inventory were built by this kind of empirical method.

The factorial strategy for constructing personality scales assumes that scales should be composed of items with high intercorrelations and low correlations with items on other scales. The scales are unidimensional and the content of the items is used as the basis for naming the scales.

An example of a logical or theoretically keyed instrument is the Tennessee Self-Concept Scale (Fitts, 1965). This questionnaire consists of ninety items and fifteen scores including self-criticism, self-esteem (nine scores), variability of response scores, distribution score, and time score. The Tennessee Self-Concept Scale clinically discriminates among variously labeled groups, such as job applicants, paranoid schizophrenics, reactive depressives, and emotionally unstable individuals.

An example of the empirical approach to personality scale construction is the California Psychological Inventory (Gough, 1966). This instrument provides a comprehensive, multidimensional description of "normal persons." There are eighteen scales classified into four groups: (1) poise, ascendancy, and self-assurance, (2) socialization, maturity, and personality, (3) achievement potential and intellectual efficiency, and (4) intellectual and interest modes. All but four of the scales were developed by item analysis procedures using external criteria. The four rationally derived scales were based on content integrity criteria and item analysis. When interpreting this test, the authors emphasize the value of a profile interpretation. They suggest that the overall profile elevation should be noted and if nearly all scores are above the mean, the client is probably functioning well. They then suggest noting the differential elevation of the four groups of scales, listing highest and lowest scales, studying any unique features of the profile, and considering the internal variability of the profile.

The Sixteen Personality Factor Questionnaire (16 Pf) is an example of an inventory which was developed by factor analytic methods. Cattell & Eber (1962) used factor analysis to identify and measure sixteen primary traits that account for covariation among surface traits. The 16 Pf was designed to measure the sixteen primary source traits and eight composite or second-level factors. Each of the sixteen factors is designated by a letter and the high and low poles by a technical name and a popular descriptive label. There are two approaches to interpretation and diagnosis with the 16 Pf. They are profile matching and criterion estimation using specification equations. Mean profiles are provided for many different subject groups.

Projective Techniques

The second major approach to personality measurement involves the projective techniques. Herman Rorschach (Shertzer & Linden, 1979) used inkblots to study personality. His assumption was that the person's responses to an ambiguous stimulus is a reflection of his or her perception. The inkblots are evaluated in terms of classes or types of associations. The Rorschach focuses on the subject's style of handling a problem.

The Thematic Apperception Test is concerned with the content of thought and fantasies. With the Thematic Apperception Test, a series of pictures is shown to a client who is instructed to make up a story to explain the situation. The plot, symbolism, and style used in the stories are used to generate clinical hypotheses about the client's needs.

System and Environmental Assessment

Another important area for which counseling psychologists need measurement tools is the treatment of couples and families. One approach to studying marital and family interaction involves individual self-report methods like questionnaires, interviews, and standardized tests. A second approach is observer (i.e., therapist) reports. Third are behavioral methods and rating scales that provide data based on observations of marital and family interaction. Behavioral self-reports rely on clients to count their own or others' specific behaviors as they occur in day-to-day interactions.

Since the marital dyad and family system are social groups, measurement tools need to assess the characteristic properties of these groups. Thus, many helpful procedures are found within the fields of social psychology, sociology, marriage and family, and other social sciences.

Cromwell, Olson, and Fournier (1976) described four general ways of viewing a marriage, partial family, or whole family for assessment purposes: (1) Marriages and families are assessed in terms of the character of individual members with an emphasis on personality and affect. (2) An emphasis is placed on group structure and particularly on discrepancies in role perceptions, expectations, and performance. (3) An emphasis is placed upon the processes in the interchanges between and among members, particularly on any disruptive or inconsistent patterns of verbal communication. (4) An emphasis is placed upon the family's ability to function as a working unit in the performance of some task. Patterns of mutual negative reinforcement in verbal communication are then noted.

Four categories of self-report methods used in family and couple assessment are: (1) nonprojective personality tests, (2) projective personality tests, (3) perceived interaction, and (4) inferred interaction (Cromwell et al., 1976). The traditional approach to family assessment has been to test each member of the family with a conventional personality measure.

The Taylor Johnson Temperament Analysis is an example of a nonprojective personality inventory used in marital counseling (Taylor & Morrison, 1966–1974). Each person fills out the inventory for self and spouse. Discrepancy scores are then used to infer interactions.

A number of interpersonal measures have been developed to assess marital relationships, family and marital problems, and parent–child interactions. Some of the instruments deal with perceived interactions while others focus on inferred interaction. An example of a perceived interaction instrument is the Interpersonal Checklist (La Forge & Suczek, 1955), on which both a husband and wife check items that they perceive as descriptive of their behavior. With the inferred interaction instruments, self-reports of interpersonal situations are subject to projective interpretations by the counselor. The Thematic Apperception Test can be used to infer interaction patterns.

Observational methods can be used to describe actual interactions. The purpose is to elicit interactions which are characteristic of typical behaviors. The interactions may involve simulation of four different situations: problem-solving, decision making, conflict resolution, and naturalistic. These tasks elicit approximations of typical family behaviors.

Problem-solving tasks involve interactions observed under standardized conditions without the necessity of joint or family decisions. Most techniques are games that force the participants to respond to situations rather than to each other. Decision-making tasks are generally simulations that involve a standardized task to accomplish any joint decisions to be made. These tasks do not confront the family with real problems. Conflict-resolution tasks confront a family with issues needing resolution in order to obtain observations about the family's handling of conflict. The goal is to observe the process of resolving conflict in order to gain some insights regarding typical interactions. The tasks require joint decisions. Naturalistic situations allow observations in the family's natural setting. An example of this kind of observation is the "Supper Meal." The observer has a meal with the family and records interactions as they occur.

There are four major assessment questions regarding marital functioning (Jacobsen & Margolin, 1979). The first question concerns the beliefs that each spouse holds about the relationship. For example, the Locke-Wallace Marital Adjustment Scale (Locke & Wallace, 1959) is a widely used inventory of global marital adjustment which assesses marital satisfaction, amount of disagreement, mutual activities, and retrospections about the decision to marry.

The second assessment question concerns the nature of the day-to-day interaction of the couple. The Spouse Observation Checklist (SOC) is a listing of specific pleasing and displeasing relationship behaviors (Patterson, 1976). Each spouse identifies how beneficial each item would be if it occurred and how costly it would be to provide each behavior to one's partner. Each spouse identifies the subset of pleasing items that would be a benefit to receive and rates them. The partner indicates the cost of giving these behaviors along a similar scale.

A third type of assessment concerns identifying the factors that contribute to the central relationship problems. The behavioral diary can be used to obtain information about the environmental variables that control a specific behavior and data on the strength of a specific behavior. The Anger Checklist (Margolin, Olkin, & Baum, 1977) describes the types of angry responses exchanged during disagreements. Pleasant Thoughts About the Spouse (Patterson & Hops, 1972) assesses cognitive correlates of specific behaviors.

The final assessment question concerns the strategies used by spouses to bring about change in their relationships. Typical measures explore the use of aversive and rewarding change mechanisms. The most commonly used method is to have spouses engage in problem-solving discussions.

The Circumplex Model of Marital and Family Systems has two major dimensions: cohesion and adaptability (Olson, Sprenkle, & Russell, 1979). Family cohesion has two components: the emotional bonding members have with one another, and the degree of individual autonomy a person experiences in the family system. Variables used to assess family cohesion are emotional bonding, independence, boundaries, coalitions, time, space, friends, decision making, and interests and recreation. The four levels of cohesion are called disengaged, separated, connected, and enmeshed.

The second major dimension in the Circumplex Model is adaptability. Positive feedback provides the family system with constructive, system-enhancing behaviors that allow the system to grow, create, innovate, and change. Negative feedback attempts to maintain the status quo. Both change and stability are seen as necessary for a viable family system. Adaptability is the ability of a marital/family system to change its power structure, role relationships, and relationship rules in response to situational and developmental stress. Variables used to assess adaptability are family power structure, negotiation styles, role relationships and relationship rules, and feedback. Four levels of adaptability are called rigid, structured, flexible, and chaotic.

In the Circumplex Model, sixteen types of couples or families are identified. These types were developed by classifying the two dimensions into four levels: very low, low to moderate, moderate to high, and very high. The four central and four extreme types are most common. The four central types represent more functional marital and family systems. In these types individual family members have the freedom to be more alone or more connected as they wish. The four extreme types represent very high or low levels of adaptability and cohesion and are most dysfunctional.

The Circumplex Model provides a framework for diagnosis and treatment of couples and families. A self-report scale called The Family Adaptability and Cohesion Evaluation Scales (FACES) can be used to obtain data from each adult family member on her or his perception of the family in terms of the two variables adaptability and cohesion. If a couple or family is extreme on either cohesion or adaptability, the model suggests that the family might function more adequately within a more moderate position on that dimension.

Two basic ways are used for making a diagnosis using the Circumplex Model. The therapist can rate the marital or family system on each of the variables related to cohesion and adaptability using clinical interviews and direct observations. It is also possible to do an empirical assessment based on an objective scale or interaction method that assesses the variables related to the two dimensions. FACES were developed for this purpose.

Environmental Assessment

The development of methods of the systematic description and classification of environments is an important advance for community mental health. These tools allow the psychologist to adapt a more contextual view of client diagnosis and to develop preventive as well as therapeutic interventions.

Moos (1974) identified six approaches to the assessment and classification of human environments. The first approach identifies the ecological variables by which environments can be classified. Categories of ecological variables are (1) geographical and meteorological variables and (2) physical design and architectural characteristics. Some meteorological factors that are related to behavior are extreme temperatures, barometric pressure, cyclonic and anticyclonic storm patterns, and oxygen, nitrogen, carbon dioxide, and ozone concentrations in the atmosphere. Man-made physical environments also influence psychological states and social behavior.

Behavioral mapping of designed environments assesses the frequency of different types of activities in different locations. Variables such as behavior density (the frequency of all types of activities at a particular place), diffuseness (the range of different activities occurring at a place), and activity profile (the frequency of specific types of activities occurring at place) have been analyzed.

Behavior Settings

The second approach to assessing human environments focuses on behavior settings (Barker, 1968). Behavior settings are natural phenomena having a self-generated space-time locus and are real rather than perceived ecological entities. A behavior setting has two components: (1) behavior and (2) nonpsychological objects with which behavior is transacted. Behavior settings are stable, extra-individual units that have control over the behavior occurring in them. Undermanned and optimally manned behavior settings have been identified, and there have been interesting comparisons of the behavior of inhabitants in the two settings. For instance, students in small schools compared to those in large schools performed in more than twice as many responsible positions and reported more satisfaction in terms of developing competence, being challenged, and being valued.

A behavior setting is a unit in the ecological environment. Aspects of a behavior setting include: (1) nonbehavioral factors such as space, objects, and times, (2) standing behavior patterns such as patterns of play, and (3) relationships between behavioral and nonbehavioral factors. A basic relationship between the milieu and the behavior is that of "synomorphy," or the relationship between behavior patterns, milieu boundaries, and the interior structure of the milieu.

Organizational Structure

A third approach to measuring human environments emphasizes aspects of organizational structure such as size, staff–consumer ratio, and average salary levels. Seven dimensions of organizational structure are size, tall or flat organizational hierarchy, centralized or decentralized shape, number of organizational levels, line and staff hierarchies, span of control, and size of organizational subunits. These structural variables seem to have more impact on attitudes than on behaviors. They are discussed further in chapter 9.

Demographic Assessment

A fourth strategy for assessing human environments is to describe the average background characteristics of the individuals functioning in a particular environment. This approach assumes that the character of an environment is dependent on the dominant characteristics of its members. Variables include background characteristics, biologically defined characteristics, factors related to geographic position or socioeconomic status, family and marriage group factors, and group membership factors.

Interest and Activity
Environmental Assessment

Two typologies of environments have been developed by Holland (1966) and Astin (1968). Holland argues that vocational satisfaction stability and achievement depend on the congruence of personality and environment. The six environmental models and personality types are called realistic, investigative, social conventional, enterprising, and artistic. They are further discussed in chapter 10.

Astin (1968) developed a typology of defined college environments. Included in the types are any factors capable of changing the student's sensory input. The Inventory of College Activities was developed by Astin as a technique for describing environmental stimuli.

Social Climate Assessment

The fifth method of assessing environments emphasizes psychosocial characteristics and organizational climate. Perceived climate scales have been developed to measure the general norms, value orientations, and psychological characteristics of different types of institutions. Moos (1973) developed scales to assess perceived climates of different social organizations. The results indicate that conceptually similar dimensions seem to be relevant in a wide variety of environments.

Three types of dimensions are:

1. Relationship. Type and intensity of personal relationships.
2. Personal development. The exact nature of these dimensions varies in different environments.
3. System maintenance and system change dimensions. Order, organizations, clarity, and control.

These dimensions appear to be related both to morale and outcomes of treatment. In general, information about organizational climate is based on the perceptions of individuals in a system rather than on objective or physical characteristics.

Functional Analysis or Behavioral Assessment of Environments

Another strategy for assessing human environments is a functional analysis of environments. The assumption is that behavior varies from one setting to another primarily because the reinforcement consequences for particular behaviors vary considerably. Stimulus changes that produce and maintain behavior and behavior change are analyzed. Situations can be classified in terms of the major types of reinforcements likely to occur in them. For instance, psychiatric programs vary widely in their organizational characteristics and these variations may be related to the types of behaviors that are rewarded in them (Cohen & Filpzak, 1971). (See chapter 6.)

Institutional Assessment

The work of Moos and his colleagues is particularly significant to community mental health (Moos, 1971; Moos & Houts, 1968). They developed a Ward Atmosphere Scale which assesses a psychiatric ward's social environment as perceived by patients and staff. There are ten different dimensions reflecting relationship variables, treatment program variables, and administrative structure variables. This scale differentiates between inpatient psychiatric wards (Moos, 1971). Moos (1972) also developed a Community Oriented Programs Environment Scale which assesses the environments of transitional community-oriented psychiatric treatment programs. This scale has ten subscales: program involvement, support, spontaneity, autonomy, practical orientation, personal problem orientation, anger and aggression, order and organization, program clarity, and staff control.

Moos' methodology and scales make it possible to compare treatment environments over time, with each other, and cross-culturally. Knowledge of treatment environments may allow the psychologist to determine the effects of different environments upon patients and possibly match patients and treatment settings.

Conclusion

Our discussion of test results does not imply that the counseling psychologist in a community mental health agency merely is a "tester." Instead, the proper role for the psychologist, as a professional who provides information through psychological reports, is that of consultant (Tallent, 1976). Although there is no consensus regarding the appropriate content of psychological reports, almost all of them are likely to include test information. Moreover, a psychological report can provide a description of the important client and environmental variables needed to interpret test information adequately.

No cookbook rules exist for writing psychological reports, because the mission of different institutions employing the counseling psychologists will influence the purpose of any psychological reports written. For instance, the mission of the "community mental health movement" will effect the content of reports in related settings. Here, as Tallent (1976) points out, naturalistic observation takes on increased importance because concern is likely to center on environmental rather than only on intrapsychic phenomena. Still, even in this situation, psychological instruments can be a valuable resource as long as the psychologist does not neglect the unique factors in each client's situation.

The primary content of a psychological report often refers to the conclusions that are transmitted to the person who made the referral. Secondary content tends to round out a report and develop and support the conclusions.

In writing psychological reports, test-by-test reporting seems less than useful (Tallent, 1976). Instead, the focus is on conclusions derived with the help of tests. Test results may be subdivided for reporting purposes into "intellectual aspects" and "personality factors."

Tests can be useful in analyzing intellectual functioning of clients and identifying assets and liabilities as well as quality of thinking.

In discussing the "personality" area, psychologists should refrain from overreliance on jargon or labels loosely derived from personality theories and abnormal psychology. It is usually safer and more useful to adhere closely to the actual observations available and to relate these to actual functioning in relevant environments in the community.

References

Ammons, R. B. *Provisional manual for the full range picture vocabulary test.* Missoula, Mont.: Psychological Test Specialists, 1949–1950.

Anastasi, A. *Psychological testing* (5th ed.). New York: Macmillan, 1982.

Astin, A. W. *The college environment.* Washington, D.C.: American Council on Education, 1968.

Barker, R. *Ecological psychology.* Stanford, Calif.: Stanford University Press, 1968.

Bennett, G. K., Seashore, H. G., & Wesman, A. S. *Differential aptitude tests—Administrator's handbook.* The Psychological Corporation, 1973.

Betts, E. A. *Foundations of reading instruction.* New York: American Book, 1957.

Betz, N. E., & Weiss, O. J. Validity. In B. Bolton (Ed.), *Measurement of evaluation in rehabilitation.* Springfield, Ill.: Charles C. Thomas, 1975.

Biggs, D. A., & Keller, K. A cognitive approach to test interpretation. *The Personnel and Guidance Journal,* 1982, *60,* 528–531.

Campbell, D. P. *Handbook for the Strong Vocational Interest Inventory.* Stanford, Calif.: Stanford University Press, 1971.

Campbell, D. P. *Manual for the Strong-Campbell Interest Inventory* (Format 325). Stanford, Calif.: Stanford University Press, 1974.

Carroll, J. B., & Horn, J. L. On the Scientific Basis of Ability Testing. *The American Psychologist,* 1981, *36,* 1012–1020.

Cattell, R. B., & Eber, H. W. *Manual for Forms A and B. Sixteen Personality Factor Questionnaire.* Champaign Institute for Personality and Ability Testing, 1962.

Cohen, H. J., & Filpzak, J. *A new learning environment.* San Francisco: Jossey Bass, 1971.

Crites, J. O. *Theory and research handbook for the Career Maturity Inventory.* Monterey, Calif.: California Test Bureau/McGraw-Hill, 1973.

Cromwell, R. E., Olson, D. H., & Fournier, J. S. Tools and techniques for diagnosis and evaluation in marital and family therapy. *Family Process,* 1976, *15:* 1–48.

Cronbach, L. J. *Essentials of psychological testing* (3rd ed.). New York: Harper & Row, 1970.

Cronbach, L. J. Five decades of public controversy over mental testing. *American Psychologist,* 1975, *30,* 1–94.

Dolliver, R. H. Strong Vocational Interest Blank versus expressed vocational interests: A review. *Psychological Bulletin,* 1969, *72,* 95–107.

Dressel, P. L., & Schmid, J. *An evaluation of the tests for general educational development.* Washington, D.C.: American Council on Education, 1951.

Droege, R. C., Shorober, W., Bemis, S., & Hawk, J. Development of a non-reading edition of the General Aptitude Test Battery. *Measurement & Evaluation Guidance,* 1970, *3,* 45–53.

Ebel, R. L. Must all tests be valid? *American Psychologist,* 1961, *16,* 640–647.

Fitts, W. H. *Manual: Tennessee Self-Concept Scale, counseling recordings and tests.* Box 6184, Acklen Station, Nashville, Tenn., 1965.

Garcia, J. The logic and limits of mental aptitude testing. *The American Psychologist,* 1981, *36,* 1172–1180.

Gough, H. Manual, California Psychological Inventory. Palo Alto, Calif.: Consulting Psychologist Press, 1966.

Heider, *The psychology of interpersonal relations.* New York: Wiley 1958.

Holland, J. *The psychology of vocational choice.* Waltham, Mass.: Blasedell, 1966.

Messick, S. Test validity and ethics of assessment. *The American Psychologist,* 1980, *35,* 1012–1027.

Moos, R. Revision of the Ward Atmosphere Scale (WAS) (Tech Report). Palo Alto, Calif.: Department of Psychiatry, Social Ecology Laboratory, University of California, 1971.

Moos, R. H. Assessment of the psychosocial environments of community oriented psychiatric treatment programs. *Journal of Abnormal Psychology*, 1972, *79*, 9–18.

Moos, R. *Evaluating treatment environments: A social ecological approach.* New York: Wiley, 1973.

Moos, R. H. Systems for the assessment and classification of human environments: An overview. In R. H. Moss, & P. M. Imsel, (Eds.), Issues in Social Ecology. Palo Alto, Calif.: National Press Books, 1974.

Moos, R., & Houts, P. Assessment of the social atmosphere of psychiatric wards. *Journal of Abnormal Psychology*, 1968, *73*, 595–604.

Olson, D. H., Sprenkle, D. H., & Russell, R. S. Circumplex Model of marital and family systems. Cohesion and Adaptability Dimensions, Family Types and Clinical Applications. *Family Process*, 1979, *18*, 3–28.

Otis, A. S., & Lennon, R. T. *Manual: Otis Lennon Mental Ability Test.* New York: Harcourt Brace Jovanovich, 1976.

Patterson, G. R., & Hops, H. Coercion, A game for two: Intervention techniques for marital conflict. In R. E. Ulrich & P. Mountjoy (Eds.), *The experimental analysis of social behavior.* New York: Appleton-Century-Crofts, 1972.

Patterson, G. R. Some procedures for assessing changes in marital interaction patterns. *Oregon Research Institute Research Bulletin*, 1976, *16*, No. 7.

Holland, J. L. *Professional manual for the Self-Directed Search.* Palo Alto, Calif.: Consulting Psychologists Press, 1973.

Holland, J. L. The influence of vocational interest inventories: Some implications for psychological testing. *The Counseling Psychologist*, 1980, *9*, 83–86.

Jacobsen, N., & Margolin, G. *Marital therapy: Strategies based on social learning and behavioral principles.* New York: Brunner/Mazel, 1979.

Jastak, J. F. *WRIPT: Wide Range Intelligence and Personality Test, supplement to manual.* Wilmington, Del.: Guidance Associates of Delaware, 1971.

Jastak, J. F., & Jastak, J. R. *Manual: The Wide Range Achievement Test.* Wilmington, Del.: Guidance Associates of Delaware, 1965.

Johansson, C. B. *Manual, The Career Assessment Inventory.* Minneapolis: National Computer Systems Interpretive Scoring Systems, 1976.

Kuder, G. F. Some principles of interest measurement. *Educational and Psychological Measurement*, 1970, *30*, 205–226.

Kuder, G.F. *Kuder occupational interest survey revised: General manual.* Chicago: Science Research Associates, 1979.

La Forge, R., & Suczek, R. F. The Interpersonal Dimension of Personality, III. An Interpersonal Checklist. *Journal of Personality*, 1955, *24*, 94–112.

Landis, C., & Katz, S. E. The validity of certain questions which purport to measure neurotic tendencies. *The Journal of Applied Psychology*, 1934, *18*, 343–356.

Linden, K. W., & Linden, J. D. *Modern mental measurement: A historical perspective.* Boston: Houghton Mifflin, 1968.

Locke, H., & Wallace, K. M. Short Marital Adjustment and Prediction Tests: Their reliability and validity. *Marriage and Family Living*, 1959, *21*, 251–255.

Margolin, G., Olkin, R., & Baum, M. *The Anger Checklist*. Unpublished inventory. Santa Barbara: University of California Press, 1977.

Mathis, H. The Disadvantaged and the aptitude barrier. *The Personnel and Guidance Journal*, 1969, *47* (5), 467–472.

Pepinsky, H. B., & Pepinsky, P. N. *Counseling theory and practice*. New York. Ronald Press, 1954.

Shertzer, B., & Linden, J. *Fundamentals of individual appraisal*. Boston: Houghton Mifflin, 1979.

Super, D. The dimensions and measurement of vocational maturity. *Teachers College Record*, 1955, *57*, 151–163.

Super, D., & Forrest, D. J. Career Development Inventory, Form One: *Preliminary Manual for Research & Field Trial*, New York: Teachers College. Columbia University, 1972.

Tallent, N. *Psychological Report Writing*. Engelwood Cliffs, N.J.: Prentice-Hall, 1976.

Taylor, R. M., & Morrison, L. P. Taylor-Johnson Temperament Analysis (T-JTA). Psychological Publications Inc., Los Angeles, Calif. 1966–1974.

Terman, L. M. *The measurement of intelligence*. Boston: Houghton Mifflin, 1916.

Tyler, L. E. The intelligence we test—An evolving concept. In L. B. Resnick (Ed.), *The nature of intelligence*. Hillsdale, N.J.: Erlbaum,, 1976.

U.S. Department of Labor. *Manual for General Aptitude Test Battery*, Sec. III, Development. Washington, D.C.: Government Printing Office, 1967.

Wechsler, D. *The measurement and appraisal of adult intelligence* (4th ed.). Baltimore: Williams & Wilkins, 1958.

Wiggins, J. S. *Personality and prediction—Principles of personality assessment*. Reading, Mass.: Addison-Wesley, 1973.

Wonderlic, E. F. *Wonderlic Personnel Test Manual*. Northfield, Mass.: E. F. Wonderlic & Associates Inc., 1970.

PART IV

INTERVENTION WITH INDIVIDUALS AND ENVIRONMENTS: TWO EXAMPLES

9

Marriage and Family Counseling

In chapter 1 we noted that a unique role of the counseling psychologist involved what may be called "developmental human ecology." This professional role in a sense involves facilitating an optimal quality of interaction between growing human beings and developmentally crucial aspects of their physical, social, and psychological environments. Obviously, no parts of an individual's developmental interactions are more crucial than are those that occur within the family.

As counseling psychologists in community practice, we are especially concerned with two kinds of outputs from family systems. We seek to optimize developmental processes, and so help people realize their fullest potentials, and we are also interested in preventing the occurrence of obstacles to psychosocial development.

Unfortunately, it seems at times that both developmental and primary preventive interventions are numbered among those things that everyone talks about and no one ever does anything about. Primary prevention, particularly, is a sadly neglected activity in most community-based human services programs. Human services workers, like firemen, seem to take greater satisfaction in putting out fires than in preventing them. Blau (1979) pointed out that the identification of at-risk children is one of the most important problems confronting psychology. Garmezy (1974) has shown that the identification of vulnerability and risk factors is a feasible and necessary first step in the prevention and remediation of psychopathology.

Unfortunately, it seems clear that many of the traditional approaches to the delivery of human services, as well as many of the instruments and techniques developed around them, offer relatively little help when we shift our efforts into the enterprise of primary prevention (Bloom, 1971).

Despite the obvious cost effectiveness and humanitarian benefits of primary prevention as a goal for human services programs, relatively little real effort and few resources have been expended on its behalf. Kramer (1976) estimated that as many as 12 million children and adolescents under eighteen years of age are suffering from mental health problems, and that 90 percent of these young people do not receive the services they need. As Cummings (1979) pointed out, the resources needed to provide remedial services to these people alone are many times greater than those made available in all of the governmentally funded programs put together. The development and application of primary prevention programs thus seems to be virtually the only economically viable approach to the improvement of human psychological functioning in our society.

One of the basic problems confronting work in primary prevention is that psychology has not devoted the same energy and attention to developing a conceptual and theoretical base for prevention that it has given to creating a lexicon for psychopathology. Yet many of the problems involved in research on primary prevention are resolvable (Albee & Joffe, 1977) and much of the knowledge needed to mount effective programs is currently available (Kazdin, 1979).

Certainly one of the places in which efforts at primary prevention must begin is in providing psychological services to families experiencing stress and disorganization.

The Rise and Fall
of the Nuclear Family

The contemporary ideal model of family life in America is called the nuclear family. It consists of husband, wife, and their joint offspring living together in a single dwelling in a more or less stable neighborhood and community environment. As we noted in chapter 2, one of the interesting features of patterns of social behavior is that they very quickly become institutionalized within communities, and internalized within individual personalities to such an extent that little awareness exists about the existence of alternative realities and possibilities. Such is the case with the nuclear family.

Far from being the only model for family organization, the nuclear family model is less than a century old and, indeed, attained its preeminence because of the decline in the extended, multigenerational family as people rapidly increased their social and geographic mobility over the past eighty years of American life (Goode, 1963). The increase in importance of the nuclear family and the decline in significance of the extended family, which we take for granted, has created very important changes with compelling implications for human development in our culture.

The nuclear family has emerged into what is called the "conjugal model" of family life (Goode, 1963). The conjugal model is one in which family functioning is almost totally dependent upon the quality of the emotional relationship between husband and wife. In this family life pattern, relatively little importance is attached to values that for centuries were keystones upon which notions of family cohesiveness, achievement, and stability were based. The family as an economic unit devoted to insuring the material needs of members, with the long-term accumulation of family land and property, has declined in relative importance. Through the first three-quarters of this century, the proportion of families subsisting through farming has steadily declined to a low of less than 10 percent of the total population. Accompanying declines in numbers of small family businesses has almost completely erased the family as an important economic unit. With this shift have come marked changes in the patterning of family relationships. The role of the father as a kind of authoritarian shop foreman, or even as the primary wage earner, has changed. The nuclear family has become less self-contained and increasingly dependent on non-kinship relationships or social institutions for services such as education, religious instruction, recreation, and health care.

The conjugal family has become a more and more highly specialized organization, primarily concerned with the personal satisfaction and emotional needs of its members. In a sense, the ideal represented in this model is of the conjugal family as a kind of sanctuary designed to provide love, warmth, and security amid the depersonalizing and isolating anonymity of mass urban living.

As the family changed from an economic to a relationship-centered unit, the pattern of role differentiation built upon an economic model has been altered. Shifts away from sharply defined sex differentiation in division of labor, in responsibility for decision making, and for spending and earning money have occurred (Bernard, 1981). These changes were both a cause and a result of changes in the number and spacing of children. This shift involves the concentration of childbearing within the earlier years of marriage. By 1970 the average age of mothers for completion of childbearing was twenty-six. This tendency has been accompanied by steady increases in numbers of married women in the thirty to fifty-five year age ranges returning to active participation in the labor market (Kievit, 1972). This tendency, in turn, has contributed to the blurring of the once economically based sex role differences in families.

The family is obviously the group with the earliest and probably most profound impact upon developing human beings. Changes in patterns of family organization, nature of family relationships, and ideals and expectations about family functioning in turn produce important effects upon developing human beings in terms of their values, attitudes, and aspirations.

The focus within the conjugal or companionship model has tended to be primarily upon the optimal development of family members as opposed to the older economic values. Where the model has worked well it has afforded children and adults unparalleled opportunities for personal growth and accomplishment. The child-centered middle-class family with its emphasis upon achievement and accomplishment has been a powerful and often very positive environment in which to nurture high aspirations and high levels of personal accomplishment. As Hill (1960) pointed out twenty years ago, the model has worked best in middle- and upper-middle-class settings, where levels of affluence and formal education are relatively high.

Even in such settings, however, the conjugal model has come under heavy stress. Marriage within this model has moved increasingly in the direction of becoming a kind of joint career that requires careful and intensive preparation to provide the insights and skills necessary for success. The index of the quality of a marriage within this model appears to be in the degree to which the marital relationship contributes to the overall development of the partners. These kinds of expectations put an unprecedented set of demands upon family relationships. The degree of matching that is maintained in the rate and directions of the individual partners' development becomes a vital factor. The simple test of this matching factor is usually seen in the quality and character of the communications patterns between husband and wife.

As marriage partners develop their relationship around these factors, they also ultimately redefine the ways in which the family assumes responsibility for the development of children. The conjugal or companionship-oriented family's primary contribution to the growth of its children rather naturally focuses in the area of its own greatest concern, that is, on the capacity for close interpersonal relationships. The conjugal family has largely surrendered its role of providing formal vocational training as it has shifted its identity away from an economic basis. Instead, it concentrates upon education and socialization in the area of interpersonal relations.

At its best, the conjugal family becomes a powerful shaping force in the interpersonal or social development of children. The conjugal family model thus places great emphasis on preparing children "to get along" with others. It attempts to provide human-relations role models for children in terms of the roles and relationships and attendant communications patterns that define the marital interactions of parents. When these socialization processes function optimally, they help to establish aspirations to seek out opportunities for deeply involving, lasting relationships in both career and marriage. The successful implementation of the conjugal family model in which mutual growth and development is the primary goal of intimate relationships may help to stimulate children to seek out opportunities for such involvements and commitments in personal, educational, and career relationships.

Problems of the Conjugal Family

Unfortunately, the somewhat rosy picture that we have painted above of the conjugal family at its best is more an ideal than a reality. The very focus of this family pattern upon the quality of interpersonal relationships may become distorted to deny important values of freedom, independence, individuality, and creativity. Sometimes the socialization patterns in this family model may be centered around external and perhaps superficial patterns of interpersonal functioning. Dressing, grooming, acceptability of language, and impulse control may be accorded far greater importance than more fundamental notions of honesty, caring, and spontaneity. Any pattern of behavior that may be interpreted by someone as socially abrasive may be promptly squelched by parental disapproval.

In its most extreme form, the central ethic behind this kind of family socialization process becomes a sort of parody of the deodorant commercials on television. The primary commandment is that "thou shalt not offend thy neighbor." In the face of this kind of preoccupation with superficial acceptability, other deeper values may be submerged. Sometimes the counselor in community practice is faced with adolescents who are rebelling against the superficiality and hypocrisy inherent in this kind of socialization process with every weapon at their command. At times, behavior that involves delinquency, truancy, drug or alcohol abuse, or sexual promiscuity may be the weapons used by adolescents in intergenerational warfare. In one sense the long-haired, unantiseptic flowerchild of the late 1960s perfectly captured the passive antithesis of the socialization goals of the conjugal family model gone awry. Today, the drug-abusing, sometimes violent or delinquent adolescent represents the active opposition. In both cases the acting out of this kind of resistance to somewhat mindless aspects of the family's and community's socialization efforts may exact a terrible developmental price from all concerned.

Social Class and the Conjugal Family

An important consideration that must be attached to this discussion of American family life is to note that in practice the conjugal model is heavily rooted in the middle class. Despite the fact that the conjugal model seems to have been the sole inspiration for forty years of family situation comedies (or sometimes more accurately, situation tragedies) in the movies and on television, it has never represented a universal reality for the whole of our society (Uzoka, 1979).

In one of the relatively few comprehensive studies of marriage and family relationships among working-class people, Komarovsky (1962), for example, found that many of the trends that define the conjugal or companionship model were much less apparent in that population. In working-class families, patterns of verbal communication between husband and wife appeared to be more limited and less central to their relationship. The extended family was seen as relatively more important. Wives sought advice and support from female relatives more frequently. Recreational and social activities were less centered around the interaction of husbands and wives. Apparently, marriage partners met fewer of their social needs within the marriage relationship than is the case in the middle-class pattern described earlier. Gans (1962) described similar phenomena in his classic study, *The Urban Villagers*.

Similar differences in family patterns have been found in studies of black families. Bernard (1972) found that the trend toward the conjugal or companionship model was precisely reversed in data from lower-class black families. A study of what Bernard termed "the marriage trajectory" or trend indicated that in ghetto cultures, proportionately fewer and fewer families were organized around stable long-term relationships.

The picture that emerges from studies of marriage and family patterns is one of great diversity and relatively rapid social change in both values and practices in American family life (Bernard, 1972). It is clear that the conjugal family model that most Americans would view as the traditional and perhaps the only proper way of organizing family life is by no means universal in our culture and indeed may be entering its own declining stages (Bernard, 1981).

The traditional nuclear family model has received its share of critical reactions from students of family organization. Scheflen and Ferber (1972) attack the mystique of the nuclear family as a "sacred cow." They criticize the basic concept on three grounds. First, they maintain, the tasks imposed on the nuclear family are simply too numerous, too complex, and too varied to be managed by two ordinary adults. They call the ideal of a family meeting all of its members' needs around the marital relationship an impossible dream. When this dream is not realized, members are filled with guilt, remorse, and a deep sense of personal failure. They view the successful marriage as a kind of virtusoso performance that is a matter of exceptional skill and circumstances rather than something to be expected as a matter of course.

Second, they contend that the nuclear family is simply too small to meet all of the social needs of its members. The number of role models open to children is too few to allow for the fulfillment of varied human potentials. The nuclear family as they see it is an enclosure that walls out people, stimulation, and opportunities needed for the full development of members.

Finally, according to Scheflen and Ferber, the nuclear family is ecologically unsound because it is wasteful of scarce resources in its emphasis on family independence and separateness.

Carl Rogers (1971) joined in this criticism by declaring that the nuclear family constitutes a failing institution and a failing way of life. He foresaw a need for vigorous exploration of alternative styles of marriage and family life to develop new possibilities for family organization. Major criticisms of the nuclear family have also come from feminists who view the reality of the conjugal family model as a trap that encapsulates women and, rather than enhancing their development and fulfillment, actually stifles and represses them (Bernard, 1972).

While the criticisms above may be valid, it can also be said that the nuclear family has represented demands for an adaptation to major realities of American life. In situations in which expectations for social and geographic mobility are high, and when individual economic success is the most highly prized goal, the nuclear family has provided a major psychological anchor and refuge in a kaleidoscopic world. Perhaps the most remarkable aspect of the phenomenon is that the nuclear family model has worked so well, so long, under such trying conditions with so little community help or support.

Family Problems in the Community

As psychologists in community practice encounter the needs of contemporary families, they realize that the conjugal nuclear family living together in peace, tranquility, and mutual enhancement of development is *not* the only reality of community life.

David and Baldwin (1979) point out that dramatic changes in patterns of childbearing seem to be occurring. A very recent trend toward later marriage and childbearing along with smaller families may well be under way. One factor, however, that is of great importance to community human services involves what is termed adolescent childbearing. Births to women under twenty years of age now comprise a higher proportion of total births than ever before. The numbers of births to women under age sixteen was 42,000 in 1977. Eleven thousand of these mothers were under fifteen years of age. There has been a substantial increase in the number of births out of wedlock to women under twenty. In 1977 one-half of all births out of wedlock were to teenagers, and about a quarter of a million children were born out of wedlock to teenage mothers (David & Baldwin, 1979).

The physical and psychological problems of children "born to children," as it were, are obvious and well-known. The needs of these infants will have to be carefully considered and eventually met to avert a veritable disaster over the next few years.

One of the most obvious populations for which community services are desperately needed is single-parent families. The divorce rate among families with children has increased markedly since 1965. One estimate (Westman, 1972) is that three out of four divorces occur in families with children. Predictions are that as many as 50 percent of all children born in the decade of the 1970s will reside in a single-parent family, with the average stay in the single-parent situation lasting about six years (Hetherington, 1979). If the two-parent nuclear family is at risk because of the multiplicity of tasks and needs concentrated within it, the single-parent family is at least doubly vulnerable.

A link between children's behavior disorders and parent conflict has been well-established in the literature (Minuchin, Baker, Rosman, Leibman, Milman, & Todd, 1975; Rutter, 1979). Research has also found that while children in single-parent families tend to function better than children in conflict-ridden so-called intact families, divorce presents children with a particularly stressful set of circumstances, which may result in severe developmental disruptions or psychopathology (Hetherington, 1979; McDermott, 1970; Wallerstein & Kelly, 1976). Hetherington, Cox, and Cox (1978) pointed out that family conflict actually increases in the year following divorce. In that situation, behavior disruptions are more common or at least more obvious in boys than in girls. Boys tend to become noncompliant and aggressive in this kind of stress situation. McDermott (1970) found a significantly higher incidence of delinquency and other aggressive behavior among children of divorce when he examined the intake records of children evaluated at a children's psychiatric hospital. He noted that these children also tended to be more often depressed than other clinical groups. Psychological testing suggested that these children personalized or interpreted parental conflict as caused by their own "badness" or misbehavior. McDermott also observed in these children fears of being overwhelmed by external forces. He viewed acting-out behavior as defense against sadness and depression.

Certainly, divorce sets in motion a set of complex psychological processes that affect the well-being of all family members. Many children in the studies reported by Wallerstein and Kelly (1975) were maintaining fantasies of parental reconciliation as long as four years after the divorce. The findings suggest that for many children divorce is not merely a single traumatic event but also represents a chronic stress situation with very long-term implications for overall growth and development.

Rutter's (1979) research on risk factors associated with child psychopathology has indicated that increased vulnerability for severe emotional and behavioral problems is found among children whose family is characterized by a high level of parental discord and the presence of psychological disorders in the parents themselves.

A child's placement in foster care is also associated with increased psychiatric risk. Apparently a child's "at-risk" status increases exponentially when factors such as parental discord, parental mental disturbance, family breakup, and similar situations are added.

These kinds of findings are of tremendous significance to community service programs interested in primary prevention. The availability of adequate services to families in crisis probably represents the most important kind of primary prevention program available in communities.

While most children eventually manage the crisis of divorce, the problem does not end there. As we noted, the continued stress associated with parental separation and conflict may well have serious and lasting consequences on the child's psychological, social, and health status. The long-term adjustment of children appears heavily influenced by the quality of life in the custodial household. Shifts in financial resources, demands on mothers to seek outside employment, and changes in the maintenance routines of the home have all been found to contribute to family stress and so impact on the developing child (Hetherington, 1979). Older children are often called upon to provide their custodial mothers with emotional support during and immediately following separation or divorce crises. They also are generally required to take a more active and responsible role in managing the household (Weiss, 1975). These emotional and behavioral demands, if too sudden or intense, may overtax the child's developmental capabilities and may also encourage premature emotional detachment from the family situation. This process of overinvolvement of the child, called "parentification," is seen to be potentially damaging (Wallerstein & Kelly, 1975).

It seems clear from this research that adequate services must be available to families, not only during the crisis of separation and divorce, but also as the family deals with the many problems that follow. Similarly, community services must not be limited to purely psychological assistance, but must also help the family with the many practical problems of housing, day care, employment, financial needs, social support, and family relationships that continue to trouble many single-parent families.

Research has also demonstrated an inverse relationship between the child's psychological functioning and the custodial parent's need for support and alliance in the battle against the former spouse. When enacted, this kind of coalition, in effect, replicates and perseverates the family conflict situation prior to divorce or separation with similar negative consequences for the children. Sometimes the battle is between the custodial parent and the memory of the ex-spouse and the hurt, guilt, or anger associated with that memory. The stress on children can be perpetuated even when the former spouse is no longer in the immediate environment.

Wallerstein and Kelly (1975) found somewhat surprising changes in parent–child relationships following divorce. About one-half of the divorced fathers whom they studied actually developed better relationships with their children in the year following divorce. Deterioration in the father–child relationship was observed in only about one-fourth of the cases. A very important research finding in this area is that other things being equal—for example, the father's own emotional adjustment—the continued availability of the father is associated with positive adjustment in children (Hetherington, 1979). This finding has significant implications for the nature and focus of community family services. Counseling services should be available to *both* parents in a divorce situation to help them to continue their parental functioning in an atmosphere of cooperation and responsible concern for the offspring. Services should not be restricted either during or after separation and divorce to the custodial parent. Where joint custody is an outcome, services should be available to both parents to help make such arrangements work in the best interest of children.

Shifts opposite to those reported above for father–child relationships were reported for mother–child relationships. Nearly 50 percent of these relationships were reported to grow more strained in the period following divorce. Mothers and sons appeared to be particularly vulnerable to this kind of conflict situation. Hetherington (1979) in reviewing this research suggested that while both boys and girls initially respond to the divorce situation with an increase in dependent and affection-seeking behavior, boys tend to receive less support and affection from the custodial parent, usually the mother. Hetherington further pointed out that custodial parents are, in the long run, more influential in terms of children's development and well-being than even highly involved noncustodial fathers in the post-divorce situation.

Extrafamilial supports including peers, extended family, school, and neighborhood contacts and other relationships may often be very important to the well-being, particularly, of older children. Family services should be aware of these resources and help to mobilize them on behalf of children. In this sense divorce is not merely a family problem but a community problem. When school, neighborhood, and community combine to ignore the existence of single-parent families and to organize community life solely around the model of the nuclear, two-parent family, severe and unnecessary distress to many lives may result.

Research further indicates (Hetherington, 1979) that following divorce parenting skills may sharply deteriorate. As the custodial parent begins to recover from her or his own emotional trauma, these skills may improve markedly. Higher incidences of mother–son conflict, however, appear to persist long after divorce. This research strongly suggests the need for immediate, crisis-oriented therapeutic interventions to help parents deal with their own post-divorce trauma, *and* parent-education programs to help these parents deal with difficult responsibilities as sole heads of families.

Models of Family Therapy

Helping family systems deal with the stresses of modern community life is a complex and difficult problem, as we have seen in the preceding pages. Families are complex human systems with powerful and unique sets of dynamics. Glib generalizations or labels attached to families in terms of "broken homes" or "intact families" or "working-class families" are easily misused and misunderstood.

A sophisticated model for assessing important family dynamics and characteristics is described in chapter 8. The FACES System looks at the dimensions of cohesion and adaptability as these relate to family functioning.

Three major approaches or traditions in the area of family therapy appear to dominate the literature. Each is oriented around a somewhat different focus in terms of family functioning and family dynamics.

The Family Communications Approach

The first of these major foci for family counseling could be termed the Communications Approach. This approach is centered around the task of teaching family members to communicate more effectively and so increasing the sensitivity and awareness of family members to each other's needs and concerns. Treatment models based upon this approach have been described by therapists such as Satir (1964) and Gordon (1970).

Family counseling interventions within this approach emphasize structured communications exercises, direct analyses of family communications processes, and teaching of models of communication based upon open and honest two-way communication. The communication approach to family counseling is based upon a number of fundamental concepts and assumptions about social interaction processes.

The Impossibility of
Not Communicating

One of the primary concepts of the communications approach is the impossibility of *not* communicating. When two or more individuals are in some kind of sensory contact—that is, they are able to see or hear or touch each other—they are inevitably communicating. Sometimes we refer to an interpersonal difficulty as a "breakdown in communication." Actually, the people having difficulty are communicating, but in a way that exacerbates rather than ameliorates their difficulty.

The ways in which interpersonal communication occurs are varied and complex. Although language is perhaps the most remarkable of human inventions, it is by no means our only way of communicating. Much human communication is subtle, indirect, and nonverbal. An inflection of the voice, the twitching of an eyebrow, the nervous drumming of fingers on a table top are all forms of communication. Unfortunately, much human communication is imprecise and confusing to the receiver. When communication is confused and confusing, people have difficulty in sustaining patterns of cooperative behavior and so meeting each other's needs in mutually satisfying ways.

Some of the difficulty in human communication is caused by the imprecision of language itself. Words are symbols that have not only specific meanings, or *denotations,* but also *connotations,* or sets of associations, connected with them. Since these connotations tend to be idiosyncratic to the receiver, they may serve to distort the message intended by the sender. For example, the word "mother" may carry a wide range of connotations across individuals that range from warm, supportive associations to angry, hostile, or fearful images and memories.

Functional and Dysfunctional Communicators

A second important concept in the communications approach is that patterns of communication and, in a sense, specific communicators themselves can be classified as "functional" or "dysfunctional" in terms of the outcomes or consequences associated with them. A functional communicator is able to establish patterns of interaction that facilitate and sustain need satisfaction. A dysfunctional communicator is likely to establish patterns of interaction that are destructive and self-defeating.

Satir (1964) identified several characteristics of dysfunctional communicators. She suggested that such communicators tend to overgeneralize across contexts and situations and to refuse to specify the situational meaning of remarks or assertions. The dysfunctional communicator thus makes very sweeping and untestable assumptions that are difficult for others to understand fully or deal with. Common examples of this kind of dysfunctional communication include remarks such as "Everybody is like that" or "Nobody likes me" or "All women are . . ." or "You are just like everyone else."

Each of these statements overgeneralizes and universalizes some specific feeling or experience so that it is difficult for the receiver to trace it back to the specific perception or event to which it was originally attached.

Another type of dysfunctional communicator is one who assumes that all other people share fully his or her own feelings and perceptions. This person, therefore, assumes that personal perceptions, evaluations, and judgments are complete, final, and self-explanatory. Such a highly egocentric pattern of communication is sometimes jokingly referred to as the doctrine of "immaculate perceptions." Examples of this kind of dysfunctional communication include:

"How could you care about him?"

"Why didn't you do it right?"

"That's the way she is."

This kind of dysfunctional communication is based upon a simplistic view of the world that causes the communicator to assume that his or her own perceptions are totally accurate, that the external world and the people in it are unchanging, and that one's own judgments and opinions are based upon data so obvious that they require no interpretation or explanation.

Another aspect of dysfunctional communication is that it is often rooted in assumptions about other people that imply a kind of omniscience on the part of the communicator. In this pattern the dysfunctional communicator seems to believe that it is possible to get inside the skin of another person and really *know* what his or her motivations, thoughts, and feelings *are,* rather than having to *infer* them from limited and imperfect observations. Such people act as though they possessed a sort of crystal ball that reveals others' true thoughts and feelings. They often "play psychologist" in the popular sense of interpreting others' needs and motives.

Examples of this kind of dysfunctional communication are statements such as:

"I know what you are thinking."

"You say that because you don't like me."

"You know what I really mean."

"I don't have to explain that."

In summary, then, the dysfunctional communicator typically *overgeneralizes,* considers his or her perceptions to be *universally valid,* fails to distinguish between *personal inferences* and *self-evident* facts, and expects others to know what is going on inside another person.

When two or more dysfunctional communicators meet, unless their individual perceptions and opinions happen to coincide, they tend to engage in very unproductive and irreconcilable conflicts and disagreements. Their conversation may be ultimately reduced to a set of assertions such as:

"The world and the people in it are, always have been, and always will be this way."

"No they aren't, they are all like this."

Two dysfunctional communicators are relatively unlikely to develop positive long-lasting relationships or evolve effective cooperative problem-solving strategies. In this model one of the goals of the family counselor is to help to change dysfunctional communication patterns within the client system. The counselor essentially attempts to teach family members to become functional communicators in problematic situations.

The functional communicator uses approaches that are the antithesis of dysfunctional patterns. The functional communicator does *not* step into the assertive, agree–disagree trap. Instead he or she seeks to *identify, clarify,* and *understand* the specific situations, experiences, or perceptions on which the other person's communications are based. The functional communicator then *confronts* the other with the inferred or probable basis for his or her own opinion or perception. The functional communicator listens carefully to the other's explanation. Out of this two-way process comes a kind of negotiation of meaning that allows both partners to share the full personal meaning of the other's messages.

Meta Communication

Another important concept in the communications approach to family counseling is the notion of meta communication. This concept is based upon the fact that when people communicate they simultaneously send many different kinds of messages in different ways. Many times receivers are unable to respond clearly to all of these messages. The verbal message may be received as garbled or incomplete unless it can be interpreted in the context of the total set of messages, some of which may not be communicated verbally. The sender's vocal inflection, volume, tone, rate of speaking, facial expressions, posture, and gestures are all relevant to the full context of communication. This overall context, then, constitutes the "meta communication" pattern.

Often, particularly in stressful situations, it is difficult to receive fully the meta communication pattern. We may respond only to the verbal messages and consequently lose many of the most important aspects of the total message. The meta communications, or messages about a message, are very important because they often convey the emotional state of the sender such as anger, hurt, disappointment, or pleasure. The direct verbal message may actually contradict or distort the full communication. For example, the message, "Of course I'm not angry that you forgot our anniversary!" may be interpretable as meta communication only within a full context of cues.

The role of the family counselor within this model is heavily concerned with observing and participating in natural patterns of family interactions in order to help members to become aware of dysfunctional or incomplete patterns of communication and to learn to replace them with more effective and complete ways of exchanging important messages in order to facilitate effective problem solving and improve the quality of interpersonal relationships.

Family Rules

Another important idea in the communications approach is family rules. The process of establishing and maintaining a family is to a considerable degree one of defining a set of relationships so that family members can live with each other in reasonable harmony and be able to solve mutual problems. Obviously, it is wasteful of both time and emotional energy to treat each of the myriad problems and tasks that confront a family in the course of daily living as an utterly new and unknown situation. Instead, as family relationships develop, certain norms or procedures for solving problems, making decisions, or accomplishing tasks gradually evolve. These are called "rules" (Haley, 1963). Some of these may be quite explicit and operate at a high awareness level, while others may be implicit and operate in a subtle and almost unconscious way.

The system of rules that is evolved in a family defines the themes that govern interpersonal relationships. Relationships may be defined around "complementary" or "symmetrical" themes. "Complementary" themes involve dynamics of dominance and submission—that is, of one member exerting control over another—while "symmetrical" themes tend to reflect egalitarian or cooperative problem-solving dynamics.

Meta-rules

One of the most difficult problems in family life concerns the question of who makes the rules in new situations. Rules about making rules are called meta-rules and are obviously very important in defining family relationships. Examples of meta-rules are that father makes the rules about the use of the family car or that mother makes the rules about when and where the children do their homework. Both of these meta-rules imply a set of complementary rather than symmetrical relationship dynamics.

When sets of family rules and meta-rules are confused, contradictory, or incompatible, they may give rise to needless conflict or dissension. Similarly, when they define relationships in terms that are unacceptable to family members, they may lead to the ultimate breakdown of family cohesion.

Resistance to Change

A final and in many ways most compelling idea drawn from the communication model of family counseling concerns resistance to change (Haley, 1963). Perhaps the most important benefit derived from looking at the family as a social system comes from the fact that family systems have tremendous power to maintain steady-state outputs of behavior from their members.

Another way of putting this is that family systems resist change and tend to operate to maintain consistent behavior in family members even when that behavior is clearly viewed as problematical or even pathological by all family members, including the identified patient or patients.

This basic paradox is the reason that family counseling is a treatment of choice in so many kinds of behavior change situations. Problems of alcoholism, drug abuse, delinquency, and many other kinds of dysfunctional behaviors are often seen both as originating in and being maintained by family dynamics. Effective intervention in this wide range of problems, hence, often involves working with the entire family constellation and attempting to change the dynamics of family living. Certainly when counselors are concerned with the development of children or early adolescents, family interventions are indicated whenever feasible.

Families, no matter how dysfunctional in terms of the ultimate development of members, have this power to maintain equilibrium in part because of the cohesive forces that operate within them as they provide for basic needs of food, shelter, and companionship. Partly, however, this high degree of stability or resistance to change arises out of the low levels of awareness that members have of the nature of family interaction processes. Basic patterns of interpersonal communication, rule making, and relationship definition are first learned in the family of origin and tend to be blindly perpetuated as spouses and parents build their own family systems. Often alternatives to those deeply habituated patterns are perceived dimly or not at all. Failures in family living are treated with a person-blame mentality that focuses on the "badness" of other family members rather than on the faulty premises and processes around which family life revolves.

Much of the function of a family counselor in the communications model is to help members become aware of the dynamics and processes operating in their family systems so that they can exercise some degree of conscious choice and control over their interactions. The family counselor also actively teaches new skills and understandings to family members to help them communicate and relate in more humane and effective ways.

The Family Structural Approach

The structural approach to counseling of families is a logical extension of the application of general systems theory to the study of family life. In a sense, the structural approach looks at family functioning in terms of basic organizational principles. Family structure refers to the pattern of roles, relationships, rules, and responsibilities established for accomplishing family tasks.

A considerable body of research has examined the relationship between structural properties of families and the well-being and development of children. Perhaps the most seminal and significant research on family structure is that done by the Philadelphia Child Guidance Clinic group led by Salvatore Minuchin. These researchers have studied family structural problems in relation to a wide variety of health and adjustment problems in offspring (Minuchin, 1976).

Much of both research and treatment in this approach involves the observation of families engaged in working on semistructured tasks. This observation identifies maladaptive patterns used by families in dealing with responsibilities and conflicts.

Counseling interventions drawn from this research tend to emphasize the family as a hierarchical system with parents or parent surrogates being responsible for the managerial or executive functions. In families experiencing difficulties, the exercise of these functions is often observed to be confused and inappropriate. In particular, many such families are found to involve children in parental conflict to the detriment of both the child's emotional well-being and the overall effectiveness of the family.

Treatment generally includes a careful analysis of family decision-making processes and prevailing ways of handling conflict. Parents are often taught child-management techniques and attitudes that clearly differentiate between the roles and responsibilities of children and parents. Children are encouraged to play age-appropriate roles and to stay out of parental conflict situations as much as possible.

Family counselors in this model serve, in a sense, as organizational consultants who analyze family interaction processes and present new and more effective organizational arrangements.

Behavioral Family Therapy

Behavioral analyses of family functioning constitute another set of family counseling approaches related to structural approaches. In this approach the counselor is especially concerned with the reward and punishment contingencies that exist within a family system. These contingencies are viewed as being responsible for maintaining deviant or undesirable behavior in children. Gerald Patterson (1976) and his associates have studied the relationship between family functioning and both aggressiveness and school achievement of children. This research supports the proposition that much undesirable behavior in children is unwittingly maintained by parental reinforcement.

Treatment in this variant of family counseling is centered around teaching parents to manage the behavior of children by increasing their awareness of contingencies for reinforcement or punishment, identifying "menus" of rewards, negotiating behavior contracts with children, and using conflict-resolution strategies in dealing with family problems.

In the behavioral approach, the delivery of family counseling services ranges from rather simple training procedures provided for parents alone to more global interventions dealing with the entire family constellation. Similar procedures involving reinforcement contingencies are used in treating marital dissatisfaction and discord (Patterson, Hops, & Weiss, 1975).

Family Networking

A third basic approach to family counseling concerns what can be called family and community transactions (Bronfenbrenner, 1979). This approach is especially relevant to the counseling psychologist in community practice in that it focuses on the degree to which families are able to utilize and contribute to needed resources that exist in the community. In our earlier discussion we noted that the nuclear family and, to an even greater degree, the single-parent family was dependent on community resources for many of its vital needs.

Research has supported this view of the family as dependent on opportunities and services available within the larger community for their growth and survival (Stack, 1974). Personal growth of children is stimulated and nurtured by interactions within school, neighborhood, church, and other community institutions. The network of community relationships is an important lifeline in the optimal functioning of almost all families. The nature and quality of transactions between families and these institutions are often influenced by basic family values, goals, and orientations (Lee, 1979; Powell, 1979). Many families may view schools, churches, police, courts, or welfare agencies as essentially hostile intruders who invade their privacy with no real intent or capacity to help. They may similarly view these agencies as unconcerned and unresponsive because of perceived or real racial or cultural bias or political orientations.

Research has demonstrated negative relationships between family isolation and the adjustment of children (Jackson & Yalom, 1966; Moos & Moos, 1975). Apparently in many families the occurrence of highly stressful situations such as the mental breakdown of a family member, child abuse or neglect, a criminal conviction, or even a divorce or separation is accompanied by a disengagement from community interaction.

Out of this kind of research an approach to providing family services has been developed that is sometimes called "family networking." This approach emphasizes helping to break down barriers between families and community resources. It often involves building positive, cooperative relationships between parents and teachers. It may concentrate on helping families relate positively to neighbors or to restore extended family relationships. It may involve helping to organize support or action groups around the specific needs of single parents, tenants, insecure neighborhoods, or others. The approach may help families utilize the services of already organized community groups such as Parents Without Partners, Big Brothers, Big Sisters, or other community resources.

Sometimes this approach involves bringing significant others such as friends or extended family into counseling groups (Aponte, 1976; Rueveri, 1979). The focus of this approach is on the development of a healthy, positive, natural environment within which family processes can thrive and prosper to enhance the growth of all family members.

An Ecological Approach to Family Counseling

If we integrate elements of the counseling approaches outlined above, it is possible to obtain a broad, ecologically oriented view of a family as it functions within a community. Out of this view we can establish goals for counseling interventions and choose alternative counseling strategies.

Essentially, we are concerned with three major sets of variables that have been shown by research to be related to the growth and development of family members. First, we are concerned with optimizing family communication patterns in order to enhance the quality of family relationships, facilitate cooperative problem solving, and model positive human relations principles within the family. Second, we are concerned with the development of optimal family structures based upon rational and realistic assessments of the developmental stages and resources of family members. We are concerned with helping adults within the family resolve their own areas of conflict and disagreement without imposing emotionally damaging stresses upon developing children. We are further concerned with helping parents understand each other's needs and the needs of children and to learn to use clearly defined and reasonable systems of limits, rewards, and sanctions in order to establish a secure and healthy climate within the family. Finally, we are concerned with helping families utilize the resources and opportunities within the community to enrich the lives and prospects of family members.

The above statement of goals sounds like a big order to fill. If, however, we believe that families are the basic building blocks out of which a positive and vital community can be built and developmental and preventive goals realized, no higher priority for our energy and activity can exist.

References

Albee, G. W., & Joffe, J. M. (Eds.). *Primary prevention of psychopathology: The issues.* Hanover, N.H.: University Press of New England, 1977.

Aponte, H. J. The family-school interview: An ecostructural approach. *Family Process,* 1976, *15* (3), 303–311.

Bernard, J. *The future of marriage.* New York: World, 1972.

Bernard, J. The good provider role: Its rise and fall. *American Psychologist,* 1981, *36,* 1–12.

Blau, T. A. Diagnosis of disturbed children. *American Psychologist,* 1979, *34,* 969–972.

Bloom, B. L. Strategies for the prevention of mental disorders. G. Rosenblum (Ed.), *Issues in community psychology and preventive mental health.* New York: Behavioral Publications, 1971.

Bronfenbrenner, U. *The ecology of human development.* Cambridge, Mass.: Harvard University Press, 1979.

Cummings, N. Funding for children's services. *American Psychologist,* 1979, *34,* 1037–1039.

David, H. P., & Baldwin, W. H. Childbearing and child development: Demographic and psychosocial trends. *American Psychologist,* 1979, *34* (10), 866–871.

Gans, H. J. *The urban villagers.* New York: Free Press, 1962.

Garmezy, N. Children at risk: The search for the antecedents of schizophrenia. *Clinical Psychologist,* 1974, *9,* 55–125.

Goode, W. J. *World revolution and family patterns.* New York: Free Press, 1963.

Gordon, T. *Parent effectiveness training.* New York: Wiley, 1970.

Haley, J. *Strategies of psychotherapy.* New York: Grune & Stratton, 1963.

Hetherington, E. M. Divorce: A child's perspective. *American Psychologist,* 1979, *34,* 851–858.

Hetherington, E. M., Cox, M., & Cox, R. The aftermath of divorce. In J. H. Stevens & M. Mathews (Eds.), *Mother–child, father–child relations.* Washington, D.C.: National Association for the Education of Young Children, 1978.

Hill, R. The American family today. In E. Ginsberg (Ed.), *The nation's children* (Vol. 1). *The family and social change.* New York: Columbia University Press, 1960.

Jackson, D. D., & Yalom, I. Family research on the problem of ulcerative colitis. *Archives of General Psychiatry*, 1966, *15*, 410–418.

Kazdin, A. E. Advances in child behavior theory. *American Psychologist*, 1979, *34*, 981–987.

Kievit, M. B. *Women in the world of work*. Columbus: Ohio State University Press, 1972.

Komarovsky, M. *Blue-collar marriage*. New York: Random House, 1962.

Kramer, M. *Report to the President's Biochemical Research Panel*. Washington, D.C.: U.S. Government Printing Office, 1976.

Lee, G. R. Effects of social networks on the family. In W. R. Burr, R. Hill, F. I. Nye, & I. L. Reiss (Eds.), *Contemporary theories about the family* (Vol. 1). New York: Free Press, 1979.

McDermott, J. F. Divorce and its psychiatric sequelae in children. *Archives of General Psychiatry*, 1970, *23*, 421–427.

Minuchin, S. *Families and family therapy*. Cambridge: Harvard University Press, 1976.

Minuchin, S., Baker, L., Rosman, B., Liebman, R., Milman, L., & Todd, T. A conceptual model of psychosomatic illness in children. *Archives of General Psychiatry*, 1975, *32*, 1031–1038.

Moos, R. H., & Moos, B. S. Families. In R. H. Moos (Ed.), *Evaluating correctional and community settings*. New York: Wiley-Interscience, 1975.

Patterson, G. The aggressive child: Victim and architect of a coercive system. In L. A. Handrlynck, L. C. Handy, & E. L. Marsh (Eds.), *Behavior modification and families*. New York: Brunner-Mazel, 1976.

Patterson, G. R., Hops, H., & Weiss, R. L. Interpersonal skills training for couples in early stages of conflict. *Journal of Marriage and the Family*, 1975, *37*, 290–303.

Powell, D. R. Family–environmental networks and neighborhoods. *Journal of Research and Development in Education*, 1979, *13*, 1–11.

Rogers, C. R. *Becoming partners*. New York: Delacorte, 1971.

Rutter, M. Protective factors in children's responses to stress and disadvantage. In M. W. Kent & J. E. Rolf (Eds.), *Primary prevention of psychopathology* (Vol. 3). Hanover, N.H.: University Press of New England, 1979.

Rueveri, D. *Networking families in crisis*. New York: Garland, 1979.

Satir, V. *Conjoint family therapy: A guide to theory and technique*. Palo Alto, Calif.: Science and Behavior Books, 1964.

Scheflen, A., & Ferber, A. Critique of a sacred cow. In A. Ferber, M. Mendelsohn, & A. Napier (Eds.), *The book of family therapy*. New York: Science House, 1972.

Stack, C. B. *All our kin: Strategies for survival in a black community*. New York: Harper & Row, 1974.

Uzoka, A. F. The myth of the nuclear family: Historical background and clinical implications. *American Psychologist*, 1979, *34*, 1095–1106.

Wallerstein, J., & Kelly, J. The effects of parental divorce: Experiences of the pre-school child. *Journal of American Academy of Child Psychiatry*, 1975, *14*, 600–616.

Wallerstein, J., & Kelly, J. The effects of parental divorce: Experiences of the child in later latency. *American Journal of Orthopsychiatry,* 1976, *46,* 256–269.

Westman, J. C. Effect of a divorce on a child's personality development. *Medical Aspects of Human Sexuality,* 1972 (January), 38–55.

Weiss, R. *Marital separation.* New York: Basic Books, 1975.

10

Career Counseling and Life Planning

One of the unique contributions of counseling psychologists to community services arises out of their interest and expertise in the area of career counseling and life planning. This is obviously an area of tremendous importance in community life. We live in a society in which even the most basic levels of self-esteem, autonomy, and independence arise out of success in work and the accompanying self-sufficiency that it provides. A great many of the most pernicious problems encountered by human services professionals have roots in histories of chronic failure to cope with vocational demands and problems.

Many problems of alcoholism, marital disruption, child abuse and neglect, delinquency, criminal recidivism, depression, and so forth are triggered or exacerbated by chronic unemployment, underemployment, job-related stress, and other problems that revolve around the vocational life of community members. Most major life crises have a heavy vocational component. School-leaving, death or divorce of a spouse, chronic illnesses or disabilities, the end of child-rearing, mid-life crises, and retirement all involve massive changes and readjustments in vocational life.

In many ways any attempt at providing counseling or psychotherapeutic help to an adolescent or adult functioning in the community without considering or dealing with his or her vocational life is virtually bound to be a partial, palliative, and artificial approach that ignores or denies one of the most elementary realities in the client's life situation.

Similarly, when we look at the human environments represented in our communities and the opportunities for human growth and quality of life that they succeed or fail in providing, we cannot rationally ignore the workplace as a center and focus of human development and human success or failure.

Unfortunately, in recent years we have seen a strange and often irrational disparagement of the importance and relevance of career counseling and life planning functions among counseling psychologists themselves. Some of this rejection of career counseling as a primary tool of counseling psychology comes from a muddle-headed view of human needs and services that has seen fit to attempt to dichotomize something called "personal counseling" from "career counseling." Much of the fascination with "personal counseling" seems to arise out of an adolescent, voyeuristic view and value system that seems to imply that counselors are really successful when they can get clients to talk about "taboo" areas such as sexual behavior or to focus upon the expression of powerful negative feelings of hostility, fear, or jealousy.

Actually, there is very little that is more "personal" or involving that clients can bring to a counselor than questions, hopes, fears, doubts and aspirations about those activities in which they will spend nearly half of their waking hours for most of their lives.

Career counseling, when it is done well, is a deeply involving and complex activity that entails, for both client and counselor, a voyage of discovery into the former's life space and psychological structure. This exploration is no less personal, intimate, or significant than anything attempted in the name of psychotherapy.

Much misunderstanding of the nature of career counseling arises out of primitive and simplistic notions about vocational counseling processes that stem from antiquated and inadequate views of early formulations of trait and factor psychology. The days of "test them and tell them" vocational counseling are long since past, yet many students of counseling psychology still seem to equate modern career counseling with the "square peg and round hole" analogy.

Career counseling today is certainly not a mechanistic process of matching test profiles to job requirements and then browbeating clients into accepting the results of supposedly omniscient psychological tests and inventories. That view is a total parody and complete prostitution of the career counseling and life planning process.

Career Development Theory

The essence of modern career development theory rests on assumptions about vocational life which are, in a sense, almost diametrically opposed to the simplistic notions drawn from the misinterpretation of trait and factor personality theory that was discussed above. Basically, these assumptions of career development theory maintain that careers are *not* characterized by a series of discrete, isolated and independent choices, events, or decisions, but rather that such choices are interrelated and interdependent manifestations of one or more basic psychological threads or themes. In other words, a real and observable thread of psychological realities provide order and, consequently, predictability and meaning to the events of an individual career. In this sense, then, the concept of career is a psychological construct used to search out coherence and some degree of consistency and order within a lifelong pattern of vocational and vocationally related behaviors.

The construct of career behavior is a broad and pervasive one. It is a lifespan-oriented concept that is focused around the order and consistency to be found within sequences of specific jobs or job-training activities. The notion of career is also held by some theorists to embrace coherent patterns of leisure and volunteer activities as well as activities that are popularly defined as "paid work" (Katz, 1973; Wrenn, 1974).

The concept of career is a *psychological construct,* not simply an economic or sociological reality. Career counseling, consequently, *is psychological counseling;* that is, it is focused around the relationships between the cognitive, emotional, and behavioral needs of human personalities and their development, fulfillment, or frustration over the life span in the activities of work and leisure.

As a field of psychological inquiry, career development theory is heavily concerned with how people think and feel about their work and leisure choices, goals, values, and activities. Human beings are purposive, planful, and goal-directed organisms, at least in terms of their needs and potentials. They actively reach out to organize information about their environments. They seek meaning in their interactions with the world.

In career psychology, we do not really seek or expect to predict or control all of the individual's specific choices or behaviors, or to fundamentally control all of the events that define his or her work and leisure life. Instead, we recognize that few people could provide a fully plausible or satisfying *psychological* explanation for *all* of the events that have shaped their vocational histories and present vocational situation.

For all of us, the overriding social, economic, cultural, and political events of a fantastically complicated and interdependent world move and shape our lives with tremendous force. Wars, recessions,

social revolutions, and technological breakthroughs all have dramatic effects on the specific opportunities and avenues open to us. The
roads we travel, the distances we move, and the destinations we
reach are all the results of complex interactions between ourselves as
individual human beings and the realities of the world outside us.
The fact that our vocational lives are no different in this regard than
our family life, our network of friendships, or our physical location or
circumstances does not imply its lack of psychological reality. Neither does it imply that systematic counseling to give people greater
understanding of their career lives and to help them to exercise
control through planning those aspects of their lives that are amenable to control is impossible or unneeded.

If we abandon the antiquated view of vocational assistance as a
simple, one-time matching process between measured aptitudes and
interests and job requirements, where does a modern, developmentally oriented focus take us as counseling psychologists in community
practice? The most pervasive force in defining the field has been the
steadily broadening emphasis upon facilitating the lifelong process of
career develpment. This involves counseling across the life span,
rather than merely interviewing in a specific decision-making situation, usually confined to the point of initial full-time entry into the
labor market. Career counseling is now seen as appropriate in a wide
range of life situations and life stages from elementary school
through retirement from full-time employment.

The shift in focus away from a psychology confined to "vocational
choice" toward a psychology of "career development" has been a
challenging and often frustrating one. While it has rescued career
counseling from the stigma of being a mechanistic, test-centered
process, always suspect in terms of latent authoritarian tendencies, it
has often become such a vague and ambiguous process that it has
sometimes seemed to float along without any visible means of intellectual or scientific support.

The Concept of Discontinuity

If career development is to be more than a catchword or slogan,
clinging to intellectual respectability by trading on the good name of
developmental psychology, it must relate in some clear way to the
mainstream of knowledge about developmental processes. One of the
primary principles that has been generated out of contemporary

behavioral science is that the process of human development represents a dynamic interaction between a set of biological tendencies inherent within the genetic structure of the organism, and the cultural and social conditions present in its environment.

In very simple or primitive societies, cultural influences may impinge on developing individuals at rates that closely approximate those biologically regulated processes that tend to determine readiness for such cultural experiences. For example, preparation for economic self-sufficiency, or work, in such cultures proceeds at approximately the same pace as the development of physical strength and dexterity. As the child becomes physically able to perform work tasks in the family and community, he or she is given increasingly difficult and important tasks and responsibilities. Thus, the developing child experiences a basic *continuity* between physical and vocational development. In other words, in simple societies biological and cultural clocks tend to keep the same time.

In complex industrial societies, however, many cultural clocks are ticking, none of which necessarily keeps the same time as the others, or as does that measured by the biological clocks that govern physical development. Attaining adulthood in a modern, urbanized, and industrial society, for example, is not a simple matter of the biological onset of puberty and an accompanying tribal rite. Instead, the attainment of adult status is variously measured by a number of cultural timetables that are read in terms of measures such as "school-leaving age," "working age," "drinking age," "voting age," and so forth. None of these is necessarily adjusted to the rate of physical, emotional, or social development of any particular individual. Similarly, the time of retirement is governed largely by cultural rather than individual decisions.

In industrialized societies, many individuals thus experience *discontinuity* between various aspects of their development and the expectations and demands placed upon them by social and economic forces. These discontinuities are by no means confined to childhood and adolescence. Marriage, parenthood, divorce, end of childrearing, widowhood, and many other events within the life cycle impose the stresses associated with discontinuity. In education, institutions such as kindergarten, junior high schools, and community colleges have been invented to bridge discontinuities.

It is possible to conceive of career counseling programs within the community as performing a similar function. Career counseling is a particularly vital function because of the uncertainties of vocational life. Employment patterns are subject to the impact of technological changes, recessions, strikes, wars, population shifts, and patterns of world competition.

Systematic career counseling should be made available across the life span and should be specifically targeted to people who are at crisis points in their development. School leavers, including dropouts and "pushouts," as well as "graduates," recently divorced or widowed people, new arrivals in the community, technologically unemployed workers, veterans reentering civilian life, handicapped workers, victims of discrimination, midlife career changers, and the recently retired all represent populations with special vocational needs who are dealing with the stresses caused by discontinuities in their life situations. Addressing the needs of these populations represents perhaps the most important and unique contribution of counseling psychologists to community services.

The Concept of Life Stages

A key concept in the articulation of career developmental frameworks involves the notion that there is an identifiable sequence of events that helps to define the pattern of growth and development of career-relevant cognitions, feelings, and behaviors as these interact with forces in the environment. These are often defined as chronological or life stages, each characterized by a developmental theme that tends to dominate the pattern of person—environment interaction at that given point in the life cycle.

Central to the life-stages approach is the notion that development in a complex urban-industrial society can never be completely smooth and continuous, but that the culture and community inevitably impose a framework within which the process of development is regulated and circumscribed. Thus, in a sense, the relevance of a life-stages approach is derived at least in part from the existence of the kinds of discontinuities discussed above.

Many life-stage schemas have been proposed to elaborate the process of human development. The one chosen here has been more fully described by Blocher (1974). This particular schema analyzes development in terms of five major chronological stages, some of which are further divided into substages (see Table 10.2, p. 272).

The life-stages approach to human development assumes that one crucial dimension in individual differences is related to age or, more precisely, to position in the life cycle. A corollary of that assumption is that human behavior can be better understood and interventions better designed and implemented when they are conceived within the context of the individual's life stage.

The usefulness of a life-stages approach for counseling hinges heavily on the notion that each life stage involves characteristic *developmental tasks* which must be recognized, confronted, met, and mastered if future development is to proceed optimally. Havighurst (1953) defined developmental tasks in this way:

> A developmental task is a task that arises at or about a certain period in the life of the individual, successful accomplishment of which leads to his happiness or success with later tasks, while failure leads to unhappiness in the individual, disapproval by the society and difficulty with later tasks [p. 2.].

Many developmental tasks are obvious and simple to define. Learning to read, for example, is an obvious developmental task of education in the early elementary school years. Failure to accomplish this task in this particular period is certain to increase the probability of failure with all sorts of future school-related tasks. The result is very apt to be personal unhappiness, diminished self-esteem, and restriction of opportunities.

Part of the function of career counseling and life planning services is to help individual clients to identify and master developmental tasks related to career effectiveness. Unfortunately, we still do not know as much as we would like about the nature of career-related developmental tasks at all of the life stages. Our life-stage schemas tend to be normative and to specify types of person–environment interaction that may fit the modal situation but miss much that is relevant in the lives of individuals who have atypical situations and circumstances in their lives.

Havighurst (1964, p. 216) attempted to define a sequence of career-oriented developmental tasks that move the individual toward higher levels of career maturity and effectiveness. His schema is summarized in Table 10.1.

Obviously, as we work in career counseling with an individual client, we need to elaborate and specify with much greater precision and detail the nature of his or her idiosyncratic needs and tasks. We especially need to understand with each client the differences in developmental tasks and opportunities that are imposed by differing socioeconomic and subcultural backgrounds.

TABLE 10.1
Vocational Development: A Lifelong Process

	Stages of Vocational Development	Ages
I.	Identification with a Worker	5–10
	Father, mother, other significant persons. The concept of working becomes an essential part of the ego-ideal.	
II.	Acquiring the Basic Habits of Industry	10–15
	Learning to organize one's time and energy to get a piece of work done. Schoolwork, chores.	
	Learning to put work ahead of play in appropriate situations.	
III.	Acquiring Identity as a Worker in the Occupational Structure	15–25
	Choosing and preparing for an occupation. Getting work experience as a basis for occupational choice and for assurance of economic independence.	
IV.	Becoming a Productive Person	25–40
	Mastering the skills of one's occupation.
Moving up the ladder in one's occupation.	

The Concept of Life Space

Most human behavior can be fully understood only in terms of its social context, that is, in terms of its interactions with other significant groups and individuals. Each human being lives and grows in a world of psychological as well as physical space. Psychological space is mapped by a geography whose rivers and mountains are constituted by interpersonal roles and relationships.

The social and interpersonal interactions of people help to define their life space. So too does the actual physical environment help to define life space. The life space of a street corner gang of angry and alienated young delinquents engaging the community in a kind of civil war is as different from the life space of a luncheon group of community leaders as the environment of an astronaut walking on the moon is from that of a golfer playing the front nine at a Palm Springs country club. Career counseling framed around concepts and values drawn solely from upwardly mobile middle-class, white experiences is likely to prove sadly deficient in terms of the challenges of practice in the full range of community settings and situations.

The Concept of Life Style

Another useful concept in fine tuning career counseling processes to the needs of specific groups and individuals is life style. Life style was originally an Adlerian concept that attempted to identify the major theme that permeated the goal-oriented strivings of an individual. It has been extended to include the basic ways in which individuals tend to cope with stress in an attempt to establish mastery over the environment. The concept of general styles of coping was introduced by Lois Murphy (1962) in the study of children's reactions to difficult or stressful situations. She found that children tended to develop distinctive styles for coping with problematic situations. We now also speak of cognitive styles and learning styles in much the same vein as we attempt to identify the idiosyncratic characteristics that make each human life unique.

In a real sense, career counseling and life planning are concerned with teasing out and working with the unique and peculiar combination of values, attitudes, and coping behaviors that define the life of each individual human being. Career counseling is concerned with what Robert White (1966) called "the study of lives." He defined this kind of study and the need which it addresses when he wrote:

> Much as we have come to know about personality, there is a serious gap at the very center of the subject. Individual lives moving forward normally amid natural circumstances have received almost no systematic study and have played almost no part in our current understanding. . . . The psychologist . . . has almost never studied ordinary people as they increase their mastery of the ordinary problems of daily life. . . . The natural growth of personality and the higher flights of human achievement have been given poor representation in man's current ideas about himself. [p. 2.].

White has almost perfectly captured the essence of the knowledge base on which the practice of career counseling and life planning is based.

Table 10.2 provides a life stage–developmental task schema that attempts to specify and elaborate the stages also in terms of impor-

TABLE 10.2

**Principal Developmental Tasks and
Coping Behaviors by Life Stages**

Life Stages	Social Roles	Developmental Tasks	Coping Behaviors
Infancy (Birth–3 years)	Love-object roles; receiving and pleasing	Trust: Learning to eat solid food and feed self, control elimination, manipulate objects, walk, explore immediate environment, communicate, relate to family, accommodate to a daily life rhythm.	Approaching Receiving Accepting
Early childhood (3–6 years)	Sibling, playmate, sex-appropriate roles	Autonomy: Sense of separateness: Developing sense of self, sense of mutuality, realistic concepts of world. Learning to be a boy or a girl, manage aggression and frustration, follow verbal instructions, pay attention, become independent.	Accepting Receiving Negotiating
Later childhood (6–12 years)	Student, helper, big brother or big sister roles	Initiative-industry: Learning to read and calculate, value self and be valued, delay gratification, control emotional reactions, deal with abstract concepts, give self to others, formulate values.	Environmental-mastering Value-relevant Work-relevant
Organization Early adolescence (12–14 years)	Peer roles, heterosexual roles	Identity development: Learning to be masculine or feminine, belong in various relationships, control impulses, be positive toward work, study, organize time, develop relevant value hierarchy.	Social Sex-appropriate Achievement-oriented

TABLE 10.2 (Continued)

Life Stages	Social Roles	Developmental Tasks	Coping Behaviors
Later adolescence (15–19)	Peer roles, heterosexual roles	Identify as a potential worker: Learning to move from group to individual relationship, achieve emotional autonomy, produce in work situations.	Reciprocal Cooperating Mutuality
Exploration Young adulthood (20–30 years)	Marriage roles, Career roles	Intimacy and commitment: Generativity: Learning to commit self to goals, career, partner; be adequate parent; give unilaterally.	Sexual Risk-taking Value-consistent
Realization (30–50 years)	Leadership, helping, creative, accomplishment roles	Ego-integrity: Learning to be inner-directed, be interdependent, handle cognitive dissonance, or be flexible and effective emotionally; develop creative thought processes, develop effective problem-solving techniques.	Objectivity, intellectual, logical analysis, concentration, empathy, tolerance of ambiguity, playfulness, sublimation, substitution, suppression
Stabilization (50–65 years)	Leadership, helping, managing, creative, accomplishment, authority, prestige roles	Learning to be aware of change, have attitude of tentativeness, develop broad intellectual curiosity, develop realistic idealism, develop time perspective.	Change-oriented Value-relevant Sensitivity
Examination (65+ years)	Retirement roles, Nonworker roles, Nonauthority roles	Learning to cope with death, cope with retirement, affiliate with peers, cope with reduced physical vigor, cope with changed living conditions, use leisure time, care for the aging body.	Affiliative Productive leisure time Personal enhancement

tant social roles and coping behavior. It represents an attempt to provide a skeleton for the kind of view of the realities of the human life cycle that White clothed so eloquently in the quote above.

Cognitive Development and Career Counseling

The idea that people's life choices, approaches to problem solving, perceptions of others, and indeed their concepts of self and the world are shaped by the ways in which they organize and attach meaning to information is a central tenet of modern cognitive psychology. This view of human behavior is called the "constructivist" position. It is based upon the pioneering work of a number of theorists and researchers including Kelly (1963), Heider (1958), and Piaget (1932).

The constructivist explanation of personality essentially proposes that people should be viewed as holistic information processors and creators of cognitive structures through which stimuli are interpreted, evaluated, and acted upon. The actual behaviors of people thus are seen as events that are mediated by these structures rather than as responses that are solely determined by the external stimulus events themselves.

The constructivist approach grew out of research done in the field of cognitive-developmental psychology. Building upon the pioneering efforts of Piaget, researchers such as Kohlberg (1969), Loevinger (1976), Harvey, Hunt, and Schroeder (1961), and Perry (1968) have all built developmental theories with which to chart, analyze, and compare stages and levels of cognitive growth as these are observed in the basic structures and schemas used by developing human beings.

Developmental stage theories are based upon the assumption that as a result of people's information-processing activities, they move through a series of fairly well-defined cognitive developmental stages. These stages can be distinguished from each other in a qualitative sense by the kinds of cognitive structures typically used. Generally, higher stages of cognitive development are characterized by increasing levels of differentiation, hierarchical organization, and complexity and by decreasing levels of egocentricity and stereotyping in these schemas.

In other words, as people move through higher and higher levels of cognitive growth, they tend to differentiate more aspects or factors in situations and tend to integrate or subsume these under sets of general principles. They also tend to see multiple perspectives or aspects of a situation, including those of other people, and to rely less on simple cultural stereotypes of other people and situations in making judgments.

The cognitive developmental stages are, thus, attempts to categorize these distinct patterns of information-processing activities within some general hierarchy. While the foci and detail associated with these hierarchies differ somewhat from theory to theory, the general features of all the cognitive developmental approaches mentioned earlier are remarkably similar.

Cognitive development is assumed to be energized or motivated by an inherent human need to improve the predictability of and control over the environment (Kelly, 1963) and to reduce uncertainty (Klahr & Wallace, 1976). The creation of higher levels or stages of thinking occurs when individuals perceive that their present constructs or schemas are less able to explain accurately and so to predict environmental events than is a more complex and highly differentiated or integrated system. For example, a young person convinced that he or she wants a career in medicine might well find that simplistic stereotypes of the role of a physician based solely upon notions about prestige and income fail to predict the reaction that the holder has to the tension, turmoil, and gore witnessed in a visit to a hospital emergency room.

Information that is somewhat discrepant from existing cognitive structures acts as a stimulus for further differentiation and integration and thus further cognitive growth (Hunt, 1967). Also, novel information has been demonstrated to motivate further exploratory behavior. The integration and assimilation of old and new information made possible by higher level constructs is seen to produce satisfaction and thus to be intrinsically rewarding.

The constructivist viewpoint has already been incorporated into important approaches to counseling and psychotherapy such as those of Kelly (1963), Ellis (1962), and Beck (1976). (See chapter 3.) In these approaches a basic assumption is that therapeutic change depends upon the "restructuring" of cognitions within the phenomenological field of the client. Changes in feelings and actual behavior then follow from cognitive changes. As new behaviors are experienced or attempted by the client, they in turn serve as new sources of information that help to maintain the sequence of therapeutic change as it gathers momentum as a positive force in the client's life.

In these approaches, then, the client is helped to reorganize and restructure information abstracted and gleaned from many aspects of his or her life situation. In this process new meanings are created and new action plans made feasible. These new actions are validated in the process of implementation. Clearly, the focus of intervention is on cognition or information-processing activity.

The idea that people use structurally differentiated frameworks to abstract and organize meaning has emanated from cognitive developmental psychology and has been applied mainly in cognitive therapy. There has been increasing support for this position in other areas of psychology, however.

In social psychology and attribution theory (Bandura, 1977; Festinger, 1957; Heider, 1958; Kelley, 1971), similar ideas and explanations have been developed. Festinger and Heider both postulated that people are motivated by a desire to keep incoming information organized in a meaningful and consistent manner. Inconsistent or unexplainable information was seen to threaten existing belief systems or cognitive structures and so serve as a source of anxiety.

In order to bring about changes in personality and behavior, one must, in this view, introduce optimally discrepant information in order to induce the need to reorganize cognitive structures in the direction of greater differentiation, integration, and accuracy. In therapy, according to this view, it is of central importance to help clients alter their attributions about cause and effect relationships in their life situations. For example, Bandura's ideas about the importance of self-efficacy in the therapeutic change process are based on ideas about the motivational consequences of greater self-attributions of internalized control. Rotter's (1954) social learning theory similarly places great emphasis on internal versus external attributions about the locus of control of reinforcements.

Cognitive Career Development

Ironically enough, one of the last areas of psychology on which the emerging constructivist view has had impact is career development and career counseling. Rather obviously, if the ideas about the relationships among thinking, feelings, and acting, as well as attributions and actions, are fundamental to any area of applied psychology, that area is career counseling and life planning.

It is precisely in the area of life planning that developing human beings are confronted with extremely complex and ever-changing events, problems, and situations. In one sense the states of developmental "discontinuity" that we discussed above arise precisely when changing life situations and problems can no longer be adequately construed, explained, and anticipated by information processing schemas acquired in earlier and simpler stages of cognitive development.

In recent years the significance of the constructivist position has begun to be recognized in career development theory and research. Bodden (1970) took as a starting point in studying career decision making the cognitive developmental principle that as people develop, their cognitive structures tend to be characterized by greater complexity. The cognitively complex individual is believed to have a greater number of constructs or meaning categories than do cognitively simple individuals (Bieri, 1955). Bodden hypothesized that if cognitively complex people are able to make finer discriminations among information stimuli or inputs, and as a result have a more flexible set of responses, then such individuals should be more able to make appropriate career decisions than cognitively simple individuals. Appropriate career decisions were defined for the purposes of this research as: (1) agreement between measured intellectual ability and level of occupational choice and (2) congruence between personality style and vocational environment according to Holland's model (see chapter 8). Cognitive complexity was measured by the Bieri Repertory Test. The results indicated a moderate but significant relationship between cognitive complexity and adequacy of decision based upon these rather simplistic criteria. This finding was replicated by Bodden and Klein (1972). Again, results indicated a significant positive correlation between cognitive complexity and the choosing of an occupation in which the environment was compatible with the subject's personal coping style.

Winer, Cesari, Haase, and Bodden (1979) hypothesized that if cognitively complex individuals are more likely to choose an occupation congruent with their measured vocational preferences, then cognitive complexity should also be related to other measures of career maturity. They then studied the relationship between cognitive complexity and variables measured by the Crites Career Maturity Index Competence Test. The scales composing this instrument include (1) self-appraisal, (2) occupational information, (3) goal selection, (4) planning, and (5) problem solving. All of these scales are defined in relation to their contribution to competent career-planning and problem-solving activities. Results of the study were consistent with the prediction that cognitive development of level of complexity is associated with higher scores on the competence factor of the career maturity dimension. In general, this and related re-

search tends to support the position that level of cognitive development is a factor in both adequate vocational decision making and
general vocational maturity.

Jepson (1974) has also worked from the assumption that career
development is one aspect of general human development and that
postulates of cognitive developmental theory should also be relevant
for career-development research. In particular, Jepson has investi-
gated the relationship of developmental stage concepts to career
decision making.

He has studied the question of whether or not individuals at
different cognitive developmental stages actually use different sets of
rules for responding to vocational decisions and problems. Generally,
his research supports the view that career decision-making behavior
is related to more general cognitive developmental stages.

Perhaps the most important contribution that Jepson has made
is in recasting the whole notion of career development more clearly in
the cognitive developmental mold. Influenced by Martin Katz (1973)
and Thomas Green (1968), Jepson concluded that each of the major
thrusts in cognitive developmental research represented the operation of a particular motivational theme or tendency that energized a
particular area of cognitive activity and so led to a progressive developmental sequence. In this way, Piaget's research in childhood
cognitive processes might reflect the motivation to seek an underlying "logical" consistency or truth. Similarly, the work of Kohlberg
(1969) in his study of stages of moral reasoning may elucidate a basic
human need for a consistent and satisfying basis for moral action.
The quests for these consistent and logical rules and systems that
give predictability and relative certainty to the individual in a confusing and chaotic world are seen as providing the energy and
motivation that move individuals toward higher and higher levels of
cognitive development.

As Jepson attempted to describe the processes related to career
development to this general model, he concluded that this process
represents the quest for personal *potency* and meaning. Here, then, if
we accept his view, is one of the sources of unity that can help to tie
career development theory and research to the mainstream of developmental psychology. It can also serve to tie career counseling and
life planning to the mainstream of psychological counseling and
psychotherapy.

If, indeed, human beings are intrinsically motivated to seek
work or other structured activities in leisure or volunteer roles that
have personal meaning and convey a sense of potency or power to

effect changes in the environment, then we can expect as career psychologists to find orderly, systematic patterns of cognitive growth related to career thinking and career decisions. Similarly, as career counselors, we can expect that facilitating positive changes in career thinking, feeling, and behaving will have major effects on human health, happiness, and general well-being. This assumption is precisely what modern cognitive career counseling is all about.

At present the most thorough and articulate framework for examining the structural or constructivist model of career development is that presented by Knefelkamp and Slepitza (1976). This model conceptualizes a four-level hierarchy of cognitive development. These four levels from lowest to highest are termed: (1) dualism, (2) multiplicity, (3) relativism, and (4) commitment within relativism. Basically, the hierarchy relates to the ability to acquire and use alternative perspectives and points of view in comprehending, analyzing, and synthesizing from complex sets of information. Two or three substages are conceptualized at each of the four levels. Figure 10.1 outlines the model.

The Dualism Level.   The lowest level of development in the hierarchy is characterized by dualistic thinking. At this level individuals tend to think primarily in "either–or," "right or wrong," "good or bad," or "true or false" terms. Within the dualistic level are two substages or positions. In the lower or Stage One of these, career thinking is characterized almost entirely in relation to external forces or resources in the environment. Believing that there is only one "right" career for them, these individuals may turn to authority figures such as parents, teachers, counselors, or tests for the "right answers." Since there is only one career, individuals in Stage One experience little dissonance so long as the outside authority sources tend to agree.

The second position or Stage Two within the dualistic level marks the beginning of doubt. The possibility of wrong advice or decisions is recognized. This causes some dissonance and anxiety. The individual is almost totally dependent on others such as a counselor to formulate a decision-making or planning process and has only minimal understanding of the optimal nature of such processes.

Because the possibility of a "wrong" decision is recognized, the individual's view of the counselor and the counseling process is somewhat more open and tentative. The expectation is still, however, that the counselor or the "tests" should provide the right solution or decision.

FIGURE 10.1 Variables of qualitative change: Knefelkamp/Slepitza Model of career development

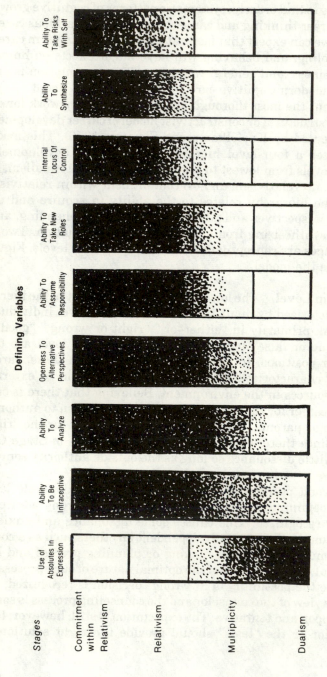

From: Knefelkamp, L. & Slepitza, R. A Cognitive-developmental model of career development: An adaptation of the Perry Scheme. *The Counseling Psychologist*, 1976, *6*, 53–59. Reprinted with permission.

The Multiplicity Level. At this level, Stage Three, the individual becomes increasingly aware of the possibility of making right or wrong choices. Anxiety and dissonance tend to be high. The client is ready to begin to use some formal elements of analysis in the planning process. The client begins to entertain comparisons between interests and abilities or between experience and skills and job requirements.

Stage Four moves the client into a more complex weighing of factors and responsibilities discovered in Stage Three. Multiple possibilities and multiple satisfactory choices can now be entertained. The decision-making or planning process is accepted as more complex. Both internal and external factors are recognized, but the self is still unable to accept full responsibility for choosing. The counselor is seen as the source of help on setting priorities and weighting factors.

The Relativism Level. Entry into this level is seen as the most significant change. In this level the individual has a fully internalized sense of responsibility for control over the planning or decision-making process. Stage Five is thus seen as an "exploring-doing" stage. It begins with the full recognition and acceptance of multiple possibilities and multiple outcomes. The self is now the prime mover. The counselor is seen only as an experienced and knowledgeable source of help, not as an unquestioned authority. The client has the ability to detach and analyze both self and environmental factors and to examine alternatives in formal and systematic ways.

Stage Six is the upper position at this level. At this stage the individual begins the process of exploration and the unlimited listing of possible alternatives. Stage Six is seen as a reflective and integrative stage that allows the client to establish and consider ties between self and career and to think about the consequences of commitment to a plan or choice. The client fully confronts the personal responsibility for making such a commitment.

Commitment Within Relativism. At this level the client has begun to assume full responsibility for planning and decision making. Clients also begin to experience the sense of career as a fulfilling and self-realizing venture. They begin to see career roles as opportunities to integrate the sense of who and what they are as individuals. They experience some degree of self consistency in terms of values, goals, and accomplishments.

Stage Seven, the lowest stage in this level, centers around the integration of self and career role. Initially individuals may feel constrained and confined by this integration. The end of this stage is characterized by a feeling of affirmation of self and a new focus on the individual style or way of enacting the career role.

Stage Eight begins with a full awareness of the commitments and responsibilities involved in following through on a career decision or life plan. This stage involves the beginning of a full integration of career role into total life style.

Stage Nine is the third and final stage at this, the highest level. At this ultimate stage of career development, individuals have a firm knowledge of who they are and how their sense of identity affects the various aspects of their lives and the significant others in their environment. They are able actively to seek out new information, take more risks to self-esteem, and make new plans to actualize talents, aspirations, and potentials.

With the Knefelkamp-Slepitza Model we have, then, a career-oriented cognitive developmental framework out of which to build a goal structure for a fully psychological and developmental approach to career counseling. In a sense, however, this model supplements rather than supplants the older models drawn from the psychology of individual differences. We have explicated a structural model involving *how* clients think about career decisions and life plans. The career counselor is still also concerned about *what* clients think about in relation to careers. A full-blown career counseling psychology must deal with both the structure and the content or substance of career decisions and life planning (Blocher & Siegal, 1981).

Person–Environment Fit in Career Counseling

Perhaps the most useful way to think about this second aspect of career counseling is with the ecological concept of person–environment fit. Just as the human motivation toward seeking a sense of potency, meaning, and personal effectiveness was a central, unifying concept in the structural or cognitive developmental aspect of career counseling, so is person–environment fit the central notion in the content aspect.

The central task of the career counselor is to help the client think, feel, and act in productive ways around relevant factors in self and environment that must be considered if developmentally appropriate choices and plans are to be formulated and pursued. If these plans are to help provide the client with increased freedom, control, and developmental opportunities, they must employ realistic considerations about psychologically relevant factors present in both person and environment. The inevitable complexity of these person–environment interactions is one of the reasons that facilitating cognitive growth to higher levels is so important.

The body of vocational theory and research that is most useful in specifying the nature of psychological person–environment interaction is that developed by John Holland (1973). (See chapter 8.) Holland has conceptualized human personality functioning in terms of a set of six basic sets of needs or preferences for specific kinds of activities. The sets of preferences are interrelated and can be arranged in terms of psychological distance to each other. The six themes that express these preferences are labeled as follows: realistic, investigative, artistic, social, enterprising, and conventional. The interrelationships or distances between these can be pictured through a hexagonal diagram such as Figure 10. 2. Adjacent themes or types are viewed as more closely related in a given personality pattern than are those occupying more distant sides of the hexagon.

FIGURE 10.2. The Holland Model. Holland's hexagonal model for defining the relationships among VPI types. The shorter the distance between any two types, the greater their similarity is thought to be. (Adapted from Holland, 1973.)

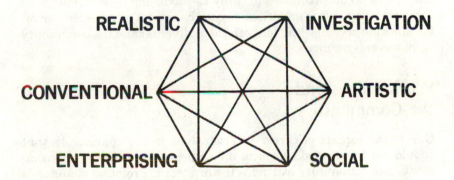

THE HOLLAND MODEL

REALISTIC   INVESTIGATION

CONVENTIONAL   ARTISTIC

ENTERPRISING   SOCIAL

Holland also categorizes occupational environments using the same typology to classify them in terms of the opportunities provided to support the activity preferences reflected in his six basic personality types. By combining information about individual personality type with information about a given occupational environment, we are able to assess, to a degree at least, the probable nature of the interaction or person–environment fit.

The Holland person–environment typology has been perhaps the most thoroughly researched theoretical approach in modern vocational psychology. Generally, this impressive body of research tends to support both the theoretical validity and practical utility of the model. Obviously, however, more research is needed to explicate and support the model fully (Thoreson & Ewart, 1976). Instruments have been developed to enable career counselors and clients to compare the relationships between personality type and environmental opportunities. (See chapter 8.)

Developmental Career Counseling

When we combine the cognitive developmental and person–environment approaches to career counseling and life planning, it seems clear that we are on the threshold of providing psychologically sophisticated models relevant across the life span and appropriate to a variety of crisis situations in the life cycle. These approaches to career counseling are as challenging as any interventions available in the psychological literature. The goals that they espouse of changing basic cognitive structures and helping clients to learn to use plans and decisions to increase freedom and control over their lives and to extend opportunities for growth-producing interactions with their environments is ambitious to say the least. The potential payoff for this kind of counseling for both the individual and the community is, however, enormous.

Work Values and the Community

One of the aspects of career interventions in the community that should not be ignored concerns the improvement of work environments and community attitudes toward work. Profound changes in work values have taken place in recent years. The centrality of work as a primary source of self-esteem and personal identity has been increasingly challenged. The "Protestant ethic" as a source for work morality has long been on the wane. As Murphy (1973) pointed out, work as a symbol of the expiation of original sin is hardly a belief compatible with contemporary attitudes. Similarly, the obvious relevance of work simply as a necessity for economic survival is, as Levenstein (1973) pointed out, simply not congruent with the facts of life in many segments of our communities. We have many families well into the third generation of life without regular work as a stable aspect of family culture. In an increasingly automated and steady-state economy, with a relatively affluent society and a welfare state, the future of work attitudes seems in doubt.

As work-oriented attitudes are no longer structured solely around either religious sanctions or economic survival, the psychological aspects of men's and women's relation to work becomes increasingly important. Work is increasingly valued or devalued, not in terms of a moral or economic imperative to work, but as a way of organizing life in some psychologically meaningful and self-fulfilling way. This is the need for potency and effectiveness that we mentioned earlier. Value systems relevant to work increasingly encompass dimensions of status, prestige, independence, power, dignity, and opportunity for satisfying interpersonal relationships. Increasingly, work is valued in terms of its opportunities for facilitating optimal personal development of the worker.

Unfortunately, many of the realities of community attitudes and opportunities militate against the fulfillment of these high expectations. Not much seems to have changed in community attitudes since Caplow (1954) pointed out many years ago that community values tend to view white-collar work, self-employment, and "clean" occupations as intrinsically superior. These attitudes also rate the importance of business occupations by the size of the organization and tend to view personal services work as degrading and unworthy. Other similar values hold that the length of time spent in formal education preparing for a job is a direct indicator of its worth and that the number of people one supervises is a measure of the importance of one's job.

When these kinds of attitudes are subtly but pervasively communicated in combination with other negative attitudes caused by social, ethnic, or sexual bias, they have a profound negative effect on the psychological relationships between people and work. When expectations are high and opportunities for fulfillment are few and far between, many people are doomed to experience frustration and defeat.

As psychologists in the community, we have an obligation to help change prevailing community attitudes and to attempt to extend and enhance genuine opportunities for psychological growth and fulfillment through work as much as possible. A tremendous challenge exists for us as career counselors in helping individuals learn to maximize their potential for obtaining self-fulfillment through work.

An even greater challenge exists for us in communicating to the society the urgency of restructuring work to provide the greatest possible source of self-fulfillment and social contribution to people from all parts of the community. If contemporary work values are to be sources of cooperation and cohesiveness rather than of conflict and divisiveness within the community, then we must find ways of organizing work and work environments in ways that allow all community members to relate to them as positive and available opportunities.

Goals for Community Career Services

Perhaps the best way to summarize this chapter is by listing a set of goals that we view as frankly utopian, yet so significant that they must be accepted at least as ideals to be pursued with energy, optimism, and enthusiasm. These goals for career services in the community are:

1. Helping all community members become aware of the alternatives available to them at particular stages of their development and to understand the probable consequences of these alternatives in terms of person–environment fit.
2. Helping all community members achieve a realistic and satisfying vocational identity that allows them to relate a productive work life to an acceptable life style.
3. Helping all community members to acquire a set of cognitive structures and work-relevant coping and mastery behaviors that enable them to choose, plan, and work with dignity, self-esteem, independence, and effectiveness.
4. Helping the total community to conceive of and organize the institutions of work and leisure in ways that offer opportunities for all members to satisfy human needs in fully human ways.
5. Helping the total community to build an opportunity structure that is devoid of racial, ethnic, sexual, and social prejudice and based upon the recognition of the unique talents and potentials of all members.

The goals defined above may seem grandiose. The adjective "all" has been used frequently and with intent. The goals themselves are guideposts through which to set directions for professional practice and social advocacy. We believe they reflect the value commitments of counseling psychology.

References

Bandura, A. Self-efficacy: Towards a unifying construct of behavioral change. *Psychological Review,* 1977, *84,* 191–215.

Beck, A. T. *Cognitive therapy and behavior disorders.* New York: International Universities Press, 1976.

Bieri, J. Cognitive complexity-simplicity and predictive behavior. *Journal of Abnormal and Social Psychology,* 1955, *51,* 263–268.

Blocher, D. H. *Developmental counseling* (2nd ed.). New York: Ronald Press, 1974.

Blocher, D. H., & Siegal, R. Toward a cognitive developmental theory of leisure and work. *The Counseling Psychologist,* 1981, *9,* 33–44.

Bodden, J. L. Cognitive complexity as a factor in appropriate vocational choice. *Journal of Counseling Psychology,* 1970, *17,* 364–368.

Bodden, J. L., & Klein, A. Cognitive complexity and appropriate vocational choice: Another look. *Journal of Counseling Psychology,* 1972, *19,* 257–258.

Caplow, T. *The sociology of work.* Minneapolis: The University of Minnesota Press, 1954.

Ellis, A. *Reason and emotion in psychotherapy.* New York: Stuart, 1962.

Festinger, L. *A theory of cognitive dissonance.* Evanston, Ill.: Row, Peterson, 1957.

Green, T. F. *Work, leisure and the American schools.* New York: Random House, 1968.

Harvey, O. J., Hunt, D. E., & Schroder, H. M. *Conceptual systems and personality organization.* New York: Wiley, 1961.

Havighurst, R. J. *Human development and education.* New York: Longmans, Green, 1953.

Havighurst, R. J. Youth in exploration and man emergent. In H. Borow, (Ed.), *Man in a world at work.* Boston: Houghton-Mifflin, 1964.

Heider, F. *The psychology of interpersonal relations.* New York: Wiley, 1958.

Holland, J. L. *Making vocational choices: A theory of careers.* Englewood Cliffs, N.J.: Prentice-Hall, 1973.

Hunt, R. A. Self and other semantic concepts in relation to choice of vocation. *Journal of Applied Psychology,* 1967, *51,* 242–246.

Jepson, D. A. The stage construct in career development. *Counseling and Values,* 1974, *18,* 124–131.

Katz, M. The name and nature of vocational guidance. In H. Borow (Ed.), *Career guidance for a new age.* Boston: Houghton-Mifflin, 1973.

Kelley, H. H. Attribution in social interaction. In E. E. Jones, D. E. Kanouse, H. H. Kelley, R. R. Nisbett, S. Valins, & B. Weiner (Eds.), *Attribution: Perceiving the causes of behavior*. Morristown, N.J.: General Learning Press, 1971.

Kelly, G. A. *Theory of personality: The psychology of personal constructs*. New York: Norton, 1963.

Klahr, D., & Wallace, J. G. *Cognitive development: An information-processing view*. Hillsdale, N.J.: Laurence Erlbaum Associates, 1976.

Knefelkamp, L., & Slepitza, R. A cognitive-developmental model of career development: An adaptation of the Perry scheme. *The Counseling Psychologist*, 1976, *6*, 53–59.

Kohlberg, L. Stage and sequence: The cognitive-developmental approach to socialization. In D. Goslen (Ed.), *Handbook of socialization theory and research*. New York: Rand McNally, 1969.

Levenstein, A. Work and its meaning in an age of affluence. In Borow, H. (Ed.), *Career guidance for a new age*. Boston: Houghton-Mifflin, 1973.

Loevinger, J. *Ego development*. San Francisco: Jossey-Bass, 1976.

Murphy, G. Work and the productive personality. In Borow, H. (Ed.), *Career guidance for a new age*. Boston: Houghton-Mifflin, 1973.

Murphy, L. *The widening world of childhood*. New York: Basic Books, 1962.

Perry, W. G. *Forms of intellectual and ethical development*. New York: Holt, Rinehart & Winston, 1968.

Piaget, J. *The moral judgment of the child*. New York: The Free Press, 1965 (originally published, 1932).

Rotter, J. B. *Social learning and clinical psychology*. Englewood Cliffs, N.J.: Prentice-Hall, 1954.

Thoreson, C. E., & Ewart, C. H. Behavioral self-control: Some clinical concerns. *The Counseling Psychologist*, 1976, *6*, 29–43.

White, R. W. *Lives in progress* (2nd ed.). New York: Holt, Rinehart & Winston, 1966.

Winer, J. L., Cesari, J., Haase, R. F., & Bodden, J. L. Cognitive complexity and career maturity among college students. *Journal of Vocational Behavior*, 1979, *15*, 186–192.

Wrenn, C. G. Hopes and realizations, past and present. *Vocational Guidance Quarterly*, 1974, *22*, 256–262.

Index